THE NOVEL AND SOCIETY

THE NOVEL
AND SOCIETY

BY

Diana Spearman

Routledge and Kegan Paul
LONDON

First published 1966
by Routledge & Kegan Paul Limited
Broadway House, 68–74 Carter Lane
London, E.C.4

Printed in Great Britain
by W. & J. Mackay & Co Ltd
Chatham

Contents

ACKNOWLEDGEMENTS

I am most grateful to Sir Karl Popper for his kindness in reading parts of this book and giving me the great benefit of his advice. Also to Miss Wedgwood for reading the chapter on Defoe and to Lord Coleraine for reading Part I.

Introduction

The relations between literature and the society in which it appears have been extensively studied; but mainly by critics and historians of literature for the light that might be thrown on books, plays, and the general process of literary development. Such studies generally assume that a relation exists, and can be traced in particular works, as well as, in movements of development and change. If the exact nature of the connection could be elucidated, it would illuminate some of the problems of sociology as well as those of literary history; in spite, however, of the amount of work devoted to it there are still a variety of opinions about it.

It is clear, of course, that there are, or at least appear to be, some sociological elements in literature. Whether women write or not seems to be related to the position of women, though not in any simple or direct way. Dorothy Osborne's remark on the publication of the Duchess of Newcastle's poems—'Sure, the poor woman is a little distracted, she could never be so ridiculous else to venture at writing books, and in verse, too. If I should not sleep this fortnight I should not come to that'—has usually been taken as showing the inhibiting effect of public opinion. For here is a woman with an undoubted command of style who, in spite of herself, has become a classic of English literature, and yet wrote nothing except private letters.

The dominance of women in the Heian period of Japanese literature and the almost complete absence of Chinese women writers can be related to certain social and cultural factors, although Arthur Waley finds them inadequate to explain the female authors of Japan. The reasons for the appearance of poetry of roughly the same form in what are called heroic ages, on the other hand, seem to be fairly clear and to be related to social conditions, though social conditions in the widest sense, including as they do the absence of writing.

This kind of evidence is reinforced by theories of social and cultural determinism deriving from Hegel, Marx and the views of anthropologists. There has always been, in every age, a tendency to connect literature with contemporary events, to regard it as a part of history, as was done, for example, in the famous seventeenth-century quarrel between the ancients and the moderns. But it was not until Hegel tried to combine every aspect of human life in his philosophy of history that a theoretical framework was provided into which literature could readily be fitted.

Lessing and Herder, it is true, had regarded literature as the expression of the spirit or genius of a nation, and Madame de Staël accounted for the differences in style and content between classical, medieval and modern literature partly in sociological terms, although race and climate also played a part in her analysis. But neither she nor those German writers explained why social conditions of the kind they postulated should thus influence literature.

This, in a sense, Hegel triumphantly did. He regarded history as the process through which some ultimate reality, sometimes translated as the Absolute, sometimes as the Idea, which Bosanquet tells us means the 'concrete world process', realizes itself in time. Art, including literature, is the way in which the Absolute reveals itself in 'the sensuous mode'. It follows that, in any historical period, every aspect of life will be connected by the Spirit which underlies them all. This is Hegel's contribution to the study of literature. Few critics or historians are today Hegelians in the sense of believing in the Absolute and its manifestations, perhaps few ever were. But many, if not most of them, are Hegelians in the sense that they believe all social and cultural phenomena, even though they appear to spring from different sources and serve different ends, are inspired by a common psychology, ethos, or outlook.

The wide acceptance of such a view undoubtedly owes a great deal to Marx's reformulation of the unitary thesis, basing it not on some untestable hypotheses about the nature of reality, but on the technology employed in particular eras of European history.

Marx's view of history as determined by technology is superior to Hegel's Absolute in that it can be, to some degree at least, tested; although even if it survived testing, this still would not explain completely why literature should also be governed by it.

For literature it has indeed become considerably more plausible than it was in Marx's lifetime; for while he could have cited the invention of printing, this only had an indirect effect on literature. The cinema, on the other hand, obviously dependent on modern technology, is often thought to have had a direct, if minor, influence on the narrative method of some novelists.

Indirect effects are, however, what really concerned Marx. In his theory modes of production mould literature through their impact on the interests and position of classes. Moreover, if the whole course of history, intellectual and artistic as well as political, is determined by the class struggle, this provides a theory of social causation, which is exactly what is lacking in most sociological theories of literature. Literature became, for many followers of Marx, and indeed for many critics and historians who were not Marxists at all, the expression not of a nation or of a period, but of a class. From the political aspect of Marxism one might think that the literature of one age, unless it was a literature of protest, could have no value or interest in another. Some Marxist critics have proceeded on the assumption that unless an author can somehow be twisted into an exponent of social wrongs, his work is worthless. Marx himself and the more serious Marxist critics were prevented from doing this by a recognition of the other aspect of the sociology of literature. An assertion that the style and content is determined by the social context may seem to account for change; it fails, however, to explain why people, even people with advanced political views, enjoy reading not only Chaucer and Shakespeare, who speak from so different a world that it is not necessary to fit them into the political spectrum, but even reactionaries like Sir Walter Scott and Balzac. It appears that Marx himself was among these people.

It was, moreover, in no way Marx's intention to depreciate cultural achievements. He thought as highly of art and literature as other educated men of his day; he was a traditionalist, in the sense that he followed a philosophic and aesthetic tradition. His attitude was misunderstood even in his own day, even by his own followers, and Engels thought it necessary to state that:

> According to the materialistic view of history, production and reproduction of real life, are in the last instance, the determining factor in history. Neither Marx nor I have asserted more than that. If anybody twists this into a claim that the economic factor is the only

3

determining factor, he transforms our statement into a meaningless, abstract absurd phrase. The economic is the basis, but all the factors of the superstructure—political forms . . . forms of law . . . political, legal and philosophic theories, religious views . . . all these factors also influence the course of historical struggles and in many cases play the dominant role in determining their form.[1]

This would allow a Marxist critic to take almost any factor as the basis for the interpretation of any piece of literature. Most of them have chosen the class conflict; indeed, the view of literature as the product or weapon of the class struggle has been accepted far beyond Marxist circles.

The influence of both Hegel and Marx in this field is vague and diffused, and shows itself in a general assumption of some kind of social determinism rather than in attempts to explain literature by any one factor; and this is true even of professed Marxists. Luckác's view, for example, of the historical novel as a product of the interest in history produced by the French Revolution and its aftermath, seems to owe little to Marx and could have occurred to anyone used to finding connections between literature and social conditions.

Today Hegelian or Marxist social determinism is fused with more modern theories derived from anthropology. Many authropologists and some historians regard any society or culture as a unified whole; although not necessarily unified by the factors emphasized by Hegel, Marx, or indeed any other nineteenth-century writer.

'Culture', according to Malinowski, 'is an integral in which the various elements are interdependent.'[2] G. and M. Wilson base their arguments about social change in central Africa on the view that 'all objective analysis of social relations rests on the assump tion that they form coherent systems, that within any one field they support and determine one another inexorably'.[3] Radcliffe-Brown believed that 'any persistent culture is an integrated unity, a system in which each element has a definite function in relation to the whole'.[4]

[1] Engels, F., letter to Starkenburg quoted in Fischer, E., *The Necessity of Art,* 1957.
[2] Malinowski, B., *A Scientific Theory of Culture,* 1944.
[3] Wilson, G. and M., *Social Change in Central Africa,* 1946.
[4] Radcliffe-Brown, A. R., *The Present Position of Anthropological Studies,* British Association for the Advancement of Science, 1931.

These writers are anthropologists and are speaking primarily of simple or primitive societies; but all concepts developed in such studies are now freely applied to modern highly developed societies. And even if they were not, sociologists and historians have produced similar theories drawn from the study of civilized societies alone. For example, H. Becker asks:

> Can historical data be torn out of their full context? Dare we assume when we begin an investigation that we can tear a closely woven tapestry apart, sew the fragments on a 'timeless' background and get anything but a crazy quilt for our labour? . . . In order for separate characteristics . . . to have meaning they must be considered with reference to the whole problem and to each other— they must be considered as a configuration united by the logic of internal relationships . . . that configuration constitutes the parts just as the parts constitute the configuration; neither can be considered in isolation.[5]

Toynbee's theory of history is founded on a similar theory of the interrelation of all elements in any one culture.

The idea of the unity of any culture is majestic and, stated in broad terms, seems unanswerable. But when applied to particular cases it does not seem so convincing.

If literature is tied to a particular social setting, how is it that no literature which is incomprehensible to us has been found? Once the language is known literature seems to find almost a readier acceptance than visual art.

The persistence of certain themes also seems hard to understand. How could Marlowe and Goethe in such different societies have both written plays based on a German medieval legend? Why do Arthur and his knights haunt English literature? The story would, if one did not happen to know the facts, seem to be tied to a particular culture and one, moreover, alien to modern ideas. That this is not so, that Malory produced his book at the dawn of the modern age, that Milton first thought of writing an epic about Arthur rather than Adam, that Tennyson wrote the *Idylls of the King* in the nineteenth century, and that a novel about Arthur, of over a thousand pages, appeared in 1958, was very popular, and has since become the basis of a musical play, is hard to reconcile

[5] Becker, H., quoted in Sorokin, Peterim A., *Social and Cultural Dynamics*, New York, 1937.

with any theory that literature is a reflection of society at any particular moment.

The study of folk stories has not always tended to the discovery of a mirror image of the culture in which they appeared. The American anthropologist Boas, indeed, said of his studies of American Iindian stories: 'Beliefs and customs in life and in tales are in full agreement.'[6] Bartlett, however, found another possibility: 'A motive may be persistently preferred in common story and rumour, largely because it has no persistent expression in any form of group culture.'[7] A similar explanation has been invoked quite independently to account for the popularity of the pastoral novel in sixteenth- and seventeenth-century France:

> The theme of pastoral romance, of shepherds and shepherdesses, of nymphs, druids and knights, of suffering, enduring, infinitely faithful love, was a theme so remote from the tone of real life that it won enthusiasm by its very contrast. To read these gentle, sentimental pages, to conjure up the theatrical pastoral scenes and costumes, was to escape from the memory of years of embittered religious, foreign and internal war.[8]

Now this can, of course, be regarded as a sociological theory in a sense, but it suggests a connection between literature and society the very opposite of that assumed by the prevailing theories of social determinism; yet when noticed it has been usually dismissed as trivial with the phrase 'escapism'.

Professor Page's conclusions about the background of the Homeric poems hardly seems to fit in with any of the prevailing theories about the relation between society and literature. 'The poems', he said, 'which Europe has most admired and felt most at home with were completed before the foundations of European civilisation were laid.'[9]

These various facts, collected somewhat haphazardly from the history of European literature, suggest that the relation between literature and society is not the simple one implied in words like 'product' and 'reflection', so often used to describe it.

Doubts about the integration of literature and society are increased by those anthropologists who are beginning to question

[6] Boas, F., 'Literature, Music and Dance', *General Anthropology*, edited Boas, 1935.
[7] Bartlett, F. C., *Remembering*, 1932.
[8] Caudwell, H., *Introduction to French Classicism*, 1931.
[9] Page, D., 'The Homeric World', *The Listener*, Jan. 19th, 1961.

the validity of the holoistic approach to their own studies. Leach, for example, says:

> When the anthropologist attempts to describe a social system, he necessarily describes only a model of the social reality. This model represents in effect the anthropologists' hypothesis about 'how the social system works'. The different parts of the model system, therefore, necessarily form a coherent whole—it is a system in equilibrium. But this does not imply that the social reality forms a coherent whole; on the contrary . . .[10]

Nadel, another anthropologist, also denies complete integration:

> Certain orders of cultural facts are without even a tacit implication of determinate social relationships and groupings . . . This as I shall attempt to show is true of language, of art (in the widest sense) and of technology and science. All that these social phenomena imply is human beings through whose actions these cultural forms materialise and for whose needs, aims, desires, they exist. They are linked to social groupings only in that they must be intelligible to and manageable by them.[11]

It is at least agreed by all schools of thought that individuals with exceptional talents are born into social situations which contain both sociological structures and cultural patterns. Opinions, however, differ widely as to how far the individual talent is moulded, if not created, by the situation.

In the main the problem has been examined by the study of either one great writer, or of a number of literatures closely connected with each other in one historical period. Sorokin has indeed included literature from different civilizations; but in his work literature is subsidiary to the visual arts and it is assumed rather than argued that it must necessarily obey the same laws.

It seems possible that more might be learned by considering one literary form, and one that has only appeared in a limited number of countries.

The novel is a form which emerged independently in modern Europe, twelfth-century Japan, and fifteenth-century China, but in other cultures never appeared at all. It is generally accepted that the society of eighteenth-century England in some way produced or moulded the eighteenth-century novel. The Japanese

[10] Leach, E. R., *Political Systems of Highland Burma*, 1954.
[11] Nadel, S., *Foundations of Social Anthropology*, 1951.

and Chinese novel ought to provide some kind of check or control on this theory. Any discussion of the Far Eastern novel involves the use of translations, and it might be thought better to concentrate on some facet of European literature; but in familiar literature and history already well known it is difficult to avoid the impression that things appearing together in time are linked by some kind of necessity. Nearly all studies of books or plays assume that this connection exists and proceed merely to elaborate it. Yet a brief consideration of the Chinese and Japanese novel may help to show at least the variety of the social conditions in which novels appear.

Any conclusion derived from this can be tested, to some extent at least, by an examination as to how far novels give an accurate picture of the society in which they were written. This means discussing their content: the early eighteenth-century novelists, Defoe, Richardson and Fielding, rather than any later writers, seem to be the best choice. Their social background will have already been described in the chapter on the theory of the middle-class novel; and it is possible to compare their picture of contemporary life with real-life documents, letters, diaries, newspapers, wills and Parliamentary debates. Much of the material culture of the eighteenth century still exists; its houses at least are familiar to everyone, and a great many people know its pictures, churches, bookbindings and carriages.

It might be thought that the nineteenth rather than the eighteenth-century novelists should be chosen because they are more familiar to most people, and because they attempted not only to reproduce the 'manners of the age' but also to delineate the condition of the people, and the relationship between classes, and thus to illuminate social problems. There is, however, acute disagreement among historians as to how far they succeeded in their aims, and this is closely involved with existing political controversies. The connection with politics, while it might make the discussion more interesting, would also make it more difficult to get an impartial view. Whether Dickens's world is or is not an accurate representation of nineteenth-century England rouses emotions which are quite untouched by a similar question about Richardson or Fielding. Another and more important reason for not choosing them is that they were themselves influenced by sociological theories of literature; and are an example of what

Popper has called 'the Œdipus effect', i.e. the way in which such predictions tend to bring about their own fulfilment.

The widely held idea that there are no elements in human life which can, even in theory, be detached from the social environment and called 'non-social' or 'pre-social' makes it impossible to discuss the relations between society and any human activity. For the purpose of examining the relations of the novel and society, it is necessary to distinguish between biological, individual, social and sociological factors, and this is true even if the latter are so much more powerful than the former that biological and individual characteristics are submerged by social and sociological.

Any human activity, as we know it, is social, because all men live in a society. Social influences act, however, on human beings who are born with certain characteristics. The basic impulses given to them are shared not only with other human beings but with the whole animal kingdom and might be described as pre-social; were it not that this might be taken as suggesting that there was a stage in human evolution in which man or his ancestors were solitary animals. The evidence seems to show that this was never so, men have always been social; but we all know that they have solitary experiences, in the sense that these are not generated by social contacts, are not simultaneously shared with other human beings and are, as experiences, immune from social influences. Many of them are physical. Pain and intense physical pleasure are examples as well as hunger. They may have social aspects: the extent to which pain is endured without complaint or the way in which hunger can be satisfied. But neither social nor sociological pressures can dissipate them. Nor can anyone who is hungry substitute the satisfaction of someone else for his own, as he can to some extent with some kinds of social experience. If you are hungry it is no use watching people eat on television, whereas a wish to dominate, to dazzle, to revolt can be partially fulfilled by watching or even reading.

Physical experiences are, however, not the only ones which are essentially solitary. There are also certain experiences that appear, in an identical form, in cultures so remote from each other that they must be immune from sociological or even social influences.

'I wonder if it is only I who have the feeling that speech which I have heard or sights which I have seen were already heard or

9

seen by me at some past time—when I cannot tell.'[12] These words were written in fourteenth-century Japan, but as a description of the experience called *déjà vu* they could be used today. It seems reasonable to call all such non-social experiences solitary.

Some kinds of literature are so universal that they seem to belong rather to mankind as a species than to any social system. The short story and the short lyric have existed, even if in rudimentary form, in every society known to us.

At the opposite pole to these impulses and experiences common to all mankind are the personal qualities of the individual. How many of these are part of his genetic inheritance and how many are the creation of his social environment has been much debated. This debate is, however, less important for literature than for many other subjects, because those historians and critics most convinced that its form and content is determined by the society in which it is written, also emphasize the talent or genius of the writer and would accept that at least a part of this is an inborn quality. They would agree therefore that there are non-social or solitary factors which affect literature, although they would contend that everything that makes it art derives from social influences.

'Social' often means simply the interaction between individual human beings. The story-teller and his audience in Oriental or medieval civilization make up a social situation, and its points of difference from the situation of a novelist writing alone for an imagined audience has important effects on the kind of literature each produces. This sense of the word has, however, been largely superseded by another. Many writers passionately believe that there exists in human society as well as human beings entities which are variously called institutions, structures, social facts, patterns, forces, which no analysis can dissolve into the men and women who establish, use or manage them. The term sociological in this book will refer to those theories which assume that the whole, whether it is taken to be a culture, a class, the spirit of the age or of a nationality, determines the nature of the units which compose it.

The circumstances of all human lives are social in the sense that they are within society and are the result of relations with other human beings; but they are not necessarily sociological in the

[12] Kenko-Boshi, quoted in Aston, W. G., *History of Japanese Literature*, 1899.

sense that they are determined by or even related to larger social units or general social conditions. If a man is prevented from marrying the woman he loves by a difference in social class the experience is dominated by sociology. If instead she dies or fails to return his love, then in the first case the obstacle arises from the nature of the universe, and is clearly non-social, although indeed it might be said that in some cultures she would not have died. We may assume, however, that she was drowned while bathing, an accident on which medical science could have no effect. If, on the other hand, she refuses to marry him, although social factors may affect her decision, they may not be present at all, and even when they are they are likely to be social rather than sociological.

The word 'social' will be reserved for those circumstances which, although they are a result of intercourse with other human beings, and may even contain sociological elements, comprise the situation in which the individual finds himself and makes it peculiar to him alone. For example, Byron's peerage was a sociological, his poverty and the sinister events in his family history, as well as his mother's temperament, social factors in his personal situation.

There was also for him, as for other writers, another and highly important element, the literary tradition. Its importance has been emphasised by T. S. Eliot in his essay *Tradition and the Individual Talent*. This seems to bring in something which is neither social nor sociological. It is indeed included in the term 'culture' and for some purposes this may be the best way of treating it; for literature, however, its influence is so great that it seems better to distinguish it from contemporary factors, either social or cultural, and call it 'historical' or 'traditional'.

Brunetière, the French nineteenth-century critic, made a similar distinction between the social and historical; but in his work the term 'historical' has a rather different connotation. In the example he gives of social and historical influences in the France of Louis XIV, he regards the structure of French society as a social factor, whereas he calls the wars of the period 'historical'. The effect of the latter, however, did not arise from the past, but was another aspect of contemporary society. A true historical influence is one coming from some event in the past, using 'event' in its widest sense to cover books as well as battles. There is, for example, nothing in English history which has more significance for

English literature than the Norman Conquest; but at some moment it surely became an historical and ceased to be a sociological influence. It is not necessary to discuss the problem of whether an historical is logically distinct from a scientific or a sociological explanation, because of the two main theories of the origin of the European novel, one stresses the sociological, and the other the historical or traditional element in its development, and arrive at radically different conclusions about the role played by sociological factors.

The theory of the novel as a bourgeois creation assumes that literature is a response to a sociological fact, institution or pattern; a response that can admittedly only be made by exceptionally talented individuals; but give the existence of such people, everything in the form and content can be adequately explained by contemporary social conditions. The idea of the romance as source and origin of the novel produces a less simple picture, in which literature becomes more and society less important. It implies that both writers and readers are influenced not only by social conditions but also by the books they read. It emphasizes the influence of Virgil and other Latin poets on the romance and the continuing influence of romance itself, and thus brings in historical as well as social factors.

There are some forms of intellectual activity which have an autonomy of their own. The subject-matter itself largely shapes its development and makes it follow a predestined course. The most convinced adherent of the sociology of knowledge would agree that this is true of mathematics; the calculus could not have been invented before the idea of a variable had been worked out. A science fiction story might be written about some other planet on which algebra had been developed before arithmetic, but it is difficult to imagine that it could have happened on this one.

Is there any of the same kind of inevitability in literature? Most people would at once answer 'No'; but traces of future development can often be seen in existing forms, and in some instances the lines followed seem somehow natural or inevitable, for example that the short story should have everywhere preceded the long romance.

Vinaver has suggested that the modern novel really began in the *nouvelle* of the fifteenth century, which, although it did not possess the length which is an essential feature of the true novel, substituted characteristically modern narrative techniques for the medieval methods employed in the romance. To some extent, he attributes this change to the tendency for episodes to become detached from the long and loosely connected narratives of which they originally formed a part, and end as separate stories complete in themselves. He cites examples from the prose romances, and also the way in which one episode of the long book *Memoirs d'un homme de qualité* has become a separate book, *Manon Lescaut*. As far as this happens there seems to be a tendency within the original form to produce something different, quite apart from sociological and social influences.

None of these theories are without elements from the others; the middle-class theory postulates certain historical influences; the evolutionary theory includes the change in social conditions in the first half of the eighteenth century and Vinaver's theory clearly depends partly on past developments. They each, however, emphasize one particular factor more than the others, and the history of European fiction looks very different viewed from these divergent standpoints.

These are elaborate and carefully developed theories. Books of many kinds are often referred to as the first European novel without any theoretical basis. Chaucer's *Troylus and Cryseyde*, for example, although it is in verse, and the Spanish *Celestina*, although it is in dialogue, if not in dramatic form, have both been called the first European novel, as has the *Ruableib* a Latin romance written in Germany about the year A.D. 1030. The rogue tale, which first appeared in a coherent and literary version in *Lazarillo de Tormes* in Spain in 1554, has also been chosen as the progenitor of the European novel. The beginning of the novel might also be ascribed to the first half of the thirteenth century, when stories previously written in verse began to be related in prose. New theories of this kind appear as often as a forgotten book is rediscovered or a particular period more extensively studied.

As the theory of the middle-class novel is not only the most widely held but is also essentially sociology, it will be convenient to discuss it before other views, because if the account it gives is accurate there would be no need to consider any earlier type of fiction.

PART I

The Novel as a Literary Form

I

The Theory of the Middle-Class Novel

Madame de Staël, Hegel, Taine, Spengler, Leslie Stephen, all the Marxist critics, a number of nineteenth-century critics quite uninfluenced by Marx, and perhaps the majority of modern critics, regard the novel as a form of literature peculiar to modern Europe and quite distinct from earlier prose fiction. The idea was inspired by the change in prose fiction which took place at the end of the seventeenth and beginning of the eighteenth century, and the absence of the novel in classical literature.

There exist, however, many pieces of prose fiction written before the eighteenth century, and some of them seem very like novels, including one of the most famous works ever written, *Don Quixote*. What, then, do critics mean when they say that the novel as a literary form first appeared in the eighteenth century? The answer can best be seen in definitions and discussions of the novel. The *Oxford English Dictionary* defines it 'as a fictitious prose narrative of considerable length in which characters and acts representative of the real life of past and present times are portrayed in a plot of more or less complexity'.

Edmund Gosse, in the 1911 edition of the *Encyclopaedia Britannica*, described it as 'the name given in literature to a study of manners, founded on an observation of contemporary or recent life, in which the characters, the incidents and the intrigues are imaginary, and therefore new to the reader, but founded on those running parallel to real history'. He added that 'with the word "novel" is identified a certain adherence to the normal conditions of experience'. In the 1946 edition this was replaced by one sentence from the original article, slightly modified, 'a sustained story which is not historically true but might very easily be so'.

Leslie Stephen, in explaining his choice of *Tom Jones* as the first true novel, gives a similar picture, but adds to it another requirement, a coherent plot. According to this 'the story is no longer a mere series of adventures, such as that which happens to Crusoe or Gil Blas, connected by the fact that they belong to the same person, nor a prolonged religious or moral tract, showing how evil will be punished or virtue rewarded. It implies a dramatic situation which can be developed without being hampered by the necessities of such representation; and which can give full scope to a realistic portrait of nature as it is under all the familiar circumstances of time and place.'[1] Saintsbury laid less emphasis on plot, but as much on ordinary life; for him the novel dealt with 'ordinary life and incident, with character, with a great deal of introduced conversation, and—in story, in talk, in comment, and everywhere—with all sorts of miscellaneous matters.'[2]

Ian Watt, whose book appeared in 1957, continues in the same tradition:

> the actors in the plot and the scene of their actions have to be placed in a new literary perspective: the plot had to be acted out by particular people in particular circumstances, rather than, as had been common, in the past, by general human types against a background finally determined by the appropriate literary conventions.[3]

The term novel in all these statements is confined to what are usually called realistic novels. Realism is an ambiguous word because it seems to imply something about the nature of the cosmos as well as about the characteristics of a piece of literature. And even when, as applied to the novel, it is obviously used in its literary sense, it can mean three different things: first a story containing incidents which might actually have happened, whether they are cheerful or sad, heroic or sordid. In this sense Jane Austen's books are realistic. In another sense the adjective is confined to novels dealing with aspects of life which in some periods would have been considered unfit for literature, extreme

[1] Stephen, Leslie, *English Literature and Society in the Eighteenth Century*, 1906.
[2] Saintsbury, George, *The Peace of the Augustans*, 1916.
[3] Watt, Ian, *The Rise of the Novel*, 1957.

poverty, crime, abnormal sexual appetites or characters without either virtue or virtuous aspirations.

In its third sense, the one used by Auerbach, realism is taken to mean 'social criticism'. He suggests, using the Satyricon of Petronius as an example, that realism in classical literature was of a very limited kind because 'the existence of society poses no historic problems; it may at best pose a problem in ethics, but even the ethical question is more concerned with the individual members of society than with the social whole . . . consequently social criticism never leads to a definition of the social forces within society'.[4]

The demand that a novel should depict, far less define, social forces was never made until criticism was transformed by absorbing Hegelian philosophy or those parts of it relating to the arts. Can one apply this definition of realism to books written long before it was thought of? It could be said, of course, that it is a mark of genius to anticipate definitions and that all truly realistic novels are concerned with social forces, although their authors may not consciously understand this. What is certain, however, is that the early eighteenth century novel was, when it first appeared, considered to be different from romance because it was thought to give an accurate picture of contemporary manners, not because it dealt with the social whole. It seems better, therefore, to use realism in this chapter in its more primitive sense. It was used thus even by Taine, himself greatly influenced by Hegel, and also to some extent by Marx. In his *History of English Literature* Taine describes the eighteenth-century novel as:

> a new kind . . . suited to the time, the anti-romantic novel, the work and the reading of positive minds, observers and moralists not intended to exalt and amuse the imagination, like the novels of Spain and the Middle Ages, not to reproduce or embellish conversation like the novels of France and the seventeenth century, but to depict real life, to describe characters, to suggest plans of conduct, and judge motives of action.

And he goes on to talk of this 'severe emanation of the middle classes'.[5] Hazlitt had said much the same thing before, and many

---

[4] Auerbach, Eric, *Mimesis* (English translation), Princeton, 1953.
[5] Taine, Hippolyte, *History of English Literature* (translated by H. Van Laun), 1890.

writers were to say it after him. Indeed, it may be said to be the accepted theory of the novel elaborated but not changed in the last ninety-eight years. The novel is still held to be the emanation of the middle classes, although the description 'severe' may have been dropped.

V. S. Pritchett describes the eighteenth-century novel 'as a plea for the middle-class virtues at a time when the aristocracy had left the country for the court and had abandoned its responsibilities in order to milk the Exchequer'.[6] Ian Watt explains the appearance of the great French novelists in the nineteenth century by an analogy between the English and the French revolutions:

> The French revolution had placed the middle class in a position of social and literary power which their English counterparts had achieved exactly a century before in the Glorious Revolution of 1688. And if Balzac and Stendhal are greater figures in the tradition of the European novel than any English novelist of the eighteenth century, it is surely in part due to the historical advantages they enjoyed . . . because the social changes with which they were concerned had found much more dramatic expression than they had in England.[7]

The bourgeoisie, Richard Church tells us, he demanded a new art form after the revolution of 1688 because the old forms were associated with the old oppressive forces . . . the Catholic Church and the feudal system, the land-owning classes'.[8] Not all authorities are agreed on either the date or the characteristics of the new form of literature. Kettle puts the rise of the bourgeois and his novel considerably earlier:

> What made these novels possible was the new attitude to life brought about by the decay of feudal society. Nashe and Defoe, separated as they were by more than a century, are both bourgeois writers, anti-romantic in their attitude, inspired by the confidence, the optimism, the enterprise of the class which acquired its wealth and culture through commerce.[9]

Sorokin, in accordance with his general theory, regards the eighteenth-century novel as an expression of the culture or intel-

[6] Pritchett, V. S., *The Living Novel*, 1946.
[7] Watt, Ian, *op. cit.*
[8] Church, Richard, *The Growth of the English Novel*, 1951.
[9] Kettle, Arnold, *An Introduction to the English Novel*, 1951.

lectual climate of the age rather than as a reflection of social conditions, and finds in it much the same values as those discovered by English critics: 'The emergence and expansion of realistic-naturalistic literature implies a shift from heroes, heroism, idealisation; from the sublime, the elevated, the romantic, the noble and the above the average to the very average level of men and motivations, and events associated with them.'[10]

Even Tillyard, who did not accept the view that the eighteenth-century novel was a new form, attributed 'the limited innovations of eighteenth century prose fiction' mainly to 'the enlarged opportunities of the middle class.'[11]

This theory of the novel has the great merit of being definite where other theories connecting literature with social change are vague; in other words it is not 'empty', but has a 'content' which allows it to be tested and falsified. Falsification can never, of course, be of the decisive kind to which experimental science can attain; but if it can be shown that the social conditions supposed to have produced the new kind of fiction did not exist when it first appeared, and that the influence of earlier forms was important, its credibility would be as much diminished as the nature of literary and historical material permits.

The foundations of the theory are unsound because England in the first half of the eighteenth century was not at all like the country described in the quotations given above.

THE POLITICAL STRUCTURE

The middle class were not 'triumphant' in England in the period in which *Robinson Crusoe*, *Tom Jones*, and *Clarissa* were written. The revolution of 1688 was not a reaction against 'feudal society' which had disappeared in England long before. Nor was it a revolt against the lingering remains of the medieval system, against the past, or some concept of the past. It was the contention of the managers of this enterprise that it was James II who was attempting to subvert the ancient Constitution handed down by our forefathers. As Hoadley, the Whig Bishop of Bangor, used to remind his hearers when he preached on the days appointed for

[10] Sorokin, Peterim A., *Social and Cultural Dynamics*, Vol. 1, 'Fluctuations of Forms of Art', New York, 1937.
[11] Tillyard, E. M., *The Epic Strain in the English Novel*, 1958.

the remembrance of the execution of Charles I and of the restoration of his son: 'Providence has restored the ancient constitution in the Revolution in 1688.'[12] The precedents appealed to were medieval: they had to be, because only in the Middle Ages were English kings deposed, to be replaced by other kings. There was a sharp dispute between the two Houses of Parliament as to whether the fact that the throne had been declared vacant in 1399 after the deposition of Richard II, 'in a parallel case to our own', was a valid precedent or not. Indeed, the eighteenth-century theory of the balanced Constitution might be regarded as a reaction against the idea, then more modern, of a centralized autocratic monarchy, back towards feudalism, in the sense, of competing centres of authority.

The House of Commons was in no way specially representative of the middle class, and if it had been, though powerful, it was not yet predominant. The King and the House of Lords were even in constitutional theory still important, and in constitutional practice more important still. In the eighteenth-century theory of the Constitution none of its three bodies—King, Lords, Commons—should be more powerful than the others, and the predominance of the House of Commons was considered as great, though not so pressing, a danger as the tyranny of the King.

The idea of middle-class dominance runs directly counter both to contemporary opinion and to the views of modern authorities. The common phrase for the more conspicuous of the nobility was 'the great', which carries with it an implication of power, as well as of rank and wealth.

According to J. H. Plumb, 'social and political life was dominated by the aristocracy'.[13] He also discerns 'a general hardening of caste during Walpole's life'—that is from 1676 to 1745, covering the period in which *Robinson Crusoe*, *Pamela* and *Joseph Andrews* appeared. Habbakuk in his essay on the English nobility, in a book on European nobility in the eighteenth century, says: 'What distinguishes the eighteenth century is that, in their partnership with the crown, the magnates were more powerful than in previous periods.'[14]

[12] Hoadley, Benjamin, *Works*, 1773.
[13] Plumb, J. H., *Sir Robert Walpole*, Vol. 1, 1956.
[14] Habbakuk, H. J., 'The English Nobility in the Eighteenth Century' in *The European Nobility in the Eighteenth Century*, edited by Albert Goodwin, London, 1963.

In the political sphere, few would dispute this; indeed, if it is disputed, the struggle over the Reform Bill of 1832 becomes incomprehensible. The House of Commons was already the more important of the two branches of the legislature. Lord Bristol, when annoyed with his son for accepting a peerage, referred to the House of Lords as 'insignificant'. This was not true; the consent of the Lords was necessary for the passage of any legis-lation; they were the highest judicial tribunal in the land, and lay peers still took part in judicial decisions. The majority of the Cabinet were drawn from the House of Lords. The Prime Minister was usually in the House of Commons because it was one of his chief functions to manage that body; but the idea that he ought to be was far in the future. No merchant or manu-facturer became a member of the Cabinet in the first three-quarters of the century.

Even if Lord Bristol's remark had been accurate, it would not have circumscribed the power of great landowners as much as might be thought because of their influence on the choice of both borough and county members. This was by no means confined to those who owned rotten boroughs. A landowner had many ways of influencing the politics of his tenants and it was considered quite right that he should do so. He also frequently had a political hold over boroughs in his neighbourhood; sometimes through the power of 'a great man' to 'oblige' the voters, sometimes through hereditary attachments and sympathies, and sometimes simply because he could get his dependants and friends made freemen or buy some property which carried with it the right to vote.

The representatives of the middle class were not the most numerous members of the House of Commons. There was a solid block of country gentlemen who, as a class, were in some ways distinct from the aristocracy. On the whole less rich, they tended to be Tory if not Jacobite. There were also representatives of the City of London and of other commercial institutions. There were a great many sons of peers, both heirs and younger sons, as well as more distant relations, friends and protégés. It appears that towns which had previously been represented by local merchants or lawyers tended as the century continued more and more to choose these aristocratic candidates;[15] no doubt because

[15] Plumb, J. H., *op. cit.*

their 'influence' was useful both to the town and to the individual voter. Even in the right to vote, the middle class in the towns often came off worse than the working class. With the variegated franchise qualifications differed in every borough, although there was a uniform franchise in the counties. There were towns with manhood suffrage, towns in which the mayor and corporation elected the member and every variation in between, including places in which only a section of the working class could vote.[16] It was the complaint of the middle-class reformers of the latter part of the century that half the Members of Parliament were chosen from the 'lowest dregs of the population', and the main purpose of the Reform Bill of 1832 was to admit 'the great, educated, rich middle class' to the franchise from which they were then excluded.

All this was sanctioned by public opinion. No one thought our liberties, which so gloriously distinguished Great Britain from every other country in the world, were the result of popular movements. On the contrary, everyone knew they had been torn from the early kings by the 'iron barons', whose descendants, in rank if not in blood, were still their best defenders. Aristocratic interference in Parliamentary elections was at times resented, even from the beginning of the century, it was clean against the theory of the constitution, but it was also defended by impartial and serious writers. Paley, for example, said: 'If certain of the nobility hold the appointment of some part of the House of Commons, it serves to maintain the alliance between the two branches of the legislature, which no good citizen would wish to see severed.' It is true that his book, *Principles of Moral and Political Philosophy*, did not appear until late in the century—1785—but such views were as widely, or even more widely, held in the earlier part of the century. Paley was an eminently 'serious' character, an archdeacon, and far from being an uncritical admirer of aristocratic legislation; he was, for instance, in favour of the abolition of the game laws.

There were, of course, even at the beginning of the century interests and classes which, though less powerful than the aristocracy, had to be taken into account in the framing of policy and in the manipulation of the House of Commons. The City of Lon-

[16] Oldfield, T. H. B., *The Representative History of Great Britain*, 1816. Porritt, Edward, *The Unreformed House of Commons*, 1909.

don was, for instance, a factor in politics, but it had been important long before the eighteenth century. Mantoux, in his book on the industrial revolution,[17] points to the part played by the City of London in the revolution of 1688 as the beginning of the political movement which ended in the triumph of the middle class in 1832, but the City had played a similar part on many occasions in the middle ages. The City, in the modern sense, of the merchants and financiers of London, had always played a considerable part in politics.

ECONOMIC ACTIVITIES AND CLASS ATTITUDES

If the middle class were far from being in a position to dictate policy, they were not dominant even in economic activities except in the sense that the bulk of the work of trade and commerce was done by men who might be described as belonging to that station of life. But the importance of agriculture, the great wealth of the English aristocracy, their readiness to marry new fortunes, and their active participation in many kinds of economic activity prevented any neat division into a landowning nobility and a trading middle class.

Agriculture was still by far the most important industry. As late as the 1760s Arthur Young calculated that half the population was employed on the land, and to these must be added the inhabitants of the country towns, from small shopkeepers to lawyers, who were also dependent on it. One of the best indications of the importance of agriculture in economic life is that Great Britain was not only self-sufficient in cereals, but an exporter of grain. These exports rather more than doubled between 1700 and 1760, and England became for a time the major surplus area in western Europe.[18] Compared with this, exports of manufactured goods increased from only £4.75 millions in the years 1706–10 to £6.99 millions in the years 1740–50. The increase in agricultural exports were a reflection of the marked rise in agricultural output in the first half of the century. The effect on incomes derived from

[17] Mantoux, Paul, *The Industrial Revolution in the Eighteenth Century* (translated by M. Vernon), 1935.
[18] John, A. H., 'Aspects of English Economic Growth in the Eighteenth Century', *Economica*, May 1961.

land must have been to make them bigger, and the larger the amount of land owned, the larger the increase was likely to be.

There were, of course, far more landowners who might be described as occupying the middle station than there were 'grandees'. But country squires are not at all the kind of person meant by modern writers when they talk of the new middle class: indeed, they were not new and their attitude to life in general, and to politics in particular, is now supposed to be the exact opposite of that of the merchant and tradesman of the time, although later in the century Wyvil appears to have included them in 'the middling rank'. Great landowners were in this period extremely rich—richer it is believed than they had ever been before; and it is also thought that they increased their wealth throughout the century. Most of the really great fortunes came from owning land, not from commerce. In 1714 the Duke of Newcastle had a rent-roll of £30,000 a year, which would represent today at least £600,000. The Duke of Bedford was said to have been richer still. There were few fortunes made from trade which could match this, and when they existed their makers ceased to be regarded as what we should now call middle class. They married their daughters to peers, bought land, and usually adopted the manners and habits of the aristocracy.

This command of economic resources meant that aristocratic taste in architecture, painting and furniture dominated these arts and it also made the aristocracy an important source of capital investment. Nor did they confine themselves to the role of rentiers or even to marrying the heiresses of rich merchants, which English noblemen had always done and continued to do in the eighteenth century. The names of many London streets and squares perpetuate the names of their builders. Harley Street, Wimpole Street and Oxford Street remind us that they were developed by Robert Harley, Earl of Oxford. Cavendish Square was built by a consortium of six peers, including the Duke of Devonshire. The Dudleys had their own ironworks, as had Earl Gower in Shropshire. The first Duke of Chandos was notorious for his eager participation in all forms of economic activity from coal, copper and alum mines to glass works, a soap works and a distillery. Most of these commercial ventures he started after he had attained the highest rank in the English peerage. He was indeed considered a somewhat odd Duke. The part played by another eccentric Duke, the Duke of

Bridgewater, in the canal construction of the latter half of the century, is known to everyone. The College of Heralds announced as early as the reign of Charles II that 'if a gentleman be bound apprentice to a merchant or other trade, he hath not truely lost his degree of gentility'.

No English aristocrat disdained business either as an entrepreneur himself, as an investor or as a politician. The historian of the Bank of England said of Henry Pelham that 'his political record is inglorious but he was a good man of business and as a financier he took his opportunities',[19] a remark that could not have been made about an aristocratic statesman in any other European country. He earned this commendation mainly by his consolidation of the various forms of the National Debt and their conversion to a 3 per cent basis—the institution, in fact, of the famous Consols.

It is just because trade was not a class preserve but an interest of the whole nation that eighteenth-century political manifestoes have such a familiar ring:

> In this situation of affairs, we should be extremely wanting to ourselves, if we neglected to improve the favourable opportunity which this general tranquillity gives us, of extending our Commerce upon which the riches and grandeur of this nation chiefly depend. It is very obvious that nothing would more conduce to the obtaining so publick a good, than to make the exportation of our own manufactures, and the importation of the commodities used in the manufacturing of them as practicable and easy as may be; by this means, the balance of trade may be preserved in our favour, our navigation increased, and greater numbers of our poor employed.

Thus Sir Robert Walpole in 1722.

Nor was this attitude to trade new: even in the Middle Ages trade held a substantial place in the esteem of Englishmen. Medieval magnates engaged in it themselves, as did at least one king, Edward IV. This esteem was, if anything, increased during the sixteenth and seventeenth centuries. The systematic consideration of economic matters was, however, greatly extended in the last quarter of the seventeenth century. Founded on the lively interest which all classes took in trade and finance, it was partly inspired by the scientific triumphs of the age. Sir Dudley North,

---

[19] Chapham, J., *The Bank of England*, 1944.

one of its exponents, attributed it to the influence of Déscartes' 'excellent *Dessertion de Methodo*, so much approved and accepted in our age'.[20] But whatever the cause, there was much writing about economic and financial questions during the lifetime of Defoe, Richardson and Fielding. This might have inspired a new form of literature; writers might have thought that a story, an allegory, or a parable would be the best way of recommending their own views. But although they might have, in fact in none of their novels do they deal with any aspect of trade, banking or commerce considered as an economic, social or moral problem. Amelia's husband was imprisoned for debt because his sister-in-law had fostered a quarrel between her mother and his wife and because he was extravagant and careless, not because he was a bankrupt merchant. Defoe's Colonel Jacques and Moll Flanders are not commercial swindlers but ordinary thieves, and from merely reading Richardson one would think that he had never heard of the balance of trade, the Bank of England or the new insurance. Peregrine Pickle's father was originally in trade and his grandfather had been Lord Mayor; but except for the use of commercial terms as a comic device in his letter proposing marriage, his business experience plays no part in the story and he had retired before it opens.

These arguments against the novel as a peculiarly middle-class product could be countered either by saying that the whole of England became middle class after the revolution of 1688, or by suggesting that although the middle class was not yet dominant, literature reveals the future, and that the novel was celebrating the coming rather than the actual triumph of the class which created it.

Some historians and literary critics maintain that there was no aristocracy, that the nobility were simply 'a richer middle class' because most of their titles dated only from Elizabeth at the earliest. This is to take a purely heraldic attitude to the concept of aristocracy, and makes it useless for sociological purposes. Moreover, it would seem to make Elizabethan England even more middle class than Georgian England.

Whatever may be thought as to the prophetic power of literature, no one could have guessed from the novels of the period that trade was going to become a more important source of

[20] North, Dudley, *Discourses on Trade*, 1691.

wealth than land, because there is no hint in them of the technological development which were to produce the change. This
is not surprising because, with the exception of the beginnings
of modern banking and insurance, neither of which figure in
any novel, these developments took place mainly after 1760.
Any contention that the novelists wrote about the middle class
because they realized that this class would dominate politics in
the next century must credit them with some mystical apprehen-
sion of the future not gained by knowledge of the present.
Writers may possess this power, but it is certainly not obvious in
eighteenth-century novels, not even in those of Defoe, although
in his other writings he did anticipate some institutions which
were to be subsequently established.

It does not follow, of course, that because the middle class
were not dominant either in politics or even in economics they
might not have created or inspired a new literary form. There is
no necessary correlation between political power and artistic
achievement, economic dominance and innovations in literature.
The statement that a book is aristocratic or middle class may mean
either that the author was himself an aristocrat or a bourgeois, or
that the book was intended for a particular audience, or that it
displays a class psychology or attitude.

In order to prove that any book is the creation of a particular
class, the first essential would be to show that it has all these characteristics. There are such books: the Japanese *Tale of Genji* is an
aristocratic novel in all three senses; so perhaps is Malory's
Morte d'Arthur; but none of the early examples of the English
novel are middle class to this extent.

THE AUTHORS AND THEIR AUDIENCE

Defoe

From constant references by literary critics to the optimism of a
rising middle class and Puritan commercial morality, it might be
supposed that Defoe was the pattern of a successful and upright
businessman. In reality, not only was he a failure in business, but
his life was so unusual as to make it impossible to regard him as
representative of any class.

Daniel Defoe, born in 1660 or 1661, was the son of a London
butcher. His father, whose name was not Defoe but Foe, was a

Presbyterian, and Daniel received a good education at a dissenting academy. These academies frequently gave a better education than the established grammar schools.

He went into business, but was unsuccessful; his first considerable work, the *Essay upon Projects*, appeared shortly after his bankruptcy. In this, together with other reforms, he proposed that of the bankruptcy laws. He was a strong Whig. He himself said he had taken part in Monmouth's rebellion and he certainly joined the army of William of Orange as a volunteer in 1688. He remained a devoted supporter of the Dutch King and among his pamphlets on economic and political subjects is a poem in William's defence, *The True-born Englishman*, which secured a considerable success. He also became secretary to a factory making pantiles and seems again to have been prosperous. This prosperity, however, was interrupted by an attack on the High Church party. Having annoyed the Dissenters by publishing a pamphlet against occasional conformity—that is, occasional attendance by Nonconformists at Anglican services to comply with the law—he produced another entitled *The Shortest Way with Dissenters*, purporting to be written by an extreme High-Churchman, ridiculing the High Church animosity towards Dissenters by exaggerating it. Unfortunately for Defoe, he did this so brilliantly that it was taken to be genuine, even by some of those whose views were satirized. This resulted in Defoe's arrest on a charge of libelling the Church of England. He was convicted, fined, sentenced to stand in the pillory three times, to be detained during Her Majesty's pleasure, and find securities for good behaviour during seven years. Although when in the pillory he was pelted with flowers, not rotten eggs, and loudly applauded by the mob, he disappeared into Newgate prison.

Up to this date, although his life had been full of ups and downs, it had been, except perhaps for some possible lapses from the path of strict commercial rectitude, plain and straightforward; but from now on it becomes more and more peculiar and devious. His fine was paid by Harley, then Secretary of State, and the Queen herself sent money to his wife and children. From then on Defoe acted as a sort of Government agent. He supported Government measures in his weekly paper the *Review*, sent reports on conditions and opinions in various parts of England to Harley, and went on a mission to Scotland during the negotiations about the Union, all the time denying that he had any connection with, or received any money from the Government. Harley had started as a Whig, but was now the head of a Government composed entirely of Tories and was, although Defoe did not know this, corresponding with the exiled court at St. Germain. It is possible to excuse and perhaps to justify Defoe's conduct, even without pleading the necessity of feeding his wife and children. Harley was a moderate man; the union with Scotland was plainly to the advantage of both countries; Defoe's activities probably substantially contributed to improving Government policy. It is perhaps more difficult to approve his continuance of these activities under the Whigs after Harley's fall, and after he himself had again been in prison; but he was essentially a Whig. He did his best to help Harley when he was impeached, by publishing an account and vindication of his conduct while in office—anonymously, of course: otherwise his support would have done little good. But Defoe soon sank to a lower rank even among secret agents; he pretended to be a Jacobite in order to 'take the sting', as he phrased it, out of first Dormer's Jacobite *News Letter* and then of *Mist's Journal.* It is hardly surprising that his contemporaries thought very badly of Defoe, although it is not difficult to understand how he had got himself into this equivocal situation. It was only after this adventure that he began writing autobiographies of shipwrecked mariners and criminals. His experience of writing as a Jacobite must have stimulated his dramatic faculties and helps to explain the extraordinary authenticity with which he managed to invest his fiction; so great was this that the *Apparition of Mrs. Veal*, a piece of straight reporting, was taken to be an invented tale until the beginning of the twentieth century, and Chatham quoted the *Memoirs of a Cavalier* as real history. When Defoe found himself debarred from both business and politics it is not surprising that he turned to humbler forms of writing. *Robinson Crusoe, Moll Flanders* and his other fictional works were not presented to the public as fiction but as authentic biography. In the Preface to *Robinson Crusoe*, Defoe represented himself to be not the author but the editor only, and stated that he believed 'the thing to be a just history of fact; neither is there any appearance of fiction in it'. Even after *Robinson Crusoe* had become famous and Defoe had been forced to admit that the story was not literally true, he followed the same formula in his last novel, *Roxana*, which, he said, was 'not a story but a history' and 'was laid of truth of fact'. This has been attributed to a Puritan disapproval of fiction which Defoe more than once expressed, but it also seems probable that the audience he was writing for wanted to read true not fictitious narratives. After all, even today there would be a much greater sale for the memoirs of a real courtesan than for a story about an invented one. The association of Defoe and the novel in general with the middle class, and the widespread belief that the working class were far less literate than they appear to have been in reality, probably gives many people a misleading impression that he wrote for sober tradesmen and respectable clerks. Sutherland, however, in his *Life of Defoe* says: 'The class to which Defoe addressed his *Robinson Crusoe* was the class that read *Mist's Journal*—the small shopkeepers and artisans, the publican, footmen and servant wenches, the soldiers and sailors, those who could read but had neither the time nor the inclination to read much', and he quotes a contemporary sneer: 'There is not an old woman that can go the price of it but buys the *Life and Adventures of Robinson Crusoe* and leaves it, as a legacy, with *The Pilgrim's Progress, The Practice of Piety* and *God's Revenge Against Murder*, to her posterity.'[21] Everyone read *Robinson Crusoe*, including Pope and Swift, who always expressed contempt for its author. But the contemporary view of the audience for Defoe's other novels is given in an epigram:

> Down in the kitchen, honest Dick and Doll
> Are studying Colonel Jack and Flanders Moll

Richardson

Richardson was a prosperous tradesman and thus fits the middle-class theory, but he, too, seems to have been led to writing *Pamela* by experiences peculiar to himself rather than by those he shared with his class or his period. There can have been few men at any time who when schoolboys composed love letters for illiterate girls. This activity, although separated by many years from his first novel, is linked to it because *Pamela* is a novel in letters, most of them written by Pamela herself. As Defoe's novels had emerged from his journalistic activities by what, three hundred years later, seems a natural process, so Richardson's arose from the union of

[21] Gildon, Charles, *Life and Strange, Surprising Adventures of D . . . . . . D . . . . . ,* 1719.

his temperament, his strong ethical views and a form of literature known to historians as the conduct book'. This was an elaborate kind of etiquette book which, with other information, gave model letters which could be adapted by the reader to his own needs. Some of them consisted entirely of letters: among the titles are *Domestic Duties, The Accomplished Woman, The Lover's Secretary—being a collection of billet-doux; Familiar Letters of Love and Gallantry* and *The Perfect Serving Maid.* All aspects of life were obviously catered for. These titles belong to the seventeenth century, but in Mrs. Rowe's *Letters Moral and Entertaining*—which appeared in 1729, 1731 and 1733—the letters are not only concerned with ordinary problems such as how to ask someone to a meal, propose marriage or request payment of a bill, but deal with more dramatic situations such as that of the girl who has retired to the country to conquer 'an unhappy passion', and the rake who has been reformed by a good and religious woman.

The idea that occurred to two booksellers of producing 'a little book of Familiar Letters on the useful concerns in common life' was thus by no means an original one, but the fact that they decided to ask Richardson to write it had momentous consequences for the development of the novel. Although not a professional writer, but a printer of such standing and responsibility that he printed the *Journals of the House of Commons,* Richardson had already produced a version of Aesop's *Fables* and written what he described as 'little thing of the pamphlet kind', including, it is believed, *The Apprentice's Vade Mecum.* The projected series of letters was written and published at the price of two shillings and sixpence. It came out after *Pamela,* and Richardson's biographers say he was by then ashamed of such a humdrum production. Richardson himself has described how *Pamela* developed out of the booksellers' idea:

Two booksellers, my particular friends, entreated me to write for them a little volume of Letters, in a common style, on such subjects as might be of use to those country readers, who were unable to indite for themselves. Will it be any harm, said I, in a piece you want to be written so low, if we should instruct them how they should think and act in common cases, as well as indite? They were the more urgent with me to begin the little volume for this hint. I set about it; and, in the progress of it, writing two or three letters to instruct handsome girls, who were obliged to go out to service, as we phrase it, how to avoid the snares that might be laid against their virtue, . . . hence sprung *Pamela*.[22]

Mrs. Barbauld, Richardson's first biographer, said that he invented the epistolary novel. This is not strictly true. Books of letters which told a story, as well as complete letters writers, had been published, the famous *Letters of a Portuguese Nun* among them, and these were immensely popular. It now seems to have been proved that the *Letters* are fiction, but even if they had been genuine they would still have presented a story which might well have suggested a plot to any novelist. *Love Letters Between a Nobleman and his Sister* appeared in 1734: although the letters were invented, the story on which they were based was real and concerned the love affair of Monmouth's Lord Grey and his sister-in-law. A real novel in letters appeared in 1731, *Lettres de la Marquise*, by Crébillon fils. Richardson apparently could not read French and he was, moreover, an extremely respectable man, while Crébillon is not a respectable writer. It does not, however, seem necessary that Richardson should actually have read the book: if someone had told him about it, it might have been sufficient to have suggested to him that fictitious letters could depict virtue as well as vice; although the idea might well have come to him, as he said it did, only when he started to compose his model letters. His narrative technique—the exhaustive analysis, the accumulation of detail—certainly owed nothing to any previous writer.

Fielding

Richardson was middle class by origin and station. Fielding, who used the double-headed eagles of the Hapsburgs (from whom his family were then supposed to be descended) on his signet ring, would hardly have cared to have been described as bourgeois and he constantly complained of those authors who tried to describe 'high life' without ever having seen it. He certainly, however, did not regard himself as one of the 'great' and he seems to have considered that he occupied a middle station. He was in the eyes of others a 'poor relation' and this explains the sharpness of the remarks made about him by his aristocratic

[22] Barbauld, Ann Letitia, *Correspondence of Samuel Richardson With An Introductory Memoir*, 1804.

connections, remarks which have shocked many historians since. When he wrote *Joseph Andrews* he was already a professional writer and, as everyone knows, the book started as a parody of *Pamela*. If the idea that Richardson incarnated the middle-class point of view is taken seriously, it must seem unlikely that this piece of mockery was meant for the same audience. Yet there is no evidence that, for fiction at least, the book market was divided by social classes at all. Chesterfield, Lady Mary Montagu and Horace Walpole read Richardson as avidly, though not so uncritically, as the villagers who, according to tradition, rung the church bells when Pamela was safely married.

When Fielding wrote *Tom Jones* he was no longer dependent solely on his writings for a living, although his earnings as a Bow Street magistrate could well bear supplementing. But however welcome the £700 he received for the copyright may have been, he meant both to inaugurate a 'new province of writing', as he himself said, and to show that prose fiction could have qualities as great as that most revered of all literary forms, the epic in verse. He was writing for educated men and connoisseurs of literature, as the dedication to Lyttleton shows. Fielding is said to have read it to Pitt and Lyttleton before it was published, and 'the princely benefactions' of the Duke of Bedford are referred to in the dedication. The gibes of Fielding's enemies were directed against this aristocratic patronage and were thus the exact opposite of those thrown at Defoe. Lyttelton was said to 'have puffed it so successfully about court, among placemen and pensioners that . . . they thought it incumbent upon them to echo it about the coffee houses'.[23] Lyttelton came into the category of the 'great' and Pitt, paymaster-general at the time, would also have been included.

Some historians of literature have found the first English novel in Bunyan's *Life and Death of Mr. Badman* instead of in *Robinson Crusoe* or *Pamela*. Bunyan's original readers might be described as middle class in a sense, but they were the humbler members and had little to be 'triumphant' or optimistic about.

The Class Background of the Novels

The English novel was indeed often about those in the 'middle

[23] *Old England*, May 27th, 1749.

station'; although, except for Robinson Crusoe, Defoe's characters are criminals or social outcasts of one kind or another. Pamela was a servant. *Clarissa* is set in the homes of country squires and men of fashion; although it is true that contemporary critics declared that Richardson had transferred the manners of his own class to the houses of the gentry. The main characters in *Tom Jones* and *Amelia* belong to the country gentry. *Tom Jones* embraces almost every section of eighteenth-century society except the successful or unsuccessful businessman, and this is the more remarkable because one of the models for Allworthy is said to have been Ralph Allen, who actually was a successful merchant.

Nor is it certain that the social milieu, of those stories, which dealt with those of 'middling' rank, come from any preoccupation with the fortunes of the middle classes or any particular interest in them. Huet, the erudite Bishop of Avranches, in his book on the origin of romance,[24] had said that the story is more acceptable in those romances in which 'the characters are in a mediocre condition, as in comic romances, than in the grand romances in which princes and conquerors are the actors . . . because it is not probable that great events should remain hidden from the world and neglected by historians, and probability, which is not always found in history, is essential to romance'. This reason may seem rather odd to us, but it was probably calculated to appeal to writers living in the atmosphere which made Defoe, for instance, pretend that his novels were real biographies. No one would suggest that English writers carefully read Huet, although he was twice translated. He meant that novels should not deal with kings, princes or others possessed of political power, but his remarks would have inevitably suggested to an English reader that romances should be about the middle class rather than the aristocracy. It is most unlikely that the English novelists wrote about this class because of Huet's theory, but they may have been inspired by similar ideas. There would have been something of the same difficulty in producing a novel about the aristocracy in England as there would have been in writing a novel about kings and princes in France, because the main characters would inevitably have been concerned in politics.

---

[24] Huet Pierre—Daniel, Bishop of Avranches, *Traité de l'origine des romans*, 1670, first published as an introduction to Madame de la Fayette's *Zaïde*.

THE EIGHTEENTH-CENTURY VIEW OF THE SOCIAL STRUCTURE

In spite of the differences in birth between the authors of the early novels, they might all express a bourgeois or middle-class ethos or attitude to life. This could not, however, have been an assertion of consciously held values peculiar to a particular class, because the modern idea of class, that of 'a number of individuals possessed of common attributes and grouped under a common or class name', does not seem to have existed in the eighteenth century. This may seem paradoxical in view of the part played by rank in every aspect of eighteenth-century life, but rank and class are not interchangeable words. Probably no one now understands how the divisions of society were then conceived, but it was certainly not in terms of three simple classes—upper, middle and lower. The first example of the word class linked with 'lower' given by the *Oxford Dictionary* is dated 1772, with 'middle' 1812, although Gisbourne's *Inquiry into the Duties of Men in the Higher and Middle Classes* was published in 1794. Johnson's *Dictionary* gives one meaning of class as 'A rank or order of persons,' but the example of its use in this sense does not relate to social class: 'Segrais has distinguished the readers of poetry according to their capacity into three classes.' The words used to express the divisions of society were rank, order, state or station, generally the two latter. Robinson Crusoe's father praised 'the middling station of life', not the middle class.

Even order does not exactly correspond with class, and station still less. A station conflict or a station war is a nonsense phrase. An essential element in the idea of class is that it is somehow an ineradicable part of the psychological make-up of its individual members and also something shared with others. Station, on the other hand, carries none of these overtones; especially where, as in eighteenth-century England, no one thought it was either necessary or particularly virtuous for a man to remain in the station in which he was born. The catechism of the Church of England refers to 'that state of life to which it *shall* please God to call me', not to that state which it *has* pleased God to call me. The example of the use of the word 'station' given in Johnson's *Dictionary* does not relate to social divisions any more than the example under class; it is from Dryden: 'I can be contented with a humble station in the temple of virtue.'

Rank has more of the connotations of class, especially when used with 'middling', as it was by Hume among others, but the two words are not synonymous. It is possible to change one's rank more completely than one's class: a self-made peer remains working class in origin, whereas in rank he is simply a peer. Perhaps the highest and the lowest ranks were conceived as more like classes, but even these do not seem to correspond exactly with the modern idea.

The English aristocracy was not a class in the same sense in which the nobility of every other European country then was. Such rights and privileges as noblemen possessed were concentrated on the actual holders of the title. The top people were peers, rich peers that is, and were known as 'the great'. The word itself conveys that it was not only the wealth and prestige, but the responsibility which high rank and great possessions brought with them, that made them great.

The prestige did not necessarily extend to their near, much less to their distant, relations; although influence might, and in contemporary opinion ought to be, exerted on their behalf by their great connections. An eighteenth-century earl thus occupied a wholly different station in life from his younger brother; but it would be difficult to maintain that they belonged to different classes. The younger brother of a country squire might easily become a merchant and the two brothers would then occupy a different station, but again it seems difficult to separate them into different classes. Macaulay remarked that it must seem strange that the enemies of Charles Montagu called him an upstart 'when he sprang from a family as old as the Conquest . . . was in the succession to an earldom . . . was cousin to three earls',[25] and explained it by saying that: 'He was the younger son of a younger brother; and that phrase from the time of Shakespeare and Raleigh, and perhaps before their time, had been proverbially used to designate a person so poor as to be broken to the most abject servitude or ready for the most desperate adventure.' This is written with all Macaulay's verve and energy and may be too strong, but the distinction which contemporary opinion made between the earl and his brother is illustrated by the end of *The*

[25] Macaulay, Thomas Babington, *History of England*, London, 1848–55.

Beaux' Stratagem. When Aimwell, who has pretended to be a lord, overcome by true love confesses: 'I am no Lord, but a poor needy man, come with a mean, a scandalous design to prey upon your fortune', the lady not unnaturally asks who he is, and he replies, 'Brother to the man whose title I usurped but a stranger to his honour or his fortune.' *The Beaux' Stratagem* first appeared in 1707; surely a viscount's brother in 1807 would not have described himself in this way.

In *The Way To Keep Him* (1760) a baronet is described as 'a younger brother, who lived a middling life, comes to a title and an estate on the death of a consumptive baronet; marries a woman of quality, and now carries the primitive ideas of a narrow education into high life'. These are quotations from plays, not descriptions of fact, and their authors were perhaps not much acquainted with viscounts or even baronets; but Lord Chesterfield and his cousin, whose son Philip Stanhope eventually succeeded to the earldom, took a somewhat similar view. Chesterfield had to break to his cousin that his brother had just married a woman, young enough to have many children and that Philip's chances of inheriting were much reduced. The cousin replied that no doubt the marriage was

> part of God's plan: He will support us to bear it, as we ought, and instead of repining, direct us to look on the comfortable side, that your Lordship will continue your tenderness and affection for our boy, and will supply his education which our little knowledge of the world could not plan, nor our narrow circumstances execute to any tolerable purpose.

Chesterfield answered this by a letter in which the following passage occurs:

> Happiness must be internal, and not depend upon the outward accidents of fortune; and providence has kindly distributed it equally among the poor as among the rich and perhaps more liberally among the former. Sturdy knows no difference, and it may be never will; for if he should have deserved a large fortune, he will know how to be content, and consequently happy with a small one.[26]

The distance between an earl and his relations has been greatly

[26] Philip Dormer-Stanhope, 4th Earl of Chesterfield, *Letters*, edited by Bonamy Dobrée, 1932.

diminished by the lessening importance of rank; but even before this modern tendency, an insistence on descent had begun to replace the eighteenth-century exclusive reverence for rank. Chesterfield said in a letter to his heir, 'You are, it is true, of a noble family, but whether a very ancient one or not I neither know nor care nor need you.'[27] There were probably few earls, however democratic, who would have used exactly these words in the first quarter of the nineteenth century.

How individual the idea of 'station' was can be seen by Bolingbroke's use of it when we should use 'position': 'On those occasions where his (Harley's) station obliged him to speak of business.'[28] Chesterfield also must have meant position rather than class when he said of Walpole that he had a 'coarse, strong wit, which he was too free with for a man of his station, as it is always inconsistent with dignity'.[29] There is no reason to suppose that Chesterfield would have thought that 'dignity' was necessary in a man of Walpole's social class, which was that of a country gentleman.

Alderman Beckford, in 1761, made a sharp attack on the nobility which has been quoted as an example of class antagonism. His actual words were: 'As to your nobility, about two hundred men of quality, what are they to the body of the nation?'[30] It is noteworthy that he said two hundred men, not two hundred families, the phrase one would have expected if he was thinking in modern class terms. The number specified seems to indicate that he was referring to actual peers; there must have been far more than two hundred men in what we should call the upper class, while the members of the House of Lords averaged round about two hundred throughout the eighteenth century. This figure included twenty-six bishops, but Beckford may have thought of them also as men of quality. Moreover, by 1761 a new period had opened, in many ways different from the age of Richardson and Fielding.

The English aristocracy was an open class: anyone who distinguished himself in politics, the Army or the law could become a peer, provided he had sufficient income to support the dignity

---

[27] *Op. cit.*
[28] Bolingbroke, Letter to Sir William Windham, *Works,* 1716.
[29] Chesterfield, Earl of, *Characters of Eminent Persons of His Own Times,* 1777.
[30] Quoted in Christie, Ian, *Wilkes, Wyvil and Reform,* 1952.

40

of his title, or was distinguished enough to be given the income as well. To own really large tracts of the countryside almost gave a man a right to a peerage and, as land could be bought, the House of Lords might also be said to be open to wealth. Men actually in trade were not ennobled, but the sons of merchants and tradesmen were quite often elevated to the House of Lords. One of the main arguments used against the Peerage Bill of 1719, which sought to limit the King's right to make peers, was that 'the shutting up of the door of the House of Lords in the manner talked of cannot but prove a great discouragement to virtuous actions, to learning and industry'. This was urged by Walpole and Steele both in pamphlets and in their speeches opposing the Bill in the House of Commons.

Possibly the lowest rank, the poor, the labouring population, the mob, was conceived of as being more of what we now call a class. It is difficult to tell, because all these words were used in varying senses; sometimes the word 'poor' means, as Mandeville explained, 'the labouring poor who are forced to get their daily bread by their daily labour',[31] while Doctor Johnson distinguished between the poor and the lower orders: 'The condition of the lower orders, the poor especially, is the true mark of national discrimination.' In this condition of life there were such innumerable gradations and differences that it is difficult even for an historian to generalize about them—how much more difficult for anyone living at the time. There was the London mob, always ready to riot, to throw dead cats and rotten eggs and to snatch the wigs from the heads of unpopular peers. There were the respectable artisans, the footmen of 'the great', generally disreputable according to contemporary authors, the village labourer, the servants of the middle class. There is no evidence that these groups considered themselves to belong to one class; indeed, it is most unlikely that they did, for there was nothing to unite them; their interests were not identical and there was no theory to persuade them that they were.

Above all, the expression 'the middling rank or station' did not convey the idea of a class bound together by a similar origin or education, which in relation to the middle class, is a nineteenth-century invention. The meaning of class, station or rank is largely

[31] Mandeville Bernard, 'An Essay on Charity and Charity Schools' in *The Fable of the Bees*, edited by F. B. Haye, 1924.

determined by the purpose for which the concept is used. Since the French Revolution class has been thought of mainly in terms of politics. When thinking of politics in the eighteenth century, either in theory or in practice, people thought of them not in terms of classes but of interests. Interests and classes are not synonymous, although some literary critics seem to think they are. A book on comedy and society from Congreve to Fielding, for example, quotes Swift as evidence for a class conflict between the middle class, represented by the merchants, and the aristocracy drawing their wealth from the land. The quotation runs as follows: 'I have ever abominated the scheme of politics (now about thirty years old) of setting up a moneyed interest in opposition to the landed.' That the moneyed interest here means not trade but finance can be seen from Bolingbroke's *Letters to Sir William Wyndham*: 'The proprietor of the land, and the merchant who brought riches home by the returns of foreign trade, had during two wars borne the whole immense load of the national expenses; while the lender of money, who added nothing to the common stock, throve by the public calamity, and contributed not a mite to the public charge.' He meant by lenders of money 'the Bank, the East India Company, the moneyed interests', and this accords with Swift, who could not possibly have believed that trade had only become important in English politics 'in the last thirty years'. In 1721, however, when the letter was written, the Bank of England, founded in 1694, was almost thirty years old; or perhaps Swift was referring to the great developments of banking itself which took place after the revolution of 1688.

The Bank was essentially a Whig creation, and had been opposed by the Tories as being only suitable for a republican state because only the Netherlands and Genoa had at that time a central bank, and as an attempt to set up a moneyed interest with Whig sympathies to counterbalance the Tory country gentlemen. Swift's remarks are really an example of party propaganda, not evidence of class conflict. The letter seems originally to have been intended for publication as a pamphlet, which strengthens the view that it is a piece of Tory economics.

Moreover, Swift meant by 'setting up' not supporting an interest which already existed but creating a new one, as can be seen from his *History of the Four Last Years of the Queen*, where he says of the introduction of the National Debt:

Artful men in office and credit began to consider what use it might be applied to; and some found it was likely to prove the most fruitful seminary, not only to establish a faction they intended to set up for their own support; but likewise to raise vast wealth for themselves in particular, who were to be the managers and directors of it . . . Thus a new estate and property sprang up in the hands of mortgagees.

Trading and financial interests cannot be simply lumped together and called 'new men, the middle class or the merchants' and opposed to the landed interest. There was a certain jealousy between the country gentlemen and the merchants and financiers who made up the City interest, but there was also jealousy and distrust of finance among traders—a distrust which can sometimes still be seen today. One of the greatest of the merchants, Sir Dudley North, was one of the most active opponents of the new banking, and the Bill establishing the Bank of England was amended to forbid it trading in commodities at the instance of some of the London merchants. Sir Dudley North is an example of how misleading generalizations about class, trade and political attitudes can be. The son of the fourth Lord North, he was 'bound apprentice' to a Turkey merchant, was highly successful in business and was a Jacobite in politics as well as an opponent of the new finance.

Many people who occupied very different stations in life are included in terms such as the middle class or the trading interest. There were merchants in London and Bristol so rich that they rivalled 'the great' themselves, and small shopkeepers so poor that they were only separated from the labouring classes because they owned some property.

Once it is realized that society was conceived of as divided into interests rather than classes, much that would be incomprehensible if considered on a class basis becomes intelligible. For instance, if merchants and financiers are thought of as exhibiting a specifically middle-class psychology, how is one to assess the attitude of a younger son of a country squire or of a peer who went into business? But if 'class' is replaced by 'interest' it is clear that while such a man would be unlikely to acquire a psychology exactly like that of a son of a merchant or a man who had risen from the lowest class, he would probably soon develop a lively sense of the interests of trade and finance.

Another mistake is to suppose that men in the early eighteenth century regarded the relations between the landed and the trading classes as either a political or a social problem. They were not thinking about conflicts between the middle class and aristocracy but about preserving the Constitution, winning wars and checking any designs of the King to extend his authority beyond its proper sphere. Such attacks as were made on peers as a body were inspired by the idea that they supported the interest of the 'Court' against the country. Quarrels between country gentlemen and merchants and satiric portraits of noblemen occur in novels and plays of the time, but these are not attempts to mirror social problems; the whole idea of a problem in this sense was quite foreign to the age. The arrogant or frivolous peer was not a piece of propaganda against the peerage as an institution; he was depicted 'as being very far from what an English nobleman ought to be'. The quarrels between country gentlemen and merchants were used for their comic possibilities. If the writers of the time had thought that they were discussing political or social problems they would have said so. No one objected to the didactic. This can be clearly seen in their treatment of what was a social problem in a real, though not in a modern sense, the question of what a Christian or even a sensible man should do if challenged to fight a duel.

Neither assertions about the happiness of the middle station nor equalitarian sentiment contradicts this. It is often said that the remarks of Robinson Crusoe's father about the happiness of the middle station are evidence of a new self-confidence in the middle classes. Bishop Hoadley also said in his sermon on the extremes of riches and poverty that 'if a wise man were to choose for himself with regard to true happiness, and the interests of virtue and religion, he would certainly choose the middle condition'. Hoadley himself did his best to escape from the middle condition, but this only makes his remark more obviously a current platitude. In 1724 it may well have seemed to many people a sober statement of fact, as it probably did to Defoe in 1719. The highest rank had, only at the turn of the century, carried with it dangers which Defoe in 1719 and Hoadley in 1724 probably thought still existed—dangers of risking one's head in politics, political involvement being very difficult, if not impossible, for the great to avoid. A duke or an earl had in the reigns of William

III and Anne to decide whether the Hanoverian dynasty would succeed to the throne as laid down in the Act of Settlement, or whether James Stuart would regain his father's kingdom. Most of them thought it sufficiently uncertain to make it necessary to insure with both sides. A man in the middle station was not faced with the same dilemma; he would hardly be singled out for blame even if there were a Stuart restoration.

No doubt, even in the first half of the century, there were merchants who detested the aristocracy, peers who despised both merchants and country gentlemen, while some of the poor have hated the rich and some of the rich feared the poor in every period; but something more is required for the development of that kind of class loyalty which is likely to inspire forms of literature. It is possible to dislike earls without loving your fellow merchants, or to despise the middle class and your fellow peers as well. The nobility probably had more *esprit de corps* than any other class but party differences appear to have been much stronger than class allegiances, simply because politics were not dominated by the idea of class. How remote the whole conception was from early eighteenth-century politics can be seen in Sir William Temple's *Essay on Popular Discontents,* when he says:

> Another cause of distempers in states, and discontents under all governments, is the unequal condition that must necessarily fall to the share of so many and so different men that compose them. In great multitudes, few in comparison are born to great titles or great estates; few can be called to public charges and employments of dignity or power, and few by their industry arrive at great degrees of wealth and fortune.

It seems that he is going on to anticipate Marxist theories; but a later sentence shows how little he is really thinking about social classes. 'The common sort of people always find fault with the times, and some must always have reason; for the merchant gains by peace, the soldier by war, the shepherd by wet seasons and the ploughman by dry: when the town fills, the country grows empty; and while trade increases in one place it decays in another.'

Egalitarian sentiment was indeed common, but it was expressed as often by the great as by those of a middle station.

*Verses written on seeing a man with a heavy load and an
oak leaf in his hat on May 29th*

Poor fellow, what is it to you
Or King or Restoration
'Twill make no difference to you
Whoever rules the nation.

Still must thy back support the load,
Still bend thy back with toil,
Still must thou trudge the self-same road
While great ones share the spoil.

This little poem was written by Sir Charles Hanbury Williams,
who if not exactly one of the great was in the phrase of the time
'a man of fashion'.

No one could ridicule the pretensions of birth with a finer
irony than Lord Chesterfield; no one complained of the stupidity,
coarseness and frivolity of high society more continuously than
Lord Hervey. Swift wrote of the Earl of Sunderland:

> In his father's lifetime when he was a Member of the House of
> Commons, he would often among his familiar friends refuse the
> title of Lord; (as he has done to myself), swear that he would never
> be called otherwise than Charles Spencer and hope to see the day
> when there should not be a peer in England.

This is certainly quite untrue and even Swift said he had fallen
away from these republican principles, but it shows what views
could be attributed, with some plausibility, to the more enlightened members of the House of Lords. Chesterfield, Sunderland
and Hervey were Whigs, but a Tory Member of the House of
Commons said when someone was taunted with his low birth:
'Every man's honour is in his own hand. Origin is nothing. It
shall never have any weight with me.'[32] No sensible man valued
himself on his rank in case people should say that he had nothing
else 'to value himself on'. There were, of course, men who were
not sensible, like the proud Duke of Somerset, and the ideas of
the time gave them more latitude than did the ideas of the nineteenth century; but on the whole the more intelligent English
aristocrats were as fond as the French of ridiculing the artificial
conventions of society. The English nobility were, however,

---

[32] Napier Lewis, *The Structure of Politics at the Accession of George III*, 1928.

aware that the laws of nature had long been superseded by the laws of England, and the privileges and possessions which these laws gave them they were determined to stick to and, as regards possessions at least, to extend.

Little as 'the great' might be inclined to surrender their privileges, their attachment to liberty was genuine and most of them not only had no resentment against the self-made man, but were prepared to help him in the work of creation. There was no division between the old nobility, or what remained of it, and the new, as there was, for instance, in Spain.

Peers were not, as far as can be seen, unpopular. Lords were often depicted as wicked or at least dissipated, but only a rather limited rationalist psychology would make anyone think this necessarily a sign of dislike. If merchants or country gentlemen had felt any hostility towards the nobility as a class, it would surely have appeared in the pamphlets and debates on the Peerage Bill in 1719. The Bill, which would have limited the power of the Crown to create peers, was strongly attacked both in pamphlets and in the House of Commons. This attack was directed by the Opposition, animated by the same motives as oppositions usually are, but they must have thought the issue was one on which they could gain support. Steele in his pamphlet *The Plebian* did indeed argue that 'too great a power in the hands of the nobility had been the ruin of many free nations', and said that 'it is well known that the great business is always carried on by men created first in their own persons', and even added that the price that could be obtained for any property was much greater if there was no lord in the neighbourhood.[33] Addison said that he was at a loss as to what Steele meant by this last observation, and it is indeed far from clear.[34] In any case these statements were merely decorations. The main arguments used by Steele and Walpole, both in their pamphlets and in their speeches in the House, were that any Act limiting the number of peers would upset the balance of the Constitution by making it impossible for the King to overcome opposition in the House of Lords; and that it would shut the door of the peerage to families who might reasonably expect with luck and industry to acquire a title for themselves. Walpole did indeed say: 'The great unanimity with

[33] Steele, Richard, *The Plebian*, 1719.
[34] Addison, Joseph, *The Old Whig*, 1719.

which this Bill has passed the Lords ought to inspire some jealousy in the Commons, for whatever the Lords gain must be acquired at the expense of the Commons'; but this, because of the composition of the House of Commons, was a sign of jealousy between two competing institutions rather than between different classes.

The theory of the Constitution with three equal and separate powers—King, Lords and Commons—itself discouraged any class or section from organizing itself on a class basis as distinct from asserting its peculiar 'interest'. There were people who doubted the surpassing virtues of the balanced Constitution, as there are people today who doubt the advantages of universal suffrage; but it was generally accepted in the sense in which universal suffrage is at present. If anyone wants to attack a measure, institution or practice, he says it is undemocratic, and this is held to be damaging. In the eighteenth century he said it would tend to aggrandize one element of the Constitution at the expense of the others, as Walpole did in his speech against the Peerage Bill.

> The strongest argument, however, against the Bill is that it will not only be a discouragement to virtue and merit but would endanger our excellent Constitution; for as there is a due balance between the three branches of the legislature it will destroy that balance and consequently subvert the whole Constitution, by causing one of the three powers, which are now dependent on each other, to preponderate in the scale.

Addison attempted to defend the Bill on the grounds that it would preserve the balance by keeping men of large property in the House of Commons. No one deploys arguments in political controversy unless they appeal to generally held sentiments and convictions. Anyone, however, who really believed in the balance would hardly be inspired to make an appeal for organization on class lines.

This hierarchical society was no doubt supported and sustained by the religious philosophy which regarded the whole creation as a great chain of being, stretching from the humblest insect to God himself. While each rank was subordinated to the one above, no one and no thing existed merely for the sake of some other species,[35] but each had a place and purpose which only he could

[35] Lovejoy, Arthur O., *The Great Chain of Being*, Cambridge, Mass., 1942.

fill. This might be said to be the accepted background for those who thought about such things, but social subordination was usually defended on utilitarian grounds.

Bishop Hoadley in his sermon 'Of the True Uses of this World' said: 'The next thing to be considered is the true uses of the honours of this world. The whole end proposed in them, nay the very nature of the thing, being only to preserve and keep up such distinctions of order accorded the members of the same body, as seemed necessary for the better carrying forward the end of human society.'[36] Bishop Hoadley was a Whig, but Dr. Johnson, a Tory, explained his deference to rank in similar terms:

> Subordination is very necessary for society, and contentions for superiority very dangerous. Mankind, that is to say all civilised nations, have settled it upon a plain invariable principle . . . A man is born to hereditary rank; or his being appointed to certain offices gives him a certain rank. Subordination tends greatly to human happiness.[37]

Gisbourne said the same thing when the French Revolution seemed to have demonstrated that God did indeed disapprove of notions of equality.[38]

This utilitarian basis might make the social structure in some ways more vulnerable to criticism, but on the whole it probably tended to make it less so, especially as an awful example of what happened once the habit of subordination was broken could be seen in the dictatorship of Cromwell.

The atmosphere of the first half of the eighteenth century thus hardly seems likely to encourage the creation of a new literary form as a sort of class manifesto, or to make people think of the relationships between classes in terms of social 'problems'. In spite of this, if the novels had been full of the clash of interests in Parliament, at elections or in the City, or even if, as so often in the nineteenth-century novel, their plots had turned on the mortgage of some gentleman's estate to a merchant or moneylender, or on a love affair interrupted because the lovers came from different classes, it would be easier to think that the novel was inspired by the desire to dramatize or elucidate the class situation. It is,

---

[36] Hoadley, Benjamin, *op. cit.*

[37] Boswell, *Life of Johnson.*

[38] Gisborne Thomas, *Inquiry Into the Duties of Men in the Higher and Middle Classes of Society in Great Britain*, 1794.

however, just in the new form that merchants, moneylenders, representatives of the trading community, do not appear.

Pamela might, possibly, be said to deal with the relationships of classes, concerning as it does the attempted seduction of Pemela by her employer, a country squire. But Pamela was a maidservant and although the servants of the great often came from what we should now call middle-class homes, Mr. B. was merely a country squire; and even servants in great houses are not generally included in the middle class by modern historians. It is hard to think that Richardson thought he was making a serious contribution to the discussion even of such class relationships as enter into the book, and his readers certainly did not take it as such.

THE NOVEL IN FRANCE AND GERMANY

The idea of the novel as specially connected with the middle class could only have developed if English novels alone are taken into account. It is clear that the social conditions and ideas of commercial Protestant England were not essential to the emergence of the novel when it is remembered that *La Princesse de Clèves* was published in 1678, in an environment in which there were none of the influences believed to have moulded Defoe or Richardson. We now leave the counting house and the printing works for the courts of princes.

French writers who might be described as bourgeois, although not so low in the social scale as Defoe or Richardson, had tried to write novels before Mme de La Fayette. These books are famous, but few, if any, critics think they are completely successful. Paul Scarron published *Le Roman comique* in 1651 and Furetière *Le Roman bourgeois* in 1665. As their names indicate, these books deal with the life of the middle class, which is held to be the inspiration and basis of the novel. It is all the more striking that the first French book still to be read as a novel should come not from these surroundings but from the Court of Louis XIV. We know as much about the genesis of Mme de La Fayette's earlier work as we do about Richardson's début, though not so much about exactly what inspired *La Princesse de Clèves* as we do about the beginnings of *Pamela*.

Sociological critics, unless they are discussing French literature, seldom mention *La Princesse de Clèves*. Ian Watt, however, does, only to say that it is not a novel. 'French fiction . . . from *La Princesse de Clèves* to *Les Liaisons dangereuses* stands outside the main tradition of the novel. For all its psychological penetration and literary skill, we feel it to be too stylish to be authentic.' This is really absurd, particularly when it is remembered that Marivaux, thought by many to have influenced Richardson, and Le Sage, known to have provided a model for Smollett, are included. But if absurd, it is also courageous. André Gide when asked by a newspaper for a list of his favourite ten French novels put *La Princesse de Clèves* third. The French are surely the people to decide whether the book is a novel or not; but it will certainly seem one to most English readers and one which is in some ways more 'modern' than the eighteenth-century English novel. It would be easier to put the story into a present-day setting than that of *Clarissa* or *Tom Jones*. There are no rapes, foundlings or duels: it is a novel about the relations between a married couple and the wife's lover, but, as Voltaire put it, set among 'honnêtes gens', which might be translated in a modern idiom as 'people with standards'. The Princess, warned by her mother against the dangers of passionate love, had married the Prince de Clèves, feeling no more for him than respect and affection. He is deeply in love with her; this is no arranged marriage and he realizes her lack of feeling for him. It is one of the important elements in the book that he does so, because it adds to his misery when she falls in love with M. de Nemours. Although she loves, she is determined to resist. And when her husband one days says: 'Sincerity touches me in such a way that I believe if my mistress or even my wife told me that someone attracted her, I should be miserable without being embittered, I should give up the role of lover or husband to advise and comfort her', she thinks that it may help her if he knows the truth and so she tells him, with the most unhappy results. The disasters are, however, due to the complicated emotions of the three characters, not to the challenges, threats or suicides which would probably have been introduced into an English novel of the period. The Prince dies from a complication of jealousy, despair and also misunderstanding, because he comes to believe that his wife is Nemour's mistress. The Princess refuses to marry Nemours, partly because she feels their love has killed her husband, but also because she cannot face the risk that Nemour's passion for her might fade with marriage.

'Do men,' she says, 'ever preserve their love in eternal bonds? Can I hope for a miracle for myself and can I put myself in a state of certainly seeing the end of that passion to which I owe all my happiness?'

The analysis of sentiment is both the object and the method of the book, but it is pursued by means the very opposite of those of Marivaux and Richardson, who may be considered Mme de La Fayette's successors. Mme de La Fayette's style is very simple, quite unlike the mixture of epigram and artifice later called Marivaudage. Nor does she pile detail on detail like Richardson. *La Princesse de Clèves* is on the contrary very short and, although it has intensity, there is a certain distance between the characters and the reader.

This is enhanced because the story is set in the court of Henri II. Some critics have seen in this merely a transparent disguise for the Court of Louis XIV. Others have regarded it as a real attempt to reconstruct a past age. Which it is does not greatly matter; the historical setting adds to the atmosphere of hopeless but distant melancholy which pervades the book, and it also links it with Mme de La Fayette's earlier work.

The exact social status of any author has become a matter of theoretical importance, and that of Mme de La Fayette has been exhaustively studied. Her family are described as of 'la très petite noblesse' and as 'très médiocre'. But whatever her origin from the point of view of the College of Heralds, from that of sociology there is no doubt that even as a girl she lived in an aristocratic society and was educated according to its standards. Her god-parents were not only fashionable but powerful, the Marquis de Brèze, Richelieu's brother-in-law, being her godfather and Mme de Combalet, his favourite niece, her godmother. Her father died when she was still a child and her mother married the Chevalier Renaud de Sévigné, a cousin of the Marquise. Her husband, the Comte de La Fayette was a genuine, though perhaps not an important, aristocrat. He was, however, a country gentleman, a species somewhat despised in Paris and at the Court, for it was the policy of the monarchy to detach the nobility from their estates and tenants and thus destroy their local influence and attach them more securely to the Crown. Nor does he seem to have had any literary or intellectual interests. Whatever the reasons may have been, and no one knows, after some years Mme de La Fayette left her husband to his country life and came to live in Paris. Here she became the intimate friend if not the mistress of La Rochefoucauld. A contemporary remarked of this relationship: 'In such cases there is always love, and even when old age has intervened there is still something left which, in the eyes of the Church, is as inadmissible as love itself.'[39]

When *La Princesse de Clèves* appeared without the name of the author gossip attributed it to La Rochefoucauld as well as to Mme de La Fayette, and she must, one supposes, have discussed it with him. Whether she necessarily paid any attention to his opinion depends on the relative strength of her affection for her book and for her friend. There seems no doubt, however, that although she lived in a circle in which she met Racine, La Fontaine and Boileau, and had known Mlle de Scudéry since childhood, it was her court and not her literary friends who stimulated her first piece of writing.

There was at the time a fashion for composing portraits of one's friends. In Mme de La Fayette's circle it was merely a kind of intellectual game, although in the *Charactères* of La Bruyère the genre produced one of the most important works in French literature. Even though it was a game, it was a game which must have encouraged the talent of any potential novelist. These portraits were criticized and discussed, and on at least one occasion a fashionable house party told stories in imitation of the Heptameron of the Queen of Navarre and critically examined each other's efforts.

Mme de La Fayette's next work was a 'nouvelle', that is, a tale too long to be a short story and not long enough to be a novel. But, more important and more directly connected with *La Princesse de Clèves*, is the book about Henrietta, the sister of Charles II and wife of Louis XIV's brother. Mme de La Fayette had known her in the days of poverty and exile and she remained her friend and confidante when Henrietta was, if not happy, at least brilliant, important and fascinating. Mme de La Fayette has herself explained how she came to write the book:

> In 1664 Le Comte de Guiche was exiled. One day she (Henrietta) told me of some circumstances extraordinary enough concerning his passion for her. Do you not think, she said to me, that what has happened to me and everything about it, would make a charming

[39] Bussy-Rabuton, Roger de, *Correspondence*, edited by L. Lalanne, Paris, 1858.

story . . . For some time, when I found her alone, she told me the particulars of which I was ignorant; but this caprice soon passed and what I had begun was left for four or five years, before she thought of it again. In 1669 she was at St. Cloud. There were not many people there and she recalled the idea of the story and told me I must take it up again.

The book leads to *La Princesse de Clèves* in two ways: by its continuance of the portrait game into sketches of characters connected with Henrietta and de Guiche, which are not unlike the description of the people in the novel; and by the court setting itself. The *Histoire de Madame Henriette d'Angleterre* begins thus:

Peace had been made between France and Spain; after a great many difficulties, the King's marriage had been arranged, and Cardinal Mazarin, full of the glory of having given peace to France, seemed to have nothing to do but enjoy the great position to which his good luck had raised him . . .

The Queen Mother, during her Regency, had left the whole of the royal authority to him as a burden too heavy to be borne by such an idle nature as hers. The King, on attaining his majority, had found authority in the Cardinal's hands, and had not the strength nor perhaps the wish to take it from him: the trouble that had been created by the bad conduct of this Cardinal was represented to him as the effect of the hatred of the Princes for a Minister who wished to set a limit to their ambitions; and had made him regard the Minister as the man who had guided the ship of state during the storm which had agitated it, and whose wise policy had perhaps saved it from wreck.

La Princesse de Clèves opens with the following paragraphs. The similarity to the beginning of *Henriette* is obvious.

The last years of Henri II's reign saw a display of opulence and gallantry such as has never been equalled in France. The King himself, charming to look at, the very flower of his race, and a worthy successor to his father, François I, was a great lover of women. His passion for Diane de Poitiers, Duchesse de Valentinois, began when he was barely twenty, but was none the less violent for that, nor were the tokens she received of it any the less dazzling. He excelled at all forms of sport and much of his time was given up to it, every day there was tilting at the ring, hunting, tennis, ballets and the like. Madame de Valentinois' colours and cyphers were very much in evidence, and so was she herself, dressed in a style which would have been more suitable for Mlle de la Marck, her own grand-grand-daughter, who was then just growing up. The presence of the Queen was her warrant. Catherine de Medici, though no longer in her first youth, was still a beautiful woman; the King had married her when he was Duc d'Orléans before the death of his elder brother the Dauphin.

She loved pomp, circumstance and pleasure, and, since she was ambitious, took great delight in reigning; she hardly seemed to mind the King's attachment to the Duchesse de Valentinois and she gave no sign of jealousy, but then she was a mistress of pretence, her real thoughts never easy to guess. In any case, it was expedient for her to keep the Duchesse closely attached to her person, since this also ensured the presence of the King.

The introduction to writing of both Richardson and Mme de La Fayette might perhaps be said to be moulded by socialogical forces in a sense, but these forces had become so narrowed down and diverted into particular channels that they became social not sociological. As far as one can see, they both began to write because they were asked to. Mme de La Fayette's impulse to write may indeed not have needed this stimulus; it must have been very strong if, as we are told, authorship was not considered a suitable occupation for a member of the nobility. This, however, does not seem to have prevented them from writing, but merely caused some of them not to sign their work. But as Richardson had not tried to compose fiction until he was fifty-four, it is doubtful whether he would ever have started without the booksellers' request.

Even if one assumes that the books were the product of the whole social structure of seventeenth-century France and eighteenth-century England, this structure was so different that consideration of each literature alone must lead to contradictory theories of the origin of the novel; theories which, moreover, have political and sociological corollaries equally divergent. Those who believe the modern novel first appeared in England and was a product of English life will feel the wind of liberty, discern the Puritan conscience and stress the importance of economic individualism. Those, on the other hand, who concentrate on French literature, will be apt to insist on the necessity of some kind of *élite*, the influence of a court, and the support which a small but educated audience gives to a writer.

Marivaux, Le Sage and Prévost, the early eighteenth-century French novelists, were, it is true, bourgeois in origin, though of the *haute-bourgeoisie* rather than of the class of Defoe and Richardson; but they were poor and in this sense may seem to resemble them rather than Mme de La Fayette. They were also professional writers, in which they were like Defoe and Fielding. It is, however, surely the first example of the novel in which social forces can most easily be traced. Once Mme de La Fayette had written a novel of psychological analysis, even though it was about great personages, it did not require much effort of the imagination to compose a similar story set in another social milieu. The rank of the characters in *La Princesse de Clèves* has, after all, no real importance; the tragic complications are in no way caused or even affected by politics or wealth. The conflict is not between private happiness and public duty, but between love and rules of morality, and feelings of affection, that would have been equally binding on bourgeois or peasant.

La Princesse de Clèves may well have influenced the English as well as the French novel. A translation appeared in 1668, another in 1722, and a second edition of the first translations in 1729. Nathaniel Lee dramatized it in 1689. His play is indeed singularly unlike the novel, but it does keep the two most important incidents—the Princess's confession and her refusal to marry Nemours. We know that Richardson had read the book, because it is criticized, adversely, in *Sir Charles Grandison*, and Lee is the playwright perhaps most quoted in *Clarissa*. The influence on Richardson, if influence there was, could only have been to suggest the idea of a novel of sentimental analysis; the methods of the two novelists were poles apart. But it is perhaps not quite without interest that the Princesse de Clèves refuses to marry her lover when the world would have expected her to accept him, and Clarissa also refuses, although the circumstances of the heroines and their motives are quite different.

Another theory could be manufactured from Grimmelshausen's *Der abenteuerliche Simplicissimus*,[40] which appeared in 1668 and 1669, even before *La Princesse de Clèves*. (The first edition, of which any examples survive, is dated 1669, but it is believed there was an edition in the previous year.) It is usual in histories

[40] Grimmelshausen, Hans Jacob, *Der abenteuerliche Simplicissimus* (translated by A. T. S. Goodrich), 1924.

of German literature to refer to this book as a novel; but any critic who may wish to reject it has much more substantial grounds than for refusing to recognize *La Princesse de Clèves*. It is a curious mixture of the picaresque tale, German folk-lore elements, and the same kind of realism, later to appear in the eighteenth-century novel, with social criticism and with what appears to be a serious social purpose. For most novels for which this is claimed there usually seems, for the uninitiated reader, to be little evidence, but early in the book Grimmelshausen says: 'The course of my history demands that I should leave to kind posterity an account of what manner of cruelties were now and again practised in this our German war.'

The very theme of the book, the vision of the world through the eyes of an impossibly simple boy brought up in isolation from the world, reveals a satiric intention. Simplicissimus criticizes, by the light both of nature and of Christian doctrine, all the institutions of seventeenth-century Germany, including the idea of birth, a concept then and long after more cherished in Germany than in any other European country. Some of this criticism is indeed, naïve, as, for example, that of the immodesty of women's dress in aristocratic circles; but that it had a serious purpose seems to be reinforced by the end of the book in which the hero retires from the world, apparently from religious motives.

Curious anticipation and strange echoes of other writers appear in Grimmelshausen. The desert island is one, although these islands were common at the time. Brecht took both the name and part of the plot of his play *Mother Courage* from the continuence of *Simplicissimus*. Reminiscences both of the German folk-story *Til Owlglas* and of Wolfran von Eisenbach's *Parsifal* have been discerned in *Simplicissimus*. The influence of the Spanish picaresque tale is also obvious; to this Grimmelshausen probably owed the autobiographical form of his novel. But picaresque tales were supposed to be funny, or at least gay, although many of the incidents seem to us far from amusing, and here Grimmelshausen's reactions are the same as ours. He did not think either the cruelties of the soldiers or the miseries of the peasants at all comic. The book is indeed a muddle, and humour, or what Grimmelshausen took to be humour, is an integral part of it. Simplicissimus himself and the other figures are caricatures rather than characters, and even as caricatures they are not altogether consistent. If, however, a mark of the novel is realistic description combined with social criticism, a good case can be made out for Grimmelshausen, rather than for Defoe, as the first realistic novelist. *Mother Courage* indeed, although it may not be long enough to be called a novel, has more psychological reality than *Roxanna*.

Little is known about Grimmelshausen's life, and this little does not seem to be connected with any of the influences which are supposed to have produced the novel. He is known to have been a soldier in the Thirty Years War and is thought to have started as a Protestant, but then he became a Catholic and, although he may be considered to have belonged to the middle station in life, the experience of a mercenary soldier is not one which readily springs to mind at the word 'bourgeois'.

The theory of the bourgeois novel can hardly be made to fit the actual facts even in England: neither the social structure, the political system, nor the class origin of the first novelists is that required by it. The circumstances surrounding the first examples of the French and German novel flatly contradict it. This does not, of course, dispose of all sociological theories, even those which claim to explain literature through influences radiating from social institutions or structures, still less of those which regard it an expression or reflection of the whole social situation. If, however, earlier fiction could be shown to have influenced both the form and content of the eighteenth-century novel, historical and traditional elements would be introduced, which would modify purely sociological theory by shifting some part of the explanation from sociological to historical factors.

Even if the whole of earlier European literature had been lost, it would be obvious from merely reading eighteenth-century novels that there had existed a number of books which the novelists were trying to rival, imitate or repudiate. This is most plainly seen in Fielding, who put on the title-page of *Joseph Andrews* 'written in imitation of the comic writings of Cervantes' and who, besides quotations from the classics and from Shakespeare, made references to earlier fiction in the introductory chapters he prefaced to each of the books into which *Tom Jones* is divided. These references would be incomprehensible if we did not already know the kind of literature he meant. For example, why should anyone discussing the theory of the realistic novel say that he purposely omitted the mention of 'elves and fairies' or tell critics not to condemn 'a character as a bad one, because it is not a perfectly good one . . . If thou dost delight in these models of perfection, there are books enow written to gratify thy taste'? Why did he call *Tom Jones* itself 'this heroic, historical, prosaic poem'? The answer is so clear to us that we do not bother to ask the question, but we should find it hard to understand if we did not know he was alluding to the surviving examples of medieval romance, the French heroic novel and the theory of the prose epic. No study of social conditions in the first half of the eighteenth century could have given the answer, and even a knowledge of the prevailing theory would hardly have made the references fully understandable without the books themselves.

Defoe and Richardson, unlike Fielding, were not trained in the classics and they are often said to have been outside the orthodox literary tradition. But Richardson at least wrote in a tradition, even if it was neither the orthodox nor perhaps the best; expressed for Richardson in the drama, it was the main tradition of European romance.

Since his novels were published as genuine autobiographies, Defoe did not indulge in literary criticism in his prefaces, but was concerned instead to defend the authenticity of his facts and the morality of his purpose, but even he observed certain inherited conventions.

As there was no catastrophic disappearance of earlier literature, there is an immense amount of material from which the influence of one writer on another can be traced, and there is no branch of scholarship which has been more intensively cultivated. There is at present something of a reaction against it, and as a method of understanding literature its usefulness is limited; but for the understanding not of literature but of the relations between literature and society, it is of the greatest importance. It is clearly necessary to disentangle those elements suggested, inspired, or simply passively taken over from writers who lived in a totally different environment from those which may be a reaction to the contemporary social situation.

It might seem as if only the immediate predecessors of the eighteenth-century novelist need to be considered, as nearly all medieval writers except Dante and, in England, Chaucer were forgotten. But any such starting-point leads back to the Middle Ages. Cervantes was the acknowledged master of Fielding and

Smollett, and *Don Quixote*, whatever it developed into, started as a parody of a tale of chivalry, the Spanish version of a kind of fiction which originated in twelfth-century France. The heroic novel had a similar ancestry, and the allegory which in *The Pilgrim's Progress* is often thought to have some influence on the emergence of the English novel, is also a medieval form.

Apart from direct influence from previous authors, it is obvious that the novel in Europe did not suddenly appear; the printed book, the long prose story and the habit of reading had all, by the beginning of the eighteenth century, been long established.

2

Medieval Romance
and its Influence on the Novel

Sociological critics refuse to accept any continuity between the eighteenth century and earlier forms of fiction. W. H. Allen, for instance, in the introduction to his book *The English Novel*, pours scorn on those historians of literature who have found such a continuity between the novels of Defoe and Richardson and medieval fiction: 'In their eagerness to supply the novel with a dignified ancestry they have behaved rather like a man who, setting out to write a history of the motor-car, should think it proper to begin by devoting a third of his space to the evolution of the ox-cart.'[1] Kettle is also convinced that romance and novel are wholly different and contrasting forms of literature. 'Romance', he says, 'was the non-realistic aristocratic literature of feudalism. It was non-realistic in the sense that its underlying aim was not to help people to cope in a positive way with the business of living, but to transport them to a world different, idealised, *nicer*, than this one.'[2] Sorokin takes much the same view, except that he approves, instead of disapproving, of the idealization, or, as he puts it, of the 'ideational' values which he regards as the inspiration of early medieval literature. 'The character of these writings shows that even in the secular world, they deal mainly with heroes, with outstanding persons and with the positive values of

No attempt has been made to cite all the editions of the French romances, but only those with English notes and glossary or, if such do not exist, those easily available to English readers.

[1] Allen, Walter, *The English Novel*, Pelican Books, 1958.
[2] Kettle, Arnold, *Introduction to the English Novel*, 1951.

empirical reality.'[3] Auerbach also calls the romances fairy tales not because of their supernatural elements but because 'the geographical, economic and social conditions on which they depend are never explained.'[4]

These writers, and those who think like them, concentrate on the content of fiction and emphasize the contrast between the prosaic stories about 'ordinary' people to be found in novels and the super natural and heroic elements in romance. The distinction was established in England before any book exactly conforming to this idea of the novel was published. Congreve, in the preface to *Incognita* (1692) laid down that:

> Romances are generally composed of the Constant Loves and invincible Courages of Hero's, Heroines, Kings and Queens, Mortals of the first Rank, and so forth; where lofty Language, miraculous Contingencies and impossible Performances, elevate and surprise the Reader into a giddy Delight . . . Novels are of a more familiar Nature; Come near us, and represent to us Intrigues in practice, delight us with Accidents and odd Events, but not such as are wholly unusual or unprecedented, such which not being so distant from our Belief bring also the pleasure nearer us.

The possible influence of romance on later forms of fiction is not, however, the only way in which a discussion of it may throw light on the development of the novel. For sociological or social determinism to be valid there should be no realistic elements in romance, far less whole romances which are realistic. There are indeed none which depict 'social forces', although it is not impossible to find in some of the them remarks on the politics of the time, as, for example, in *Escoufle*—

> Que honis soit princes que Laist
> Por ses villains ses gentix hommes.

Here Renart at least glances at political realities. In crediting romances with even superficial realism it is, however, necessary to take account of the distinction made by C. S. Lewis in *An Experiment in Criticism* between realism of presentation and realism of content. He defines presential realism as 'the art of bringing something close to us, making it palpable and vivid by sharply

[3] Sorokin, Peterim, *Social and Cultural Dynamics*, Vol. 1, 'Fluctuations of Forms of Art', New York, 1957.
[4] Auerbach, Eric, *Mimesis* (English translation), Princeton, 1953.

imagined detail', while he describes a fictitious narrative as realistic in content when 'it is probable or true to life'. As he points out, some of the wildest of medieval stories contain 'sharply observed or imagined details',[5] but there also exist romances which can be described as realistic in the same sense as Jane Austen's, though not in the same sense as Defoe's novels.

There are, besides content, other aspects of fiction—the narrative method, whether the story is told in verse or prose, straightforwardly or in some involved manner; the extent to which dialogue is used, and if used how far it is made to resemble actual speech, and how far to conform to conventions of good taste, grammar or literary theory; whether the thoughts as well as the actions of the characters are revealed. These formal aspects are as important for the development of fiction as its content. Neither changes in narrative method nor in dialogue were linked to the realistic plot, nor was the change from verse to prose. The first prose romances were less realistic than some of the stories told in verse.

Authorities on medieval literature, who have not generally accepted the idea of sharply distinct forms, include those other elements, as well as the plot, in their discussions.

Ker said of the development of the romance from the story of adventure into the story of sentiment:

> The term medieval ought not to obscure the fact that it is modern literature, in one of its chief branches, which has its beginning in the twelfth century. No later change in the forms of fiction is more important than the twelfth century revolution, from which all the later forms and constitutions of romance and novel are in some degree or other derived,

and, describing the kind of story which emerged in the twelfth century, added:

> There is little incident, sensibility has its own way, in monologues by the actors and digressions by the author on the nature of love. It is rather the sentiment than the passions that is here expressed in the 'language of the heart', but however that may be, there are both delicacy and eloquence in the language. The pensive Fénice who debates with herself for nearly two hundred lines in one place, is the ancestress of many later heroines.[6]

[5] Lewis, C. S., *An Experiment in Criticism*, 1962.
[6] Ker, W. P., *Epic and Romance*, London, 1908.

Gaston Paris held the same opinion:

> The psychological analysis, sometimes very delicate, to which after the example of Chrétien they submit the sentiments and above all the conflict of sentiments of their characters, they express in monologues, often of a wearisome subtlety, of a carefully designed form and of a tedious prolixity but which often joins to a certain insight, a real simplicity. It is here that these romances are the real precursors of the modern novel.[7]

And a German critic, Alfons Hilka, to complete the trio of nationalities, declared that 'The reflective monologue as used in these romances is identical with the method of the modern novel.' An innocent scientist who took up Dorothy Sayers's translation of Thomas's *Tristan*[8] made similar remarks, although he thought that it was the fully fledged novel rather than the precursor, in spite of its being in verse, and found it fascinating, not wearisome, If Ker and Gaston Paris seem old-fashioned, Cazamian in the *History of French Literature* which he wrote for the Oxford University Press in 1955 said of Chrétien de Troyes: 'He stands at the source of several movements, or fashions, that shaped the course of fiction directly during his age, and indirectly through the whole history of the novel.'[9] It is true that even lovers of medieval literature do not now always accept the way in which heroes and heroines of romance talk about their emotions as 'psychological analysis', finding what psychology there is superficial and, moreover, limited by artifical conventions.

Southern regards the analysis of sentiment as the application of logic, the intellectual passion of the age, to emotion rather than as 'psychology'.[10] Vinaver also rejects the similarity between the novel and the romance, although for very different reasons to those of sociological critics. He believes that as romance was written by 'clerics' or as we should say by educated men, the change from the tone and method of the *chansons de gestes* to the technique of Chrétien de Troyes, arose from the education of the time. In this education 'grammar' was one of the most important subjects. This meant not so much grammar in our sense but 'the ability to elucidate and comment on certain Latin texts'. This

---

[7] Paris, Gaston, quoted in Vinaver, Eugene, *Le Morte d'Arthur*, 1947.
[8] Sayers, Dorothy, *Tristan in Brittany*, 1929.
[9] Cazamian, L., *A History of French Literature*, 1955.
[10] Southern, R. W., *The Making of the Middle Ages*, 1953.

method was extensively used for the study of the Bible and then extended to classical literature. As this was written by pagans, it did not seem at first sight suitable reading for the faithful. It was, however, both loved and admired, and by attributing to incident and opinion, a '*sens*' in accordance with Christian doctrine the love of classical literature was reconciled with the Christian life. In Vinaver's view it led to a tendency to replace the mere relation of incidents by an attempt to interpret them, which 'meant either commenting on the story or letting the characters speak for themselves'.[11] The monologues, in which the heroes and heroines describe their emotions at length, were one of the results of this process.

The interpretation was called '*sens*', as opposed to *matière* or subject. Chrétien de Troyes himself draws attention to the distinction in the opening lines of the *Chevalier de la charette* in which he says both '*matière*' and '*sens*' were given to him by Marie de Champagne. Another example of the deliberate intention of interpreting rather than merely telling a story occurs at the beginning of *Eric et Enide*. 'Chrétien de Troyes . . . draws from a story of adventure (*Roman d'Aventure*) a very beautiful "conjuncture" by which can be proved and known that he is not wise who does not devote himself to his vocation as well as God gives him grace.'

It seems fairly plain that those characteristics which distinguish the romance from the *chansons de geste*, and also from the mere fairy story, were not introduced from the same motives which inspired later writers of fiction. Neither the origin of literary methods, however, nor the intentions of the writer necessarily determine their influence on subsequent developments. The twelfth-century themes continued to be used all through the history of European literature, and the surface resemblance which Chrétien de Troyes's methods bear to those of latter writers of fiction mean that they played some part in the evolution of the novel.

Possibly the best way to indicate what all the critics, both those who stress the continuity of fiction and those who deny it, mean, is to give a brief summary of two of Chrétien de Troyes's romances, *Cligès*, believed to have been writen about 1176, and

[11] Vinaver, Eugene, 'From Epic to Romance', *Bulletin of the John Rylands Library*, 1964.

Le Chevalier au Lion, which is dated somewhere between 1176 and 1181.

CLIGÈS[12]

There was an Emperor of Constantinople who had two sons. The eldest, Alexandre, refused to be knighted by his father, but demanded to be allowed to go to the Court of King Arthur, because this King was the mirror of chivalry and the greatest knight in the world. His father allowed him to go and after a stormy voyage, during which he suffered greatly from sea-sickness, he landed at Southampton. He was kindly welcomed by Arthur and his Court and accompanied the King to Brittany. A lady of the Court, Soredamors, falls in love with him and he with her, exhibiting all the symptoms then considered essential. There are no external obstacles, merely the lover's doubt whether she can love him, the girl's hesitation as to how to make it plain to him that she does: 'For this love he serves the Queen and the maids of honour but to her, of whom he thinks the most, he dare not address a word. If she dared to reveal to him the right she thinks she has over him she would do it gladly but she dare not.'

There is indeed, a difference between Soredamors and Alexandre. The lady knows he loves her and wonders only how she can reveal that she loves him. The knight cannot believe that he can ever win her love. This was the attitude considered proper at the time. In the middle of the love affair Arthur learns that the Regent he had left in England has rebelled against him. Before returning to England to deal with him, Arthur knights Alexandre and his companions and the Queen gives him a silk shirt stitched with gold. Soredamors had helped to make it and had put in the sleeves and neck one of her own hairs instead of a thread.

Alexandre, needless to say, performs prodigies of valour in England, only annoying Arthur by presenting some prisoners he has taken to the Queen, instead of sending them to him. Guinevere one day sees that Alexandre is wearing the shirt she had given him and, under the dark walls of Windsor Castle which the King's army is besieging, 'catching sight of a gold thread which seemed pale by the side of the golden hair which shone beside it, remem-

---

[12] Cligès, *Les Romans de Chrétien de Troyes,* edited by A. Micha, Paris, 1957. (Cligès has been translated into English by W. Wiston Comfort in *Arthurian Romances of Chrétien de Troyes,* 1928. Also separately by L. J. Gardiner, 1912.)

bering by chance who had worked it, she started to laugh, and Alexandre seeing her asked her what had made her laugh. Calling Sorcdamors . . . shc said "Damosel, look here and tell me without hiding anything who sewed the shirt this knight is wearing".' One might have expected this would have led to an avowal, but not at all. There are still some thousands of lines and a good deal of fighting before the Queen eventually intervenes, saying to Alexandre, 'Love is worse than hate when he wounds and destroys his friend. Lovers do not know what they do when they hide from each other. I wish to teach you love for I know that love is killing you.' The lovers are married, and at line 2382 their son Cligès, the hero of the romance, is born.

By this time the Emperor of Constantinople, feeling himself near to death, sent a mission to ask Alexandre to return. Unfortunately they were all drowned at sea, except one who preferred Alis, the younger son, to Alexandre. He returned to Constantinople and reported that they had been returning with Alexandre when the whole company had been lost in a shipwreck. So Alis was crowned Emperor. Alexandre heard of this and proceeded to Constantinople to claim his crown, taking ship from Shoreham in Sussex. The barons, recalling somewhat improbably the struggle between Eteocles and Polynices, urged a compromise: Alis would nominally keep the throne, but would not marry, so that Cligès would inherit and until then Alexandre would exercise effective power. This arrangement worked satisfactorily until Alexandre's death, but on his death-bed he urged his son to go in disguise to Arthur's Court, for until he had been there 'he could not know how much prowess and courage he had'.

Alis, basically not a bad man, had faithfully kept his promise not to remarry, but, urged by evil counsellors, he now changed his mind and sought the hand of the daughter of the Emperor of the West. She was already promised to the Duke of Saxony, but the Emperor said that if Alis would come with an army so large that he would be able to tell the Duke that he could not resist, he could have her. The two Emperors met at Cologne. The Duke of Saxony demanded his bride, but receive instead a challenge from Cligès, and a tournament with three hundred knights on each side, which was more like a battle than the regulated and orderly tournaments of later times, took place.

By this time, Fénice, daughter of the Emperor of the West, has fallen in love with Cligès and here occurs the debate to which Ker referred. She tells her nurse she

> would rather be torn limb from limb than that we two should be remembered as is the love of Tristram and Iseult, of whom so many follies are told it would shame me to repeat them. I could not accept the life that Iseult led, love in her was too ugly. She owed her body to two men, her love to one alone. Her whole life was thus lived refusing herself to neither. This love was not rational, but mine is completely faithful to one, neither my body nor my heart will ever be shared. My body shall never have two possessors. He who has the heart has the body too.

The contradiction between body and heart is made more striking in Old French by the resemblance between the words *cors*, body, and *cuers*, heart.

Fénice then goes on to discuss the practical difficulties of living up to these sentiments in the circumstances. Her nurse is fortunately able to provide her with a magic potion which makes Alis believe he has slept with her on their wedding night, although he has not. The Emperor, Fénice and Cligès then return to Constantinople; on the way they are ambushed by the Duke of Saxony, but Cligès saves the situation. In the end they return safely to Constantinople, but as soon as they arrive Cligès remembers his dying father's advice to go to Arthur's Court and decides to follow it. It must be borne in mind that Cligès does not know that Fénice loves him. There is another long dissertation by Fénice on the nature of love and Cligès departs for England. When he gets there he finds the King at Oxford, where he is holding a tournament. Cligès defeats all the knights of the Court including Gawain, who, at this date, was more famous than Lancelot.

He refuses to disarm after these encounters, an example followed by many a later knight of romance, including the Black Knight in *Ivanhoe*. After his final victory he consents to 'raise his helm' and everyone is overjoyed to learn that this best of all knights is Alexandre's son.

After performing many chivalrous feats in Britain, Normandy and France, he remembers Fénice and decides to go back to Constantinople, where he is received with general delight. Fénice takes a leading part in these celebrations, and being one day alone with him she asks him if there was no lady in Britain whom he loved. He replied: 'Madam, I was in love there but not with anyone from there. My body was in Britain without my heart. I do not know what has become of my heart since I left Germany except that it has followed you here.' Fénice replies: 'I have never been in Britain and yet my heart was there.' After a good deal more conversation on these lines the lovers begin to consider what to do. Cligès proposes that they both fly to Arthur's Court, but Fénice sharply replies: 'I will not go with you there for the whole world would take us to be as Iseult the Fair and Tristram.'

In the end, with the aid of the nurse, they resort to the stratagem of Romeo and Juliet, though with happier results. Fénice pretends she is ill and takes a potion which makes her appear to be dead. Cligès prepares a tower outside the town where he proposes to keep Fénice in secret: but the palace doctors, being more experienced than was expected, know very well that she is not dead and, having secured the Emperor's permission to shut out her ladies, proceed to torture her in order to make her confess. The ladies, however, watching through a crack in the door, see what is going on, rush in and fling the doctors out of the window. Fénice is buried and the next night Cligès rescues her from her tomb. She is, however, very ill from the boiling lead with which the doctors had burned her; however, she recovers under the care of Cligès and the nurse, and all comes out well in the end.

The Emperor is naturally furious when he hears what has happened, and particularly when he learns of the effects of the magic potion on what he had believed to be his loving-making with Fénice. Cligès and Fénice, whose objections have apparently been overcome, take refuge with Arthur. On hearing of their wrongs the King summons a great army, but before they set out news comes the Emperor has gone mad from grief and died. The barons summon Cligès to be Emperor. And it is because of Fénice that 'Every Empress however highly born and rich is guarded in Constantinople as if she was in prison'.

Jean Frappier says that *Cligès* is in many ways the most interesting of Chretien's poems, 'the most intellectual and theoretical';[13] but these qualities make it less representative of its genre. If one is going to read romance at all it is not unreasonable to demand that it shall be as romantic as possible. *Cligès* alone does not really give an adequate idea of why romance is regarded as so different

[13] Frappier, Jean, *Chrétien de Troyes*, Paris, 1957.

to the novel. It combines two of the most fashionable themes of its day, the Byzantine with the Arthurian, but with the exception of the magic potions it has no supernatural elements and the link with the Round Table is clearly artificial. We are told that no one would listen to any themes but the matter of France, the matter of Britain and the matter of Great Rome; and the matter of Britain was rapidly gaining on the others, so the intrusion of the Round Table into so many stories is easily understood. *Yvain* or *Le Chevalier au Lion*, on the other hand, is full of magic, enchanted fountains, giants and beings born of a woman and a fiend.

YVAIN[14]

King Arthur held the feast of Easter at Carduel in Wales, and after dinner one of the knights tells a story of a jewelled and magic fountain he once visited where a storm could be raised by dashing water on the stone, the only disadvantage being that once the storm is raised, a furious knight appears. This knight overthrew him in the ensuing fight. Yvain, who is his cousin, reproaches him for not telling him the story before and declares that he himself will go to the fountain and avenge him. Kay, the Seneschal, remarks 'it is clear that it is after dinner. After dinner every man is ready to kill Noradin' (the contemporary Sultan, Nurèdin Mahmud). Not unnaturally this makes Yvain all the more determined to go, so he is far from pleased when the Queen repeats the story to the King, who is so fascinated by the idea of the fountain that he swears that he and his whole Court will go there in a fortnight's time.

Yvain slips out alone and unobserved, arrives at the fountain, goes through the prescribed ritual, raises the storm and wounds the knight so badly that he flies to his castle pursued by Yvain. The portcullis cuts Yvain's horse neatly in two pieces. Yvain, however, was on the front piece and escapes death, but is trapped in the castle. He wanders into the great hall and is alarmed to hear a door opening and someone coming out.

Up to this point the story has been a fairy story with evident folk-lore elements. Now, although there is a ring with the power of making its wearer invisible, for about 1,360 lines it changes

[14] *Yvain, or The Chevalier au Lion*, edited with English notes and glossary by T. B. W. Reid, 1942.

into the kind of comedy which makes some critics call Chrétien the first European novelist. Through the door comes not an armed knight but a young girl. She expresses a lively sense of gratitude to Yvain, not as might have been expected for having rescued her from a dragon, but because he was once kind to her when she came to the Court with a message. She tells him that the Knight of the Fountain is dead but that she will save Yvain from the vengeance of his widow and retainers, and gives him a ring which will make him invisible. But she warns him that when the dead knight is carried into the hall and all his retinue assemble round the bier, he must not move. The knight's beautiful widow accompanies the bier and Yvain instantly falls in love with her. She, however, seems to have loved her husband and is in the greatest agony, which continues after the funeral. The damsel, however, is of a practical turn of mind, and besides wishes to do Yvain any service in her power. When she finds her lady still weeping and tearing her hair after the funeral she addresses her in somewhat hard but eminently practical words: 'It is a marvel to me, Lady, that you behave so foolishly. Can you bring your husband back by lamentations? . . . You ought to be considering how you are going to defend your fountain, and you will not stop weeping.' The lady, whose name is Laudine—the name is only mentioned once in the whole poem—is slowly brought to consider the problem of defence, which is urgent, because it is known that King Arthur will arrive the following week. Lunette, the damsel, then remarks that, for herself, if two knights have fought and one has beaten the other, she would consider the victor to be the better knight. Laudine realizes exactly what she means and is very angry; but having spent the night debating the question she decides to see Yvain. In the morning she tells Lunette that she has reconsidered the matter and will see the knight.

Lunette, having carefully dressed him in a scarlet gown lined with fur and decorated him with a gold buckle and other jewels, leads him by the hand to the room where Laudine sits on a scarlet sofa. The situation is such as to embarrass even a hero of romance, and Yvain has not an idea what to say. Lunette remarks, 'Ten thousand curses on anyone who brings a knight who has neither speech nor tongue into a lady's chamber', and says to Yvain, 'Have no fear that my lady will bite you . . . ask her to pardon you the death of her husband Eslados the Red'. Having pulled himself together, Yvain says, 'I do not ask you for mercy. I will give you thanks whatever you do to me. Nothing would displease me.' 'No, my Lord?' she replies, 'and if I kill you?' 'Madam, I would still thank you.' When she reproaches him for having killed her husband he replies, 'By your leave, Lady, when your husband attacked me, what could I do but defend myself?' According to the conventions of chivalry this was unanswerable—and even the dictates of common sense make the offence, thus explained, much less serious than it might have been. The lady finally consents to marry Yvain.

A great many irrelevant remarks have been made about this episode, comparing it with the story of the Matron of Ephesus, but Mario Roques is surely right in saying that Laudine is actuated by purely practical considerations: 'She holds a fief and she must defend it. Eslados the Red having disappeared it was necessary to replace him as soon as possible.'[15] Her barons and other retainers agree with her and when introduced to Yvain, like him very much.

Arthur comes and raises the storm, and Kay insists on meeting the knight. Yvain easily unhorses him and the Court stays at Laudine's castle for a week. Everyone enjoys this very much, including Gawain, who, much amused by Lunette's story, takes her for his *amie*.

All the week the other knights have begged Yvain to go with them to new adventures and not to stay with his wife. Gawain finally persuades him, saying, 'Will you be one of those degraded by marriage?' Laudine gives him permission to go and only stipulates that he shall return in a year, giving him a magic ring. The defence of the fountain and the fief, once so important and to be important again, is not mentioned, and this is one of the few examples of the inconsequence of romance to be seen in *Yvain*, which otherwise seems carefully designed.

It is hardly necessary to say that Yvain forgets his promise and next August, while the King is holding a tournament at Chester, a damsel appears—whether Lunette or another the scholars have not decided—and calling Yvain a traitor, a liar and a hypocrite before the whole Court, seizes the ring from his finger, and disappears.

Yvain now goes mad, as was obligatory on knights crossed in

15 Roques, Mario, 'Yvain', *Romania*, 1964.

love since Tristram. Found lying naked in a forest, he is rescued by a lady who cures him with magic ointment. He leads her retainers against an attack by an ill-disposed neighbour and she is so grateful for this that she offers to marry him or to become his mistress. Having refused both suggestions, he wanders off into a forest where he sees a lion fighting with a serpent. He decides to intervene on the side of the lion, because it is a 'noble animal'. Having killed the serpent he expects the lion to attack him, but it does everything it can to express its gratitude. When he moves off, it follows him like a dog and like a dog becomes very useful in sighting and hunting game.

They find themselves at the fountain again and Yvain loses himself in lamentations, but is interrupted by the complaints of a woman imprisoned in one of the towers of the castle. This is Lunette, who has been accused by the Seneschal of treason to her lady and will be burned unless she can find a champion to fight not one but two knights at once. Yvain naturally says that he will fight for her. However, when he seeks a lodging at a neighbouring castle he is forced to engage with a giant in order to rescue his host's sons and daughter. He only manages to kill him with the help of the lion, and this delays him so that he is only just in time to rescue Lunette; however, it does not stop him from defeating both knights.

Laudine thanks him warmly and asks him to stay with her as long as he likes, and the lion, too. This was particularly kind of her, as it had proved a difficulty elsewhere when he had been looking for a night's lodging. He replies that he will never stay long in any place until his lady has pardoned him. On being asked his name he says, 'Call me the *Chevalier au Lion.*' The failure to recognize him is not so improbable as are similar incidents in other literature, the Elizabethan drama for instance, because he is in full armour which to some extent covered his face. Wandering sorrowfully away, he is taken in at a castle and both he and the lion are put to bed and nursed until their wounds have healed.

While he is ill his host, the Lord of the Black Thorn—never mentioned before or afterwards—dies, leaving two daughters, and the elder is determined not to share her inheritance with her younger sister. Getting to Arthur's Court first, she enlists Gawain as her champion. When the younger sister comes in her turn she finds no one who is prepared to take on Gawain. The fame of the

Knight with the Lion has, however, reached the Court, and she decides to go and look for him. He is now engaged in fighting two semi-fiends in order to release three hundred maidens held as ransom for their lord. The younger sister, the disinherited, as she is called, falls ill on the way but another girls takes up the task and finally catches up with him. Thus he and Gawain are induced to fight one another.

They fight all day without either of them gaining any perceptible advantage and Yvain finally says, 'My Lord, the night is coming on. I do not think anyone could blame or reproach us if the night separates us . . . But for my part I greatly respect and admire you . . . I never thought to see a knight whom I should so much wish to know.' Gawain answers by telling him his name, and Yvain says that he would never have fought him if he had known he was the man he loved most in the world and offers immediately to yield to him. Gawain answers, with an equal disregard of the interests of the lady he is representing, saying that this is impossible because he will yield himself. While they are arguing everyone in the Court points out to the King that it would be much better if the ladies could be brought to agree as it would be a great pity if two such good knights were to do each other any serious damage. Arthur tells the elder sister that she had better give in, as if she does not, although it will distress him very much, he will declare Yvain the victor.

When Yvain is healed of his wounds, he returns to the fountain and raises such a violent storm that the castle is shaken to its foundations, which gives Lunette the opportunity of arranging a reconciliation between him and his wife. She tells Laudine she will go and find the *Chevalier au Lion* and beg him to come and defend the fountain. She is not sure, however, that she will be able to persuade him: he is in such grief and anguish because his lady is angry with him. Laudine promises that if he will come 'I will do everything he wishes to make his peace if I can'. Lunette, unsatisfied with this, makes her swear on a sacred relic. The end is obvious and not long delayed.

It can perhaps be gathered from these summaries that Chrétien's poems in many ways fit the pattern laid down for romance. They are fairy stories not only because of the giants, enchanted fountains and magic potions with which they abound, but because love is more powerful and more faithful, courage more magnificent and beauty more astonishing than is commonly met with in real life. Moreover, all the romances that Chrétien finished end happily; and, although there is little attempt to disguise the savagery of war, which at least in *Cligès* appears more unpleasant than in Froissart, what one supposes to have been the realities of life in the twelfth century are not very apparent. People die and even have their lives interrupted by illness but there is no description of disease. There are revolts but no famines.

Although individual character does appear, it is subordinated to the necessities of the plot. Fénice displays a certain individuality in her care for her reputation, but it is never explained why she thinks it is less like Iseult to live with Cligès secretly in a tower than to go to Arthur's Court with him. Jean Frappier has an explanation, but it does not seem entirely convincing. He maintains that she objected so strongly to Iseult's conduct because she slept with her husband, not because she slept with Tristran. 'The reproaches of Fénice are directed to the lover of Tristran not to the wife of Mark.'[16] But if this is correct why did she refuse to go to Arthur's Court with Cligès when he first suggested it? Lunette is a character and so is the lion, although he is depicted in a way which would be too flattering to human beings to call anthropomorphic; he is credited with all the more amiable human qualities and at one time contemplates suicide. Yvain is not, in the poem, exactly like all the other knights in the other romances; but his motives are mainly conventional; as for Laudine, we are never told what she feels about Yvain at all. On the other hand, the complaint often voiced that the hero always wins does not seem valid. The brave and successful knight was not only regarded as a credit to himself, and everyone connected with him; he occupied a position similar to that of some sporting hero today. No one would be much interested in a Test cricketer who did not make an outstanding score or a footballer who never scored a goal. But Yvain would not have won on two occasions if his lion had not intervened and Eric in *Eric et Enide* is by no means invincible.

It may perhaps also be gathered from the summaries that there are other elements in Chrétien, a kind of drawing-room comedy in the scene in which Guinevere teases Soredamors about the

---

[16] Frappier, *op. cit.*

shirt, and comedy, with more acid undertones, in the scene in which Lunette persuades her lady to forgive and marry the man who has killed her husband.

There are also elements which might be called realistic. Although Chrétien is vague about time and place, he is never vague, as is seventeenth-century romance, about details of day-to-day life. When Yvain first leaves Arthur's Court he makes certain his horse is properly shod. Fortresses, and the way one got in or out of them, are carefully described. Although no one seems to be much concerened with doing anything but fighting, there is a lot of talk about gold and other forms of wealth; and it is clear that these are highly valued by everyone, including the hero and heroine. The quarrel between the sisters in *Yvain* is about land, and the duel between the friends is judgement by battle, then as legal a method of reaching a decision as any other. When Yvain fights with the knight at the fountain, he splits his head to the brain so that 'his blood and brains stained the bright rings of his coat-of-mail'. Laudine's attitude after her husband's death is not at all romantic: she is only concerned with the problem of defending her possessions. These examples may be called presentational realism only; but in the complaint of the damsels at the castle of the Worst Adventure, realism of content seems to make a sudden and somewhat disconcerting appearance. They have arrived at their unfortunate situation because their lord had got himself involved in a fight with two fiend-like creatures and had only escaped by promising to send them thirty maidens every year. This echoes many ancient tales, but the description of their plight and their conversation is reminiscent rather of Engels than of the Minotaur. When he entered the castle Yvain saw 'three hundred maidens who were engaged in various kinds of weaving and embroidery'. Although they were handling silk and gold thread they were in such poverty that their clothes were torn at the breast and elbows and their shifts dirty at the neck, their shoulders 'bowed and their faces pale with hunger.' The statement of the unfortunate girls has a curiously nineteenth-century ring:

> Every day we make silk but we shall never be better clothed for it. We have scarcely any bread, little in the morning and less at night, for from the work of our hands each has only four deniers of a livre to live on. And on this we cannot have sufficient food and clothing . . . There is not one of us that does not produce the

value of twenty sous which would be riches for a duke . . . But those for whom we work are rich by our disinheritance.

All authorities are agreed that it was not Chrétien's deliberate or conscious purpose to produce a picture of contemporary manners, although Jean Frappier says: 'The mysterious charm of the Breton themes and the extraordinary adventures did not prevent Chrétien de Troyes from being an accurate and sometimes malicious observer of the society of his time.'[17]

The realistic or sentimental vignettes are then incidental only. But from the point of view of the social origin of literary forms and conventions, it is surely the earliest examples or the first signs which are the most important, because in them the social forces are easier to isolate from other possible factors, such as imitation or literary tradition. Chrétien did not have models in the Classical literature available to him, either for society comedy or for such realistic descriptions as that of the weaving girls. Nor is anything of the kind to be found in his supposed Celtic sources, at least if they were anything like the Celtic literature that has survived.

While such details as Yvain's care to see his horse was properly shod, or the unpleasant result of cleaving someone through the skull, could be regarded as examples of presentational realism, the description of the weaving girls is not calculated to bring the story closer to us, but rather to bring us up with a jolt, and it must have had the same effect, one would suppose, on the original audience. Even if they were indifferent to the sufferings of the poor, it is an intrusion of real life, which, as it were, breaks the dream. This scene, the wooing of Laudine, and the scene in which Guinevere sees the hair which Soredamors had sewed into the shirt, were not so much sharply observed details as evocations of real life which contained the germ of a very different kind of fiction. One feature of Chrétien's writings is intensely realistic—the dialogue. This is naturally difficult to assess, but the talk at Arthur's Court and the conversation between Lunette, Yvain and Laudine in which the marriage is arranged seems, in spite of being in verse, to have the ring of authentic speech.

The theory of *sens*, the necessity of interpretation, gave a deliberate seriousness, an intellectual weight to the romance, which distinguishes it from mere fairy story and also from

[17] Frappier, *op. cit.*

Oriental romance and makes it the true ancestor of the novel. The romance may seem to us frivolous, but it is this underlying seriousness which separates it from the *fabliaux*, the comic and frequently indecent tale of contemporary life.

In considering the romance either as a product or as a reflection of a particular state of society, it is essential to remember that it was only one among many forms of literature. As well as *fabliaux*, *chansons de geste* and saints' lives continued to be written after the appearance and wide diffusion of the romance. The *pastorale*, the animal fable, and the allegory emerged when the romance was at its height, as entertainment, if not as literature. There is therefore little point in attempting to translate a tendency to idealization in the romance to a corresponding tendency in society, when the opposite characteristics can be found in other kinds of fiction. No doubt the particular attributes found in romance can tell us something about the period in which it was written, but only when cross-checked by other and different stories.

The difficulty presented by the co-existence of romance and *fabliaux* was for long resolved by ascribing them to different classes. No view used to be more firmly held, and not only by critics committed to class theories of politics or society, than that the romance was written for the amusement of nobles and that the *fabliaux* were a bourgeois creation.

All this has now been questioned and the arguments against it seem powerful. *Fabliaux* are found bound up with romances in the most elaborate and expensive manuscripts. There are allusions to reading of *fabliaux* to courtly audiences, and scenes in the courtly romances where this happens.[18] It is known that the bourgeoisie in the thirteenth and fourteenth centuries devoured romances as eagerly as the knights and ladies. Even before the modern discussion of the problem, Bédier, the French medievalist, had said: 'The castes of the middle ages, so sharply divided in social life, mingled in everything that had to do with literature, a strange promiscuity mixes the audiences and the forms, knights and merchants, romances of the Round Table and *fabliaux*.'[19]

Why English critics ever believed in the class division is hard to see, as romances and *fabliaux* are mixed in *The Canterbury Tales*. It has always been known that Chaucer wrote for the highest

[18] Lykrog, Per, *Les Fabliaux*, Copenhagen, 1957. Review *Speculum*, 1958.
[19] Bédier, Charles, *Les Fabliaux*, Paris, 1893.

social circles, and he continues to be reproached, from time to time, for being a 'Court' poet. The *fabliaux* were realistic and satirical, dealing with those aspects of medieval life ignored in the romance. It may then well be asked why literary historians have seen the origin of the novel in romance rather than in *fabliaux*. The answer partly lies in the seriousness which romance shares with the novel. Although both were essentially entertainment, the authors of romance generally tended to take themselves very seriously indeed. It was romance also which inspired vast books written in prose, and these versions outlived the Middle Ages, directly influencing the fiction of the sixteenth and seventeenth century. Moreover, French critics and historians of literature consider that some of the thirteenth-century romances, even those in verse, tended to become more realistic, and to have a distinct affinity with the later novel of manners. Bossuet, for example, in the history of French literature, edited by J. Calvet, says of them: 'Distant ancestors of the modern novel, they attempt like it to evoke contemporary reality and introduce us to a living milieu. They show us . . . a complete picture of the manners, the ideas and the tastes of high French society during the course of the thirteenth century.'[20] Their invocation of contemporary reality is indeed limited, and resembles Madame de La Fayette rather than Chaucer. What exactly is meant can best be seen by the description which the editor gives of a poem by Jean Renart called by its contemporaries *Le Roman de La Rose*, but by modern scholars *Guillame de Dole*, to distinguish it from the more famous poem called after the rose. The basic plot is the same as the story of Imogen in Shakespeare's *Cymbeline*, which may seem romantic enough; but Professor Lejeune who edited it describes it as

> not strictly speaking a roman d'aventure. Neither complicated situa-
> tions, nor extraordinary feats of arms, are found in it. The marvellous
> is completely absent from this work, which aims from the beginning
> to the end at naturalism, at realism.
>
> Neither is it a novel of psychological subtleties in which the
> characters analyse themselves minutely or discuss themselves freely.
>
> It is in truth a novel of manners following a formula already
> modern, depicting the manners of an aristocratic society with those
> who composed it, great lords, bourgeois and servants.[21]

[20] Bossuet, Robert, *Le Moyen Age*, Paris, 1931.
[21] Lejeune, R., Introduction to Jean Renart's *'Guillaume de Dole'*, Paris, 1936.

There are romances which resemble the novel of manners even more closely. The incidents in *Guillame de Dole*, although not 'marvellous' in the sense of being in any way supernatural, are not exactly probable. Another of Renart's works, *Le Lai de l'Ombre*,[22] although written within a convention, has no improbabilities at all. Nor does it seem to have any particular '*sens*' unless that 'love will still be lord of all'. Nothing unpleasant, however, happens to the knight who does not pay homage or tribute to love, in spite of his charm and prowess. He is only forced by the God of Love to worship a charming and beautiful lady. She rejects his addresses, but he manages to slip a ring on her finger before he leaves her castle. She sends a message after him to demand his return and when he comes insists on his taking the ring back. 'Which', he says to himself,

> is the least bad of these alternatives? I know perfectly well that if I leave it she will say I do not love her . . . This request has so struck me that to leave it is not worthy of me. I believe it would be more worthy and honourable in me to take it back if I do not wish to commit a great fault against my honoured and gentle lady and the faith I owe her . . . But if I do as she asks I shall not have honour from her.

Then he says, 'Lady, I shall hold you to a pact. I will do according to your will if I may do what I like with the ring.' The lady readily agrees to this condition. He is sitting at the side of a well and in the water is the reflection of the lady. 'No,' he says, 'I shall not take it back at all, since I have there my sweet friend. I love nothing better after you.' 'God,' she says, 'there is only ourselves here, where will you find her so quickly?' He replies, 'In the name of God, see there your fair shadow that waits." He takes the ring and throws it down and says, 'Take it, my fair friend. Since my lady does not want it you will take it without any arguing.' This graceful act wins the lady.

The point does not lie in the slight story but in the way in which it is told. The *Lai de l'Ombre* has been compared both with De Musset and Marivaux, but it is not so much like either as like a development of the drawing-room comedy of Chrétien, which is probably what it is.

[22] *Le Lai de l'Ombre*, edited with modern French glossary by J. Orr, 1948.

La Chastelaine de Vergi[23] is not a comedy but a tragedy of courtly love. It is concerned with people bearing contemporary titles, although the story does not seem to fit any actual holders. The Duchess of Burgundy has fallen in love with a knight of the Court, and, being repulsed, accuses him to her husband of attempting to seduce her. The Duke, instead of immediately revenging himself on the knight as his wife had expected, asks him instead if the story is true. This puts the knight in a dilemma, as he is having an affair not with the Duke's wife but with his niece, the Chastelaine de Vergi; and, quite apart from the practical inconveniences likely to follow, it was one of the strictest rules in the code of courtly love that the lover must never divulge the name of his mistress. The knight, however, also owes a duty to the Duke as his lord. He tells the truth to the Duke, who tells his wife, and she shows the Chastelaine, by insinuation, that she is aware of it. The Chastelaine dies of grief, the knight on finding her dead kills himself, and the Duke, on discovering the truth, kills his wife.

Although in reality people seldom die of grief, this type of romantic dénouement is not always absent from novels which are called realistic. After all, Clarissa did something of the same thing in the eighteenth century.

The moral, as expressed in the final verses, is that from this example one ought to hide one's love; but although the *sens* arises out of the story in a way, there is no feeling that the poem was written to illustrate this rather obvious point. It seems rather to have been inspired by a kind of 'pity and terror'. This is confirmed by F. Whitehead, who edited the romance for the University of Manchester, and described it as 'a work in which the action is only internal and the final tragedy completely explained by what we know of the minds and motives of the human actors involved. A work whose closely reasoned plot foreshadows (or perhaps anticipates) the romantic tragedy of later centuries.'

The *Lai de l'Ombre* has 960 verses and the *Chastelaine* 955. Bossuet defined the romance as a poem 'which seldom had less than 8,000 verses and sometimes more than 30,000'. So the *Chastelaine* and the *Lai* might be considered rather the equivalent of the later short story than of the later novel.

[23] *La Chastelaine de Vergi*, edited by F. Whitehead, 1951. (English translation, A. Kemp-Welch, London, 1903.)

Phillippe de Beaumanoir's *Jehan and Blonde*,[24] *Joufrois*,[25] the Provençal *Flamenca*,[26] the *Comte d' Anjou*,[27] *Guillame de Dole*, and Renart's other romance, *Escoufle*,[28] are long, and Beaumanoir's realism might almost be called prosaic. Except that it is in verse, *Jehan* resembles a nineteenth-century historical novel. The *sens* which Beaumanoir intended to convey is given in the opening lines; it is that poor young men should emigrate in search of honour and wealth. 'A man who lives with great difficulty and would if he went to another country be able to acquire honour and friends and riches, and loses all this by his laziness, ought to be condemned and despised by all men of worth.' The story is conducted on these realist lines throughout. The hero goes to England, taking passage on a merchant ship. He does not meet the Earl of Senefort (Oxford), who is to become his patron, in any enchanted forest but on the road from Dover to London, on which the Earl is travelling on his way to attend Parliament. He does not rescue his lady from dragons but is assigned to her, as her special squire, by her father. His duties chiefly seem to consist of carving at meals. If the love affair is considered non-realistic, squires did run away with their lords' daughters, and the lords, even kings of England, had to make the best of it.

Gautier d'Aupais,[29] although much shorter, is on similar lines. The hero, returning from a tournament where he has spent all the money he had, goes nevertheless to an inn to have a meal. When asked to pay he tries to get the money by gambling, and loses everything he has, including his horse and armour. He, like Jehan, leaves home and takes service with a great noble, and falls in love with his daughter and eventually marries her.

The *Comte d'Anjou*, also called the *Comtesse d'Anjou*, has been described as descending to 'a bourgeois realism'. It describes the adventures of a daughter of a Comte d'Anjou when she is forced

---

[24] de Beaumanoir, Philippe, *Oeuvres Poetiques*, edited by H. Suchier, Paris, 1884–5.
[25] *Joufrois*, edited by K. Hofmann, Halle, 1880.
[26] *Flamenca*, edited with text and modern French translation by Paul Meyer, Paris, 1865. (Translated into English prose by H. M. Prescott, London, 1930; into English verse by M. J. Herbert, Princeton, 1962.)
[27] Maillart, Jean, *Le Comte d'Anjou*, edited by Mario Roques, Paris, 1931.
[28] Renart, Jean, *Escoufle*, edited by Paul Meyer, Paris, 1894. (There seems to be no English or modern French translation, but there are long summaries of both Guillaume de Dole and Escoufle in Langlois, Charles, 'La Vie au France en Moyen Age', Paris, 1926.)
[29] *Gautier d'Aupais*, edited by E. Faral, Paris, 1919. (See also Longlois, *op. cit.*)

to fly from her home because of her father's incestuous passion for her. The 'bourgeois realism' is shown in detailed descriptions of bourgeois and peasant life, in detached observations such as 'After great sorrow it is necessary to eat', and in a calm acceptance of brutality. The heroine's husband finally condemns his aunt to be burned alive. It is true that she has tried to murder his wife, but he watches the proceedings with great enjoyment.

Of *Flamenca*, a love story, Nitze and Dargan say in their *History of French Literature*: 'Except for its metrical form the *Flamenca* differs little from the modern novel.' *Joufrois* is a romance of adventure, but adventure confined entirely to this world, and some of the characters have the names of real persons such as Henry I of England.

Enough has perhaps been said to show that by no means all romances transport their readers to an idealized world or deal with 'positive values of empirical reality'; at least if this phrase is interpreted to mean either Christian doctrine or conventional morality. Jehan's motives in going to England were worthy of some character from Smiles's *Self Help*. The lady in the *Lai de l'Ombre* had a husband, her duty to whom she rather feebly invoked at one point in rejecting the knight. Although it is true that courtly love had a morality of its own and was held to be the source of all virtue, it is by no means certain that this is what Sorokin meant in describing the high moral tone of medieval literature. *Flamenca* has indeed been interpreted as a criticism of courtly love from the Christian point of view, but this, even if correct, is hardly obvious on the surface.

This particular novel of manners tended to describe manners as they ought to have been rather than as they actually were, and this tendency extends also to the material background. Medieval romances, with the exception of a few passages in Chrétien and the *Comte d'Anjou*, describe mainly what people liked to read about: fine weather rather than storms, summer rather than winter, youth rather than age. They see the splendour of medieval pageantry, not what was probably equally evident, the dirt and smells of the medieval towns. There are no tortures save those of love, no descriptions of executions except in the *Comte d'Anjou*. The adventures may all belong to this world and the theme illustrated be extremely prosaic, but there is no satire; and although a French nineteenth-century critic was much shocked at Jehan's behaviour in running away with his lord's daughter, he was a worthy young man, honourable and brave. There are, however, similar limitations to the realism of some of the English eighteenth century novels, to those of Richardson, for example, and even to *Tom Jones* itself.

Are these realistic romances to be ascribed to changes in contemporary society, or are they a result of the separate development of elements that were used together in Chrétien's poems? Chrétien's influence cannot be ignored. His romances were extremely popular, were imitated, adapted and the unfinished ones continued; and he was regarded as a master. Jean Frappier says that

> For fifty years the writers of romance in verse depended more or less on him . . . Whether it is a question of the romance of adventure and of love, or of the romance of manners, or of works which mingle after his example realism and the marvellous, the influence exercised by Chrétien can always be recognised, even in the works of authors like Jean Renart, who were not attracted by the Arthurian themes.[30]

The mere existence of a 'romance of manners' should, according to sociological theories, tell us something about contemporary society; but when it is only one among a number of other kinds something perhaps should also be said about its relative popularity. Scholars assess the success or failure of any work by the number of surviving manuscripts. By this test none of the realistic romances, except *Le Lai de l'Ombre* and the *Chastelaine de Vergi*, appear to have attracted much of an audience. *Joufrois*, *Guillaume de Dole* and *Flamenca* exist in one copy only, *Escoufle* in one and the fragment of another, and the *Comte d'Anjou* in two. In contrast, there are seven manuscripts of the *Lai*, and fifteen of the *Chastelaine*, some of them dating from the fifteenth century. Orr, who edited the *Lai*, suggested that Renart's other works were not liked because 'his realism was not in tune with the times'. On the other hand, the *Lai* is certainly the most entertaining of its author's poems, and the *Chastelaine* is also considered by modern critics to have high literary quality. They are also the most original of the thirteenth-century romances, in the sense that, however much they owe to what was now a well-established literary tradition, readers are reminded of later rather than earlier writers and forms of literature.

[30] Frappier, Jean, *op. cit.*

PROSE ROMANCES

Whatever their qualities, all these romances were written in verse, and it is not unreasonable to object that a novel is essentially a prose composition. If the first prose versions of the stories of romance are the true beginning of the novel, this would have to be put in the early years of the thirteenth century.

The turn to prose might well be considered one of the most momentous in the evolution of the novel, and its relations to changes in society to be well worth studying. Bruce in his *Evolution of Arthurian Romance* suggested that it was connected with a social phenomenon, the growth of literacy, especially among women, so that romance was no longer written primarily to be read aloud. It is doubtful how far modern scholars would accept his assumptions; but the change in medium has never been considered of outstanding literary or sociological interest, because at first it simply consisted in removing the rhyme from a poem. Some of the authors explain the motives which led them to do this. Roughly speaking they were two: a desire for accuracy, and a wish to make the subject easier to understand. It is evident that there were in the thirteenth century people who found verse as distasteful a medium for telling an interesting story as we should today.

The chronology of the prose romance is far from settled, but it is known that a prose version of Robert de Boron's poem on the Grail, *Perlesvaus*, a prose continuation of Chrétien's *Le Conte de Graal*, a prose *Tristan*, and the enormous work known as the prose *Lancelot* appeared some time between 1210 and 1235. This was also the period in which the prose chronicle first appeared, and the prose romance established the chronicle form for fiction, the form which starts with the birth of the hero, and which long survived the Middle Ages.

It might have been thought that the change in medium would bring with it a greater realism, but there is in romance no simple correlation between realism and prose; indeed, the prose romances tended to lose the realistic elements of the thirteenth-century stories in verse. Romances in prose show two opposite tendencies —to drop the *sens* and to relate a mere *roman d'aventure*, what later ages were to call a tale of chivalry, and to use a story to expound not the doctrines of courtly love but those of the Christian religion, or some aspect of it preferred by the author.

The Novel as a Literary Form

The prose *Tristan*[31] is an example of the first tendency. It has not been printed since 1516, but it has been studied by scholars and is considered simpler, indeed cruder, than the poems on the same theme. By making Tristan a knight of the Round Table owing allegiance not to Mark but to Arthur, it resolves the conflict between love and feudal obligations. A corresponding simplification is made in the character of Mark: he becomes simply a villain, an enemy to knighthood, and the writer's sympathies are exclusively reserved for the lovers. This Tristan, however, is as much or more concerned with adventure as with Iseult.

Not only is the romance expanded by introducing a long prologue concerning Tristan's ancestors, but it is also enlarged by the incorporation of all kinds of incidents derived from every conceivable source: *fabliaux*, Oriental fairy stories, the Latin classics, and even the Old Testament. Two somewhat unexpected characters are introduced: a Saracen knight in love with Iseult, and Dinadan, a knight who mocks at the theory and practice of chivalry, even admitting that he has no fondness for fighting.

Those who wished to use romance to express their religious convictions, or to convert others to them, were naturally attracted to the Grail story. A writer called Robert de Boron had written a poem about the early history of the Grail in which appears the first surviving mention of the whole legend of Joseph of Arimathea and the origin of the Grail. The prose version is taken by some scholars to be the earliest of all the prose romances. *Perlesvaus, The High History of the Holy Grail*, is a continuation of Chrétien's *Conte de Graal*, but the whole spirit is changed by the infusion of a harsh, crusading ethic which all the incidents are used to illustrate and emphasize.

Perlesvaus, however, might almost be considered a discovery of the twentieth century. Much more important from the point of view of literary history is the prose *Lancelot*.[32] This is, in a way, one of the most famous books ever written, because it is this *Lancelot* which Paolo and Francesca in the *Divine Comedy* read, and

[31] Vinaver, Eugene, *Etude sur le 'Tristan' en Prose*, Paris, 1925. (See also *Introduction to Malory*, 1947, and 'The Prose Tristan' in *Arthurian Literature*, edited by R. S. Loomis, 1959.)
[32] *Prose Lancelot*, edited by H. O. Sommer under the title 'The Vulgate Version of the Arthurian Romances', Washington, 1908–13. (Much abridged and translated into English by L. Paton, London, 1929.)

reading, kissed, and it is this to which Chaucer referred as the 'boke of Lancelot de Lake, that wommen holde in ful greete reverence'. Although it has none of the qualities which make medieval romance in verse delightful—it is neither gay, amusing nor surprising—it is an impressive work and in one respect at least conforms to the most modern requirements. Raymond Williams has said: 'When I think of the realist tradition of fiction, I think of the kind of novel which creates and judges the quality of a whole way of life in terms of the qualities of persons.' This indeed is exactly what the combination of the Lancelot story with the Grail theme sets out to do and achieves, although it is rather ideal than actual ways of life, which are depicted.

The prose *Lancelot* consists of three parts, although there are no divisions in the manuscripts: the *Lancelot* proper, an expansion of Chrétien's *Chevalier de la Charrette*, which retains much of the atmosphere and motives of courtly love; the *Quest of the Holy Grail*, which has a purely religious inspiration; and the *Mort Artu*, which contains the death of Arthur and the destruction of the Round Table. By combining these themes, which were originally quite distinct, the writer or writers depicted the downfall of the Round Table as a consequence of Lancelot's sin. The first part showed the greatness of Lancelot as a knight, the second his failure in the quest of the Grail because of his sinful love, and the last the worldly consequences of the corruption of sin. Another favourite medieval idea, that what is great must fall, symbolized by the wheel of fortune continually turning, is according to Jean Frappier transformed from a pagan to a Christian symbol by making fortune an 'angelic creature'.

This book superseded all other versions of the Arthur story and continued to be printed long after other medieval romances had undergone a temporary eclipse. Seven editions were printed in Paris between 1488 and 1533, and an abridgement at Lyons in 1591. Although it is in prose, it is less like the modern novel than the poems of Chrétien or many other verse romances. This is partly, no doubt, because it can hardly have been written by one man, so different are the various sections, although they are joined by the unified interpretation of the whole story. Even if the sections are considered alone, they are much more difficult for a modern reader to understand or to enjoy than most of the romances in verse. This is because it is not the subject-matter which really separates medieval from modern fiction. No one was ever deterred from reading Chrétien de Troyes or Malory because of giants, love potions or the Holy Grail; it is far less easy to read the prose *Lancelot*, because while both Chrétien and Malory use the narrative technique to which we are accustomed, *Lancelot* is recounted in the medieval manner.

In the emergence of the novel as a literary form, it is the change in technique rather than the content of the book which is of the greater importance. Once someone has produced a long account of an adventure, a whole life, or a particular episode, related partly by narrative, partly by dialogue, whether it is laid in the far past or in some quite imaginary time and place, the further step of telling a story of contemporary life by similar methods is a less drastic innovation. The French prose romance told a story in a mixture of narrative and dialogue, which relates it to the novel, but it did not tell it in logical sequence. Logical does not mean chronological: the romance frequently starts with the marriage of the hero's parents and may end with his death. Some modern novels—Aldous Huxley's *Eyeless in Gaza*, for instance—do not move along a temporal line but the incidents have a logical relation to each other. The prose romances employ a different technique which French historians of literature call '*entrelacement*', interweaving. Lot in his *Étude sur le 'Lancelot' en prose*[33] explains that 'no adventure forms a whole sufficient in itself. On the one hand, previous episodes left provisionally on one side in it pursue their ramifications, on the other subsequent episodes near or remote are drawn into it.' The canon of Toledo in *Don Quixote* was highly irritated by this narrative method: 'I have never,' he said, 'yet seen a book of chivalry complete in all its parts, so that the middle agrees with the beginning and the end with the beginning and middle; but they seem to construct their stories with such a multitude of members as though they meant to produce a monster rather than a well-proportioned figure.'

Nineteenth-century critics took much the same view, and ascribed the rambling line of romance to mere incompetence or to the lack of logic of the medieval 'mind'. Lot and Vinaver have shown that it is, on the contrary, a literary technique and both have compared it to the making of tapestry.

---

[33] Lot, Ferdinand, *Etude sur le Lancelot en Prose*, Paris, 1918.

Just as in a tapestry each thread alternates with an endless variety of others, so in the early prose romances of the Arthurian group numerous seemingly independent episodes or 'motifs' are inter-woven in a manner which makes it possible for each episode to be set aside at any moment and resumed later. No single stretch of such a narrative can be complete in itself any more than a single stitch in a woven fabric; the sequel may appear at any moment, however long the interval. But the resemblance goes no further, for unlike the finished tapestry a passage of a prose romance has as a rule no natural conclusion; when the author brings it to a close he simply cuts the threads at arbitrarily chosen points, and anyone who chooses to pick them up and interweave them in a similar fashion can continue the work indefinitely.[34]

Thorpe in his edition of the *Romance of Laurin* has thrown a flood of light on the composition of the prose romance by point-ing out that during the time it took to read a long romance some of the members of the audience would probably have disappeared and others arrived. 'The long romance would have needed a considerable number of evenings for its recital. The sittings might not have been consecutive . . . at each sitting there must have been a possibility of new-comers.'[35] This obviously means that the episodes would have to be more or less self-contained, and the construction of the work as a whole would tend to follow the pattern of a radio serial rather than of a nineteenth-century novel.

THE FIFTEENTH-CENTURY NOUVELLE

The moment when this method was exchanged for one more like that employed in the eighteenth and nineteenth centuries was a turning-point in the development of fiction as, if not more, important than the deliberate introduction of contemporary scenes and characters. Vinaver places this in the fifteenth century and believes it to have resulted, apart from the personal idiosyn-crasies of writers, from the tendency to take episodes out of a long cycle and make them complete in themselves, thus turning them into 'nouvelles', 'the real though unacknowledged starting-point of modern fiction'.[36] In this view there are two distinct traditions

---

[34] Vinaver, Eugene, Introduction to *Malory's 'Morte d' Arthur'*, Oxford, 1947.
[35] Thorpe, Lewis, Introduction to *The Romance of Laurin*, 1960.
[36] Vinaver, *op. cit.*

of prose fiction in Europe, that of the vast complicated inter-woven romance, and that of a story with a definite beginning leading to a well-defined end. The actual story told by either method is not so important as the method itself, as can be seen by contrasting Malory, who used the new technique to tell the story, already old in his day, of the Round Table, with the Spanish writers criticized by Cervantes who wrote of heroes, whose names at least were new, in the old manner.

The influence of Malory on the subsequent course of English literature, indeed of English life, has always been fully admitted. A French critic has said: 'Without him, in the England of today, neither poetry, nor thought nor art would be exactly what they are.' But this pervading influence is usually thought to have been felt in poetry and national ideals rather than in prose fiction. Gosse in his article in the *Encyclopaedia Britannica* said: 'The great merits of this writer were that he got rid of the medieval burden of allegory, essayed an interpretation of the human heart and invented a lucid and vigorous style of narrative. But his book became . . . a feeder of poetry rather than prose and it gave no inkling of the methods of the modern novel,' and this is the usual attitude of critics who generally add something about Malory's nostalgia for the past which unfitted him for making innovations in literature. Vinaver has re-interpreted *le Morte d'Arthur* in the light of Malory's French sources.

He says of Malory's Arthurian romances that 'they effect the transition from the medieval to the modern conception of the novel', and adds:

> If . . . courtly poetry, through survivals and adaptations, became the ancestor of the psychological novel, it was because the cardinal elements of psychological fiction were there, even though they were lacking in cohesion and unity of purpose, as were the non-harmonised voices before the discovery of plural melody; and perhaps the main importance of Malory's work lies in the fact that it is an example of their gradual harmonisation.[37]

The manuscript of the *Morte d'Arthur*, found at Winchester in 1937, has led Vinaver to believe that Malory conceived the different episodes as separate stories, and that it was Caxton, his

[37] For a view dissenting from Vinaver's estimate, see C. S. Lewis, 'The English Prose Morte' in *Essays on Malory*, edited by J. R. W. Bennett, 1963.

publisher, who tried to amalgamate them into one. But even if his view is rejected, as it still is by some scholars, Malory greatly simplified his material. Vinaver has compared the *Morte d'Arthur* with the French books which Malory translated, and shows how he simplified the narrative line. This he did partly by shortening and leaving out whole stretches of the French book. He also re-arranged the episodes he kept; for example, in the Tale of King Arthur there were, in the book he translated, three main strands: (1) Arthur's war with the barons, who were unwilling to recognize his title, or with foreign enemies; (2) Merlin, his love for Nivene, and his death; and (3) the relations of Arthur with his sister Morgan Le Fay. These main episodes are interwoven with the adventures of various knights. Vinaver has listed the separate threads and the way they are interwoven by letters which may at first sight look like elementary algebra; but no one need be alarmed, it is not an attempt to apply mathematical formulae to literature. In the original the first episode concerns Merlin and Nivene. This is a preparation for Merlin's final incarceration in the rock, for Merlin tells her a story of how Diana shut up her lover Faunus in a tomb; this Vinaver calls a^1. The French *Merlin* then moves to Arthur's wars, b; then to Morgan Le Fay, c^1; then back to Merlin and Nivene, a^2, then to Morgan Le Fay again, c^2. Malory, instead of this line $a^1bc^1a^2c^2$, follows the simpler one $a^1a^2bc^1c^2$. This is only one comparatively straightforward example: an analysis of the more drastic disentangling of the themes of the French *Morte d'Arthur* in Malory's book of Sir Lancelot and Queen Guinevere must be sought in Vinaver's edition of Malory.

There are, as Vinaver has also pointed out, strongly realistic elements in Malory's subject-matter, and these are curiously like the characteristics supposed to be new in the eighteenth-century novel. Vinaver says that:

> his originality as a writer shows itself chiefly in the directness of exposition, in the substitution of simple manners for courtly etiquette and in the elimination of the supernatural and mysterious. He prefers straightforward speech to elaborate orations, human cunning to the inexplicable workings of supernatural forces, and a realistic setting to the conventional fairy-tale scenery of French romance.

Vinaver has enabled readers unfamiliar with the French sources to follow the changes made by Malory, so that it soon becomes possible to discern those sentences which he inserted or altered, even without reference to Vinaver's notes. Only one example can be given here, but the transformation wrought by 'a preference for realistic dialogue' can be seen in the following passage.

> Soo unto this counseyle these five kynges assented, and so they passed forth with hir oste thorow North Walys and come uppon Arthure be nyght and sette uppon his oste as the kynge and his knyghtes were in their pavylyons. So kynge Arthure was unarmed and leyde him to reste with his quene Gwenyvere.
> 'Sir,' seyde sir Kayyus, 'hit is nat beste we be unarmed.'
> 'We shall have no nede,' seyde sir Gawayne and sir Gryflet that lay in a lytyll pavylyon by the kynge.
> So with that they harde a grete noyse and many cryed 'Treson!' 'Alas!' seyde Arthure, 'we be betrayed! Unto armys, felowys!' than he cryed. So they were armed anone at all poyntes.

Of this the remarks of Sir Kayyus, Sir Gawayne and Sir Gryflet are not in the French, and instead of Arthur's shouts, the French says, 'When King Arthur heard the cries he knew they were all alarmed and asked for his arms and they were brought and he armed as quick as he could because he saw plainly that they had need of him.'

It has been said that one of the marks of the eighteenth-century novels was to substitute a definite locality for the vague background of previous fiction. This, however, is a constant preoccupation with Malory. He is not only certain that Arthur was King, not of a fairy-tale kingdom, but of England, he also knows exactly where the knights are in that kingdom. In the story of the Fair Maid of Astolet he says: 'Astolet, that is the English Gylforde . . .' It has been suggested that he selected Guildford because it was about a day's ride from London, and as Lancelot is going to Winchester it would have been a natural place to break the journey.

The discontent felt by Arthur's subjects with his endless wars is ascribed mainly to the people of the southern part of England; and the fiefs, which Lancelot gives to the knights who follow him overseas after the quarrel with Arthur, correspond with known places to such an extent that it has been conjectured that Malory spent some time in Aquitaine as a soldier. An example of realistic detail not noted by Vinaver is the description of Lancelot's treatment of the hawk, which a lady had constrained him to climb a tree to catch. He managed to catch the creature's jesses, found a rotten bough, tied the jesses to it, and threw the bough down. This, of course, would be the only way of dealing with a hawk, especially with a hawk which had reason for anger, as it would be quite impossible to descend the tree bearing the infuriated bird on one's wrist.

Ian Watt in his study of the eighteenth-century novel found that it was 'distinguished from most previous fiction by its use of past experience as the cause of present action'. Perhaps the word 'most' conceals an admission that Malory made the actions of his characters produce the final tragedy. This may be thought to be an integral part of the story itself, but, as Vinaver has pointed out, Malory has made it more explicit, and has completely dropped the idea of the wheel of fortune for ever turning, so that prosperity and disaster were not due to human actions but to unavoidable fate. In the French *Morte d'Arthur*, Arthur says at the last disastrous battle, 'Fortune who has been a mother to me has become a step-mother and will cause me to pass the remnants of my days in sorrow and contempt and in misery', whereas in Malory he says, 'Sir Lancelot, this day I have missed thee.'

Nor does Malory judge worldly chivalry by the light of religious truth. He is noticeably uninterested in Galahad, and his Lancelot seems hardly disturbed by his failure in the quest of the Grail. Malory interprest the tragedy of Lancelot as one of conflict between two duties both equally valid: his feudal obligation to Arthur, and the duty of a knight to his lady. Tragedy has, in English in general, followed Shakespeare in making the intrusion of evil the fulcrum of disaster. There is no evil in Malory, no sense of sin, and even no real feeling of guilt. When caught in bed with Guinevere without arms or armour Lancelot says, 'Jesus Christ be my sword and buckler', and his remorse after the catastrophe is the sorrow of a man who has made a fearful mistake, not of a man who had committed a great sin. Heaven accepts this interpretation; for the abbot of the monastery in which he passes his last years on the night of his death declares that he had seen in a dream how heaven's angels came to fetch him.

Malory also emphasizes the contribution which both Arthur and Gawain made to the final calamity, and their motives, too, were, in the circumstances, quite natural and dictated by the conventions of the time.

Whether Malory seriously thought that adultery was not of a sin or that love is its own justification, although it has been discussed by learned men, is beside the point; he has created his world without evil, for Mordred in this version is not so much a character as a necessary piece of mechanism. It would be silly to use the word 'modern', but Malory's interpretation is more in tune with today's ideas than is either the prose Lancelot or Tennyson's *Idylls of the King*.

Malory has often puzzled critics, but whatever their views on his merits as a story-teller, they have unanimously admitted his greatness as a prose writer. About Antoine de La Sale and his book *Le petit Jehan de Saintré*,[38] supposed to have been written between 1451 and 1455, there has been the widest disagreement. French critics have expressed very different views both about the intentions and the value of this work. Some have regarded it as a masterpiece and one of the first examples of the French novel; others have found it painful not to say disgusting, a clumsy melange of the medieval edifying story with the *fabliaux*. It is in any case a story, whether it is a novel or not. The plot, although Jehan de Saintré was a real character, appears to have been invented. It is set about a hundred years before the author's lifetime, in the reign of Jean Le Bon, but is generally considered to portray rather the manners of the author's own period. No attempt is made to fit the story into the facts of the King's life: there is, for example, no reference to the sufficiently striking episode of his capture at the battle of Poitiers and his four-year imprisonment in England.

The beginning of the book, though perhaps startling to modern ideas, conforms with the conventions of the time. A great lady, simply called *Belle Cousine*, or My Lady, cousin to the King of France and a widow, chooses one of the Court pages when he is thirteen, teaches him all she knows, supplies him with money and uses her influence with the King for his advancement, with the purpose both of educating a good knight and making him her lover when he is of proper age. She achieves both these ends. For thirteen years they are devoted lovers, and Jehan distinguishes himself in

[38] *Le Petit Jehan de Saintré*, edited by P. Chaufrois, and F. Desonay, Paris, 1926. (English translation Irvine Gray, 1931.) The book has been discussed by Sainte-Beuve, *Causieries du Lundi. VII*; George Saintsbury, *History of the French Novel*, 1917; Gaston Paris, *La Poesie au Moyen Age*, Paris, 1895; A. Coville, *Le Petit Jehan de Saintré*, Paris, 1927; Janet Ferrier, *Forerunners of the French Novel*, 1954.

tournaments and jousts of which there are long and no doubt accurate descriptions. At the end of thirteen years, however, he decides that he must do something to distinguish himself further and goes to fight against the infidel.

When he comes back after no very prolonged absence he finds that My Lady has taken another lover, a middle-class abbé; from this point the book changes and becomes 'realistic' in every sense of the word. It recounts Jehan's revenge both on the monk and on the lady. Strictly speaking, the conventions of courtly love did not permit action against the lady, and Jehan's treatment of the monk is hardly in the best traditions of chivalry. After having been beaten by him in a fight with their bare hands, Jehan tricks the unfortunate monk into armour in which he is, of course, helpless before an experienced knight; and when he has defeated him, pierces through his tongue and both his cheeks with a dagger and leaves him thus. His vengeance on the lady is more subtle.

> It befell one evening, after supper, the King and Queen being in a fair meadow, and with them great plenty of ladies and lords, that the Seigneur de Saintré said unto the Queen and unto the other ladies: 'Sit ye all here, and I will tell you a true tale and a marvellous history, which one hath writ unto me from afar'.
>
> —'Come,' said the Queen, 'let us hear it, perdy! Be seated, Madam', and she called My Lady her Fair Cousin; and all ye ladies, let us sit down and hearken to this tale of the Seigneur de Saintré's.'
>
> The Seigneur de Saintré began anon his tale, as well as he could, saying:—'Madam, I read of late a letter concerning a true history lately befallen which none hath yet heard tell. It befell, in Germany, that a very noble and puissant lady was pleased to take into her favour a gentle youth; and she gave him such bounty, such honours and such love that in a certain space of time she made of him a worshipful knight; and they loved one another so loyally (so the letter doth say) that never were truer lovers.
>
> 'Thus was it, Madam, with this poor wretch, who was in such favour with his lady that never was any lover in better. It came to pass that by the will of Fortune, for love of her, and to increase his honour, he journeyed into France to perform deeds of arms, out of which he came forth with honour. But whiles these things were being done, his Lady fell acquainted with a monk, tall, stout, and puissant of body, who was a Lord Abbot: and they cast such love unto each other that it was over-much.'

'And then,' said the Queen, 'she made such evil joy as to forsake, for a monk, him that so loved her?'

'Madam, it was so; for I have it by a letter that would not lie. Now hearken, Madam, and you shall hear what came of it . . .'

Then word by word he told the story: first, how the lover found them hawking; how the Abbot sent to ask My Lady whether they should bid him to sup, and the answer that she made; how the lover, to see the farce, soon assented; how the Abbot and My Lady disparaged knights and squires that went about the world to do deeds of arms, and then how they wrestled, and the two goodly falls that the Abbot gave him, their laughter and merriment, the embassy that the brethren made; and to be brief, the combat, and how he dealt with the Abbot; likewise the words that the lover spake unto his Lady, and how by cause of her blue girdle, she being unworthy to wear that colour, he ungirded her and bore it away. For this matter, which was yet hid and supposed to be in Germany, the Lady was much blamed by all that were there, and the lover much praised for the combat.

. . . Then said the Seigneur de Saintré unto the Queen and unto all the ladies there present:—

'Madam, and ye, ladies, the tale biddeth us say of this Lady whether she did well or no; and you, Madam, I ask first.'

The Queen, when she had heard tell of the love between a Lord Abbot and a lady misdoubted somewhat that it might be her Fair Cousin; but sith she wist naught of the love between her and Saintré, she knew not what to think for certain; so, to see what My Lady would say, she put upon her the task to speak first of that Lady. Then answered she: 'Madam, may't please you to excuse me, for I paid no heed to his tale. But, if you please, say yourself or let the others say; and when you and all the rest have spoken (though 'tis a thing whereof we ought to be silent) I will say what I think, if I must.'

Then quoth the Queen: 'Sith that We, as Queen, must first begin, verily Saintré, if it be as you have said, We say that such a Lady is false and evil; and We will say no more.' —'And you, My Lady de Retel, what say you?'— 'I say as the Queen saith; and moreover, that she ought to be banned from all gentle company that she was in.' . . . And there was none among them all but gave sentence before her.

Now when the Seigneur de Saintré had asked them all, he turned him unto My Lady and kneeling asked her opinion, as he had the rest. My Lady, who knew not what to say, being she whom the tale concerned, was so besought by the Queen and other ladies to speak, as they had done, that she said at length: 'Sith that I must speak, I say that this lover, be he knight or squire, was passing discourteous to have ungirded the Lady and borne away her girdle, as you did say.'

'Forsooth, Madam!' said Saintré; 'have you naught else to say, save that for having ungirded that false Lady of her blue girdle, and borne it away by reason that she was not worthy to wear such a colour, you say that he was therefore passing discourteous?'

Then drew he from his sleeve the girdle all tipped with gold, saying unto her: 'Madam, I would not be so discourteous.' And before the Queen and all, kneeling full courteously upon his knee, he laid it in her lap.[39]

Two objections can be made to describing the book as a novel. Whole chapters are devoted to such topics as Christian doctrine and Roman history, although they are given in a dramatic setting as they are part of Belle Cousine's education of her knight, and it has been suggested that her exposition of Christian ethics supplies an ironic comment on her subsequent behaviour. The treatment of the Crusade is wildly romantic. Jehan performs prodigious feats of arms and finally kills the Grand Turk himself.

Nor are the characters depicted with any particular skill. Belle Cousine's infidelity, which is more than the need for another bed-fellow when her knight is away—she has lost all interest in Jehan—does not seem to be consistent with the rest of what we are told of her. She was indeed offended that Jehan had conceived and organized his expedition without asking her advice, but this is not made a reason for her behaviour; she originally retired to the country because she was miserable at Court without her lover.

On the other hand, the plot could have been treated as a short story. It is easy to imagine it as one of the tales either of the Decameron or of the *Heptameron* of the Queen of Navarre. La Sale gives it the elaboration of background and detail, which is one of the marks of the novel, with the characteristically modern narrative technique. This very elaboration may incline modern readers to refuse it the title as the descriptions of jousts are undoubtedly tedious; but it has to be remembered that they interested the author, who was much in request as an umpire, and no doubt interested its first readers, too. We are told not much more about them than we learn in some American novels about the details of

[39] *Le Petit Jehan de Saintré*, translated Irvine Gray.

various industries, and they take up not much more space than some English writers have given to cricket or hunting. The jousts are treated also in contrast to the war in a completely realistic spirit: although the hero always wins, he wins on points only—not as he would have in the novels of some of the nineteenth-century followers of Scott, in which he would undoubtedly have knocked his opponent off his horse at the first onslaught.

The narrative method is also modern in the sense that the story is concerned only with two characters. There are digressions, but these are lessons given by Belle Cousine to Jehan, and there are no episodes unrelated to the main plot, as in the romances. Jehan's journey round Europe challenging all comers might be regarded by a strict critic as a digression, but it serves to show his prowess.

There is, however, no unity in tone between the two parts of the story. In the first part, Belle Cousine's seduction or education of Jehan, whichever word may best describe it, is treated in idealistic terms. It has been called 'gracious' by both French and English critics; while enough has been said about the second part to show that its realism would be called harsh even today. Many reasons have been suggested to explain this divergence, among them that La Sale, who was tutor to the Duke of Calabria, the son of King René of Anjou, wrote the first part as a sort of frame to the lessons he wished to impart to his pupil, and the second to amuse the same pupil when grown up. Or that one was written in the pure atmosphere of the Court of Anjou and the other at the 'decadent' court of Burgundy. Other critics have seen the book as an unsuccessful effort to join together two stories, the first a chivalrous romance, the second a typical *fabliaux*.

Two characteristics of the latter novel absent from Malory and La Sale are the conscious portrayal of contemporary life and the detailed descriptions of landscape, houses and streets. Richardson and Fielding meant 'to paint the manners of the age' and this, to their contemporaries, was what distinguished their work from earlier fiction. Johnson said, 'The works of fiction with which the present generation seems more particular delighted, are such as exhibit life in its true state, diversified by accidents that daily happen in the world.'[40]

Malory certainly had no intention of painting a picture of con-

[40] Johnson, Samuel, *The Rambler*, No. 4, May 31st, 1750.

temporary life: he thought he was writing of another age and from time to time contrasted it with his own. La Sale, on the other hand, although he says his story took place in the past, gives us only too much of the 'manners of the age'. The use of contemporary life as material for story or romance was not, however, new in the eighteenth century, unless a rigid distinction is made between poetry and prose. The pilgrimage and the pilgrims in *The Canterbury Tales* are meant to refer to scenes and characters of Chaucer's England, and many of the tales are set in it as well. Also it must be remembered that what nineteenth-century critics meant by 'accidents that daily happen in the world' was the kind of thing that might occur to the ordinary citizen of a civilized state in the eighteenth or nineteenth century. Saintsbury thought that the novel could not have emerged in a period of violence or disorder. In a book such as *Tom Jones* in which violence does occur it is purely private—duels, highwaymen and fights. The story is determined entirely by the interplay of individuals, uninfluenced by war or by the arbitrary action of tyrants, governments, barons, mobs. The Jacobite rebellion has no real effect on events, as can be seen by comparing it with *Waverley*. A book such as this, however, would not have given a true picture of the fifteenth century any more than it would give a true picture of the twentieth. Johnson and Saintsbury would not have regarded Koestler's *Darkness at Noon* as dealing with incidents that might happen to anyone.

Elaborate descriptions of the natural background are also lacking in both Malory and La Sale. La Sale, indeed, describes clothes, food and furnishing; but Malory describes these less than most other medieval writers and uses mainly evocative phrases for landscapes, such as 'a grete water that rored' and 'the cryinge and crackyin of thunder', and these phrases are often inserted in dialogue as in 'Then Sir Lyonelle espyed a grete appyll tre that stoode by an hedge, and seyde "Sir, yondir is a fayre shadow, there we may reste us and our horsys." '

Descriptions, however, hardly appear in the eighteenth-century novel until Fielding, and only in a minor degree even in his books. *Robinson Crusoe* is, of course, an exception, but the description of the desert island and of Crusoe's various implements and utensils is the story.

The absence of background does not strike us quite so forcibly as it did the nineteenth-century critics, because many of the most admired modern novelists have returned to the method of telling a story mainly in dialogue, only indicating its setting briefly and in outline.

To the *Morte d' Arthur* and *Petit Jehan de Saintrè* should perhaps be added another book, *Les Angoisses douloureuses qui procèdent de l'amours*,[41] by Hélisenne de Crenne, which appeared in France in 1530. It is, as can be easily guessed from its obscurity, not a very good book, or even interesting in the way in which mediocre books sometimes are; but it is a long prose story and deals with characters in a middle station of life in a realistic setting. It is written indeed in the aureate diction of the period, which diminishes its realistic quality, as no one can ever have talked in such a way, except as a game and for short periods.

Two if not three books thus appeared between the middle of the fifteenth and the middle of the sixteenth century which possessed at least some of the characteristics often said not to be discernible in fiction until the eighteenth century. Neither Malory or La Sale founded a school and both were isolated writers, as was Hélisenne de Crenne. Is one to assume that there were in this period social forces which stimulated a tendency towards the novel? And were these in turn suppressed by other forces which encouraged a return to a less realistic kind of fiction?

THE CONTINUING INFLUENCE OF ROMANCE

The themes of romance lived on, as is sufficiently shown by our own familiarity with them, but they were submerged, for the educated classes, by the sixteenth- and seventeenth-century passion for the classics. The earliest English novel was, however, not written for those who knew Greek or even Latin, but for a much humbler audience. These people continued to read versions of medieval stories up to, and even after, the publication of *Robinson Crusoe*.

Malory was not reprinted after 1634 until the beginning of the nineteenth century; but *Guy of Warwick*, which was among John Paston's books in the fifteenth century, had six new editions between 1640 and 1760. *Huon of Bordeaux, Paris and Vienne,*

---

[41] There seems to be no modern edition of this book, but there are copies of sixteenth-century editions in the British Museum.

Valentine and Orson were other stories which appeared again and again. These versions had indeed lost everything of the originals except the outline of the story, but they were republished for exactly the kind of readers for which *Robinson Crusoe* was written. New romances were even produced. *The Seven Champions of Christendom* first appeared in 1615. Among the evidence for the popularity of this kind of literature is one of Bunyan's sermons, in which the sinner in hell is described as saying: 'The scriptures, thought I, what are they? A dead letter, a little ink and paper— give me a ballad, a new book, George on horseback, and Bevis of Hampton.'

Mr. Badman also read romances; as Bunyan says he did himself before he was converted. Historians of literature have seen the origin of 'the valley of the shadow', in the *Pilgrim's Progress*, in 'the dark valley' of the romances, and have described Mr. Greatheart as a descendant of the knight errant. How convincing these parallels seem must depend on individual judgement.

Long after the realistic novel had been established the old romances were apparently still read. The two books which predisposed Jeremy Tugwell, in *The Spiritual Quixote*, to 'enthusiasm' were *The Seven Champions of Christendom* and Mandeville's *Travels*, and this as late as 1771.

Richardson said that he had wasted his time when young in reading romance, and romance to him seems to have meant a mixture of the medieval story with the heroic novel; at least it meant this to Miss Harriet Byron, who describes her dreams as haunted with romantic echoes: 'I am a damsel in distress. The milk-white palfrey once came in. All the marvellous takes place; and lions and tigers are slain, and armies routed by the pursuance of his high aim.'

In France, where the novel was in origin not popular but aristocratic, the influence of romance was naturally less, and has sometimes been taken to have been non-existent. But the Spanish tale of chivalry which, in the French translation of Amadis de Gaule (1540), was one of the most admired and widely read stories of the seventeenth century, continued the medieval tradition, and is indeed considered to have been derived from some version of the *Lancelot* story.

Even in the hey-day of classicism, Mademoiselle de Scudéry, in the dedication of her first book (1641) to the Duchesse de Rohan, says, 'It seems to me Mademoiselle that a stay in Brittanny is in some manner favourable to reading of this sort, and that there the great names of Tristan of Lyonesse and the incomparable Iseult dispose the mind, in a way, to take pleasure in similar adventures.'[42]

The effect of the change in technique in the fifteenth century may not be so immediately obvious as the continuing influence of the old stories, because, although completely victorious in the end, it was not adopted for long stories for a considerable time. Its importance can best be realized when it is remembered that fiction has often returned to the subject-matter of romance, more frequently still to fantasy and adventure, but never to the technique of the prose romance.

[42] Scudérey, Madeleine de, *Ibrahim ou l'Illustre Bassa*, 1641.

3

The Literary Background of the Eighteenth-Century Novel

As neither the realism, the contemporary setting nor the narrative method employed in the eighteenth century can be regarded as unique to the period, it is at first sight not easy to see why Fielding declared that his was a 'new province of writing', and why later critics and historians of literature agreed with him. To writers themselves, however, the most important part of the literary background is their immediate predecessors, and when the new was compared with the old romance in the eighteenth century it was not being contrasted with Chrétien de Troyes, the French thirteenth-century romance or with Malory, all forgotten at the time, but with *Amadis de Gaule*, *The Arcadia*, *L'Astrée*, and the French heroic novels.

Anyone who picks up one of these books will have no difficulty in seeing why eighteenth-century readers were so impressed by the originality of the novelists of their own day. The sixteenth- and seventeenth-century romances are all episodic in structure, their characters are kings and princes, they are all set in the past and the hero and heroine are idealized to suit their exalted rank. This idealization, which is not confined to the main characters, leads to a lifeless form of speech, grammatically faultless and without any idiosyncrasies either of personal character, class, profession or nationality. The Lancelot story may be the basis of *Amadis de Gaule*, but it has been changed to suit the moral and literary conventions of the sixteenth century. This Lancelot would never have entangled himself with another man's wife, particularly if that man was a king. The realistic element of the older romance, even in the form of vivid description has, however the original Spanish may read, vanished in the French version, as well as in Southey's translation.

Although *L'Astrée*, *The Arcadia* and the French heroic novel are very different from each other, they were all inspired by the idea of the prose epic.

THE THEORY OF THE PROSE EPIC

It was believed not only by critics but also by Cervantes, Sir Philip Sidney and Fielding that an epic might be written in prose. Sir Philip Sidney's statement is the best known to English readers:

> The greatest part of Poets have apparelled their poeticall inventions in that numbrous kinde of writing which is called verse: indeed but apparelled, verse being but an ornament and no cause to Poetry; sith there have beene many most excellent Poets that never versified, and now swarme many versifiers that neede never aunswere to the name of Poets. For *Xenophon*, who did imitate so excellently as to give us *effigiem iusti imperii*, the portraiture of a just Empire, under the name of *Cyprus*, made therein an absolute heroicall Poem. So did Heliodorus in his sugred invention of that picture of love in *Theagines* and *Cariclea*. And yet both these writ in Prose: which I speak to shew, that it is not riming and versing that maketh a Poet, no more than a long gowne maketh an Advocate; who though he pleaded in armor should be an Advocate and no Souldier. But it is that fayning notable images of vertues, vices, or what els, with that delightfull teaching, which must be the right describing note to know a Poet by.[1]

There seems little doubt that Sidney conceived his *Arcadia* to be such an heroic poem. Subsequent generations on the whole have, however, regarded it as a romance; but if any reader approaches it expecting anything like either twelfth-century fiction, or like Malory, he will be struck mainly by how very unlike the older romance it is, in structure, in language, and in characterization.

L'Astrée is generally described as a pastoral novel. In this kind of fiction ladies and gentlemen go and live as shepherds and shepherdesses in an idyllic landscape. Several critics have lately been at pains to argue that this convention is not as pointless as

[1] Sidney, Philip, *An Apologie for Poetry*, 1595.

was at one time believed and that the love affairs are not without psychological truth, even if they have no social reality. Its artificiality, however, separates it from the early eighteenth-century novel, and even the psychology is weakened by the strongly moral purpose of the author. There are two opposing ways in which a writer can attempt to influence his contemporaries for their good: by depicting the manners of the age as they are and insinuating that they are in need of change, or by painting manners *Moral* which have never existed as a pattern to which men and women might aspire. D'Urfé, like most of those who told of Arthur, took the second course, and in his moral purpose he was as successful as any writer has been. He contributed to a refinement of manners and sentiment; but there is no denying that this method does not make for exciting reading. It requires poetry rather than prose, and even when it is moving and delightful it certainly makes a book less like a novel. This is not surprising when it is remembered that d'Urfé himself thought he was writing not a romance but an epic. Since an epic is generally defined as a poem relating the deeds of a hero, this may seem an odd judgement, because the pastoral necessarily excludes the heroic and because d'Urfé's book is mainly in prose. At least one Renaissance critic, however, included the pastoral among the epic kinds, and d'Urfé so far observed the conventions of epic as to set his novel far in the past and to people it with kings.

Both *L'Astrée* and *The Arcadia* may have been among the books Richardson and Fielding protested against, but Sir Philip Sidney's work always retained a certain reputation—at least in England. It is believed that Richardson took the name of his first heroine 'Pamela', then almost unknown, from it.

The real target for the slighting remarks about 'strange tales' and 'heroical adventures' were the heroic novels of La Calprenéde and Mademoiselle de Scudéry. These authors were also inspired by the idea of writing a prose epic. La Calprenéde remarked, 'I have conducted my heroes to battle in a manner a little too near to that of Homer, Virgil and Tasso.' and Mademoiselle de Scudéry said that the only masters she had imitated were d'Urfé's and that same Heliodorus to whom Sidney referred. There is certainly nothing epic about the heroic novel except the intention of their authors, Mademoiselle de Scudéry included in her's portraits of her contemporaries, depicted, it is true, in the most flattering colours; but this clearly led away from the heroic towards a more realistic conception of the novel. She, as well as La Calprenéde, took over from epic theory the idea that the hero should be some historical character, and that the example of his actions should inspire virtuous aspirations in the reader. From the romance came the preoccupation with love. Whatever his name—Cyrus, Alexander or Ibrahim—the main concern of these heroes is not war, politics, or conquest, but the woman he adores, woman not women, for these heroes are strictly monogamous.

The vast range of epic, including as it does whole segments of history, gave sanction to the episodic structure of these books, which itself was probably inherited from the prose versions of medieval romance. There are in the heroic novel many subplots neither necessary nor strictly relevant to the main design, but the technique is not the medieval technique of interweaving. In this form, known as the 'intercalated romance', fresh characters do not wander in as they do in medieval romance, take charge of the story for a time and then wander out again only to be encountered later. In heroic romance they tell the story of their lives instead. A reminiscence of this technique can be seen in the story of the Old Man of the Hill in *Tom Jones*. An American author has counted the pages of La Calprenéde's *Pharamond* and formed the following estimate:

Number of pages devoted to the main group
of characters   1,000

Number of pages devoted to those characters
who figure in the episodic action which is not
related to the central action   2,500

Number of pages of direct narrative given to
matters not immediately important to the
central action   500[2]

Madmazelle de Scudéry's books are the antitheses of the twentieth-century novel in ideas, and in the conception of character; but the structure of the most famous, *Le Grand Cyrus*, is curiously modern, employing as it does the technique of the flash-back. It opens with a description of the assault and burning of a sea-port. The characters are simply there, they are in no way explained and we only learn how they got there and their relations

[2] Pitou, S., *La Calprenéde's Pharamond*, Baltimore, 1938.

to each other considerably later. This is done by one character explaining the situation to another; it is not shown as memory or reminiscence as it would be in the modern use of the method. It is, all the same, a warning not to assume too easily that particular ways of constructing a novel are necessarily the result of a particular social or cultural situation. Indeed, by the beginning of the eighteenth century almost every way of telling a story had been tried: starting with the birth of the hero and proceeding straight on, plunging into the middle of a situation with full explanations, plunging into the middle of a situation without any explanations, and then proceeding to the end of the adventure, and plunging into the situation and only elucidating it by moving backwards in time.

Richardson and Fielding reacted against both the content and the narrative method of the heroic novel; although Fielding was himself influenced by the theory of the prose epic. They objected to the impossible virtue, as well as to the high rank of the characters, and probably also, although they did not explicitly state this, to the lifeless dialogue. A character in the beginning of *Le Grand Cyrus* starts to persuade the hero to rescue a princess, whom he has in charge, from imminent death by fire or massacre in the following words: 'My Lord, if the name of Thrombulas has not escaped your memory, grant him the grace of exercising your authority to prevent the death of an illustrious personage.' It is hardly necessary to point out the complete unreality of this sort of conversation in the middle of a town which was being sacked by one army and burnt by another.

The theory of the prose epic must have had some influence in shaping the modern novel, because what would a prose epic be but a kind of novel? We know that the concept moulded Fielding's ideas, because he tells us so both in the Preface to *Joseph Andrews* and in the introductory essays in *Tom Jones*: 'A comic romance is a comic epic-poem in prose; differing from comedy, as the serious epic from tragedy: its action being more extended and comprehensive; containing a much larger circle of incidents, and introducing a greater variety of characters.' The word 'comic' here does not have exactly the connotation it has today: one must think of comedy, not of farce, as Fielding himself indicated.

Indeed, no two species of writing can differ more widely than the comic and the burlesque: for as the latter is ever the exhibition of what is monstrous and unnatural, and where our delight, if we examine it, arises from the surprising absurdity, as in appropriating the manners of the highest to the lowest, or *e converso*; so in the former, we should ever confine ourselves strictly to nature, from the just imitation of which will flow all the pleasure we can this way convey to a sensible reader.

THE SPANISH PICARESQUE TALE

If the eighteenth-century novelists' reaction against the heroic novel is the aspect of their work most emphasized, as it generally is, their realism seems more revolutionary than it was. If they are placed not against selected authors but against the whole background of European fiction, it is doubtful whether the new element they introduced can be said to be realism at all; or, if it is called realism, it is realism of a peculiar kind.

The Oxford Dictionary defines this word as 'fidelity of representation, rendering the precise details of the real thing or scene, often with the implication that the details are of an unpleasant or sordid character'.

This sort of thing was not introduced into fiction by the English writers of the eighteenth century, but by the Spanish authors of the picaresque tale. This is realistic in its contemporary setting, its choice of characters drawn not only from the lowest strata of society but also from semi-criminals, and its acceptance not only of poverty, brutality and meanness but also of the physically disgusting as well. The form had a long ancestry in the tales of cheating and trickery which were current in the Middle Ages as they are in all countries and periods. One species of these were books about the stratagems and tricks of beggars. Just as legends and stories originally quite separate clustered round the figure of Arthur, and were finally organized into a long and coherent narrative, so these tales of rogues, vagabonds and beggars tended to coalesce round some famous ruffian or jester: in Germany, Till Eulenspiegel, and, in England, Scroggins, Henry VIII's jester. These remain, however, a series of anecdotes only.

The first writer to combine the adventures of a rogue in such a way that we now recognize the result as a novel was the author of *Lazarillo de Tormes*, whoever he may have been. Published in 1554, this book marks an innovation in form as well as in content, for it is the first important novel to be autobiographical, although at least two of the later Spanish romances took this form.

The early picaresque novels are all stories of an unscrupulous but not of a criminal character, of a man whom we should now describe as never having had a chance. He is always born of very poor and degraded parents or else he is illegitimate. In either case his parents are indifferent to him. The story describes his shifts to live as he passes from one master to another. *Lazarillo de Tormes* has been described by a modern critic as an 'epic of hunger'; and if nothing were known about the background of the picaresque tale, it would undoubtedly be taken as a literature of social protest. This, however, does not seem to be correct. Those who know most about these books tell us that they were meant as entertainment only, that the earliest examples had no serious satirical intention, let alone any reforming aim, and that such satire as they display arose out of what was regarded as the fun. They were not written by poor men, rogues, or social reformers, but, in the words of Chandler, the American critic who devoted several books to the genre, 'their creators standing high in the State, the professions or literature, simply assumed the rags for the moment'.[3]

There are two theories of the origins of the picaresque tale, one maintaining that it arose from the peculiarities of Spanish society, the other that it was essentially a parody of the romance. The way in which the hero passed from master to master and place to place has, for instance, been described as a reflection of the drifting, aimless character of a society in which both social institutions and economic life were decaying. Earlier critics, on the other hand, saw it as a parody of the wanderings of the knight errant. There is no doubt that there is some truth in the parody theory. The rogue wandering about in search of food, destitute of any good qualities except wit and ingenuity, is too much the exact opposite of the noble and ever-victorious knight, too much of an anti-hero for the contrast to be accidental. Anyone who chooses can also believe that the disorganization of Spanish society in the sixteenth century inspired this reaction from the ideals of chivalry.

The first picaresque tales offered no excuses for their appearance; but as they multiplied, their authors found it necessary to say that they were writing in order to warn people against the

[3] Chandler, F. W., *Romances of Roguery*, New York, 1899.

vices they depicted. It seems to be believed, however, by most historians of Spanish literature that their real object remained to amuse only. Certainly the heroes or anti-heroes are not treated with sympathy, compassion, or psychological subtlety. The tricks, the devices and the unedifying adventures of the rogue are the point, not why he became one, or what effect his life had on him. There is not the slightest attempt to present the criminal as a hero, as was done in later literature: he remains an anti-hero in every example of the genre. To quote Chandler again, 'the rogue is an artful dodger, with too much good nature and humour as well as too little resolution to wear the tragic mask'. In reading the picaresque tales, it must be remembered that they were meant to be funny, however little some of the incidents may appeal to the present-day sense of humour. The comic intention may to some extent dilute the realism; but the absence of sympathy or of social indignation gives the greatest possible scope to realism, in the sense of willingness to depict the harsher aspects of society, the more humiliating attributes of humanity, although oddly enough these do not include sex. Neither love nor lust is a motive in these books.

When contrasted with the picaresque novel instead of with the heroic romances, the contribution of Richardson and Fielding to the development of fiction looks rather different. They did not, as is so often said, introduce realism. This had already been done, and was perfectly well known to anyone interested in literature in England, indeed to anyone who could read. *Lazarillo de Tormes* and many others of the same genre had been translated soon after they appeared and frequently reprinted. Whether the novels of Defoe, Richardson and Fielding are regarded as more or less realistic depends on what one considers to be real. The world depicted even in Defoe is much less harsh than that shown in *Lazarillo de Tormes*, still more so that depicted by Richardson and Fielding. Only Smollett, in the eighteenth century, came anywhere near the sordid side of the picaresque tale, and although there is both brutality and coarseness in his books, his main characters are not anti-heroes. Although they fall far short of what the nineteenth or even the twentieth century regards as admirable, Smollett seems to have considered them decent young men. Even before he tried to paint the portrait of a Christian gentleman, Richardson's Clarissa is a heroine indeed and the wicked Lovelace has heroic qualities. Although Fielding was reproached at the time for the 'lowness' of some of his scenes and characters, Tom Jones is like a medieval hero in his courage, recklessness and generosity, these qualities merely being adjusted to eighteenth-century conditions.

Don Quixote

It is to be supposed that *Don Quixote* is not regarded as a novel by those who maintain that the novel first appeared in the eighteenth century, because the events in it could hardly have taken place in the real world exactly as narrated. But whatever it is called, its influence on the development of the novel was enormous, especially in England. The first play that Fielding wrote, although not the first one to be acted, was called *Don Quixote in England*. The words on the title-page of *Joseph Andrews*, 'Written in imitation of the comic writings of Cervantes', have already been quoted, and Fielding returns to his debt in *Tom Jones*. There were more direct imitations by minor authors: *The Female Quixote* by Fielding's sister is one, *The Spiritual Quixote* by Richard Graves another; and Smollett not only referred to Cervantes in the Preface to his first novel, *Roderick Random*, but actually tried to put the story into eighteenth-century dress in *The Adventures of Sir Lancelot Greaves*. Smollett's Preface to *Roderick Random* enables us to see what *Don Quixote* meant to eighteenth-century writers:

> The world actually began to be infected with the spirit of knight errantry, when Cervantes, by an inimitable piece of ridicule reformed the taste of mankind representing chivalry in the right point of view, and converting it to purposes far more useful and entertaining, by making it assume the sock and point out the follies of ordinary life.

That Cervantes' attitude towards chivalry and its literature was not as simple as Smollett supposed, but highly ambiguous, makes it a greater book than Smollett realized and rendered its influence more profound. The irony of Don Quixote was never matched even by Fielding, and certainly by no other writer, but it offered a standard and a model. Spain cannot be denied a share and a large share in the development of modern fiction.

ANOTHER ASPECT OF THE HEROIC NOVEL

What might be called the unheroic aspect of the theory of the heroic novel also tended to realism. Although these books are generally considered merely as examples of how not to write a novel, their influence, even in England, cannot be entirely discounted, because of their great popularity. The anonymous author of the first (1672) translation of Huet's book on the romance said in his Preface: 'It is not my province to plead for them, be they good or bad, since they are so much in vogue in the world, as to make a considerable part of the polite learning.' In the Introduction to the 1715 translation by Stephen Lewis it is said: 'Romance has of late convey'd itself very far into the esteem of this nation, and is become the principal diversion of the retirement of people of all conditions.' Both Sir William Temple and Sir George (Bloody) Mackenzie wrote heroic romances in their youth, and Chesterfield was still warning his son against them in 1721. Mrs. Delaney borrowed *Pharamond* for her sister from Lady De la Warr in 1726, and the lender desired that 'you will take great care no accident happens to it'. In Leonora's library (Spectator 37) there were *Astrée*, the *Arcadia* and the *Grand Cyrus*. Richardson's and Fielding's repudiation of their methods would not have been necessary, indeed would have been hardly intelligible, unless they had been widely read. Fielding's own knowledge of them seems to have been profound, and there are passages in Richardson's books which strongly recall them. The faultless character of Sir Charles Grandison, although depicted in contemporary scenes, recalls the heroes of Mademoiselle de Scudéry; and surely in the description of the attitude of Clarissa's neighbours to her virtues, Richardson is allowing the heroic novel of his youth to influence him rather than portraying anything he had ever seen for himself: 'Your elders I have seen declining to offer their opinions on a subject till you had delivered yours, often to save themselves the mortification of retracting theirs when they heard yours.'

The heroic novels probably encouraged realism, not only by creating a reaction against their subjects and methods, but because nothing struck English readers more than the absence of the marvellous. The first translator of Huet remarks in the Preface, 'Giants, dragons and enchanted castles, which made so much noise in romances of former times, are no longer heard of. The composers do now consult nature and endeavour to exhibit her true and lively portrait in all their books.' Mademoiselle de Scudéry dilated on the necessity of having the utmost regard for probability:

Among the rules that must be observed in the composition of these works, that of probability is without doubt the most necessary. It is the cornerstone of the building . . . For myself I hold the more natural the adventures the more pleasure they give, and the ordinary light of the sun seems to me more marvellous than the strange and sinister rays of comets.

This is from the Introduction to *Ibrahim ou L'Illustre Bassa*,[4] not the most famous but the first of her works, and she adds: 'I have observed for this reason, the costumes, laws, religions and the inclination (we might say psychology) of peoples.' And in a sense this is quite true; for example, she warns the reader that when her Turkish characters address the Sultan as 'Thou', this is not improbable because in Turkish 'Thou' is not only used to indicate intimacy and affection but also high respect. This is accurate. As a realistic manifesto, the passage comparing the light of the sun and of the comets could hardly be bettered, and the way in which Mademoiselle de Scudéry talks about probability is very similar to the way in which Fielding discusses it in the introductory essays in *Tom Jones*. The contrast between theory and practice in these novels might have suggested to any young writer that following the precept, rather than the example, would lead to an important new contribution to prose fiction.

The literary background seems to suggest that even if James II had retained the throne as an absolute monarch and the trading, dissenting middle-class element in English life had been suppressed, there would still have been factors making for realism in English fiction, and that the impact of writers on each other was as important as the influence of sociological forces. It must be remembered that revulsion is as much a sign of influence as admiration and that it is just as, or even more, likely to produce a new form or a change in content than admiration leading to imitation.

THE INFLUENCES OF DRAMA

The innovation of the eighteenth-century novelists was not so much to introduce realism as to fuse realism with romance. They differed from writers of prose epics in choosing characters in

---

[4] Published under the name of her brother, and thought by some to have been written by him. The authorship, however, makes no difference to the present argument.

private life instead of historical figures, from the picaresque tale in placing them in a much higher station and giving them many amiable, if not heroic, qualities. These characteristics, although innovations at the time, had not been unknown in medieval fiction; but the eighteenth-century writers introduced something really new in European fiction when they transformed story into plot. Instead of a series of adventures, Richardson and Fielding constructed books in which all the incidents contribute to the central design. This reaches its height in *Tom Jones*, which is as carefully thought out as the most finished detective story, and in which every incident, except perhaps the Old Man of the Hill, seen at the end of the book to have been part of the general plan. The strong plot was regarded, before the twentieth century revulsion from it, as so peculiarly characteristic of the novel that pre-1914 critics generally considered the first true novel to be *Tom Jones* just because of the skill in construction which it displayed.

Although Richardson's plots are less complicated, they are equally strong, not to say melodramatic. Their details are not so clearly inseparable from the main design as those in Fielding's books, but that few have tried and none have succeeded in producing a shortened version of *Clarissa*, is some evidence that the slow pace and innumerable details are necessary to Richardson's main idea.

The dovetailing of incidents into a rational pattern might be attributed to a new psychological attitude akin to the careful experiments of the scientist or the methodical accounting of the tradesman, but it was first seen in poetry and the drama. It seems reasonable to think that it was the drama, itself a form of fiction, which led the novelists to the kind of structure before only seen in plays.

Fielding himself was a playwright before he became a novelist, and although it may be objected that Fielding's own plays are not masterpieces of construction, any play, however desultory it may seem compared with the well-made drama of the nineteenth century, must be more concentrated than the seventeenth-century romance. The number of separate themes with which it can deal are limited and it cannot lose sight of characters for long periods at a time. Fielding wrote a number of burlesques including his best-known theatrical piece, *Tom Thumb*, a parody on heroic tragedy, and adaptations of two of Molière's plays. In order to parody it is necessary to understand, and in order to adapt to read the original with care. Fielding had had a classical education and was familiar with the Greek dramatists; he was, moreover, interested in literary theories, and well aware of the dramatic theory which French critics had drawn from Classical authors. This laid the main stress on the famous unities and must have encouraged anyone bred in its tenets to give more importance to a clear design than had previous writers of fiction.

Richardson never wrote plays and the effect of his knowledge of the theatre is obscured by his preference for writing novels in letters, and by the slow unfolding of his story; but the way in which he subordinated everything to the thoughts and actions of his principal characters, if not due only to himself, a possibility which should never be forgotten, would appear to be drawn from the stage. He has often been called a Puritan, but he seems to have had none of the Puritan dislike of the stage. The virtuous Clarissa was quite prepared to go to the theatre, merely having a preference for tragedy; and Richardson constantly alludes to and quotes from plays and playwrights in all his books.

The drama was a powerful force in the period between the publication of *Robinson Crusoe* and the publication of *Tom Jones*, because everyone read plays as well as going to see them. This habit is attested by references in literature and also in letters and diaries.

The idea that the influence of the drama was important is supported because Defoe and Smollett—the least susceptible of eighteenth-century novelists to plays and players—did not construct their books in the new manner, but simply followed the old tradition of a series of adventures unified only because they happen to one person. Defoe shared to the full the Puritan abhorrence of the stage: he referred to the theatres as 'those nurseries of crime' and in 1709 proposed a scheme for suppressing them which, with characteristic humanity, was to provide a sum to compensate displaced actors. Smollett, it is true, wrote plays, but they were extremely bad and he was an unsuccessful playwright; he was also a Scotsman and there was no Scottish dramatic tradition. He himself tells us his novels were modelled on *Don Quixote* and on Le Sage's picaresque novel *Gil Blas*, both of which he translated.

This dramatic influence makes it plain why the early novels

were so unlike the *Spectator* essays which, especially the Sir Roger de Coverley series, seems to want only slightly more organization to become novels. Textbooks usually mention them as forerunners of the novel and as a powerful influence in its development, but any novel which arose from them would have been a domestic novel resembling those of Jane Austen or perhaps Mrs. Gaskell. The early novel was, in contrast, full of violent incidents and complicated plots: it was not until 1778, when Fanny Burney published *Evelina*, that the *Spectator* attitude to character and manners flowered into a complete novel, and even in *Evelina* there is a repudiated marriage.

It was obviously not the Elizabethan dramatists, themselves not worried by a few loose ends, a few striking but irrelevant events, who taught the novelists the art of plotting: this they learned from Restoration comedy and from the theatre of Corneille, Racine and Molière; if not directly, then through their English imitators, and through French theories. Where the Elizabethans, especially Shakespeare, were probably important, was in offering a model of realistic dialogue. The use of different kinds of speech to indicate difference of character, class or profession was introduced into storytelling mainly by Fielding, although there are slight examples in Richardson. Defoe in his novels hardly employs it, his characters all talk alike, although real criminals no doubt had their own slang. This is rather strange, as he used dialogue to illustrate character in his more serious writings. Richardson uses the method, in a slight degree, to distinguish the talk of his servants from that of gentlefolk, but mainly to indicate states of mind. In Clarissa's dream, for instance:

> Methought my brother, my uncle Antony, and Mr. Solmes, had formed a plot to destroy Mr. Lovelace; who discovering it, and believing I had a hand it it, turned all his rage against me. I thought he made them all fly to foreign parts upon it; and afterwards seizing upon me, carried me into a church-yard; and there, notwithstanding all my prayers and tears, and protestations of innocence, stabbed me to the heart, and then tumbled me into a deep grave ready dug, among two or three half-dissolved carcases; throwing in the dirt and earth upon me with his hands, and trampling it down with his feet.

This has been highly praised by modern critics for its use of symbols, it is also reminiscent of Elizabethan drama.

It is impossible to prove that the prose dialogue of Shakespeare suggested to Fielding that the speech of the lower orders might be copied or heightened for comic purposes in the novel; but it was there as a model if he needed one.

Although the stage may have inspired the transformation of story into plot and the introduction of contemporary idiom, their transference to prose fiction was a real innovation, which had far-reaching consequences for the future of the novel.

4

The Rise of the Far Eastern Novel and the Beginnings of Romance in Europe

The evidence for the influence of earlier literature, especially the earlier forms of fiction, on the character of the new novel and the moment when it appeared, is overwhelming, and any attempt to separate completely the various types of fiction fails as decisively as attempts to link the novel with any particular class. This does not eliminate the effect of social conditions; but introduces another factor, the influence of past events. This is the influence both of older writers, summarized in the term literary tradition, of culture patterns or attitudes deriving from the past and of the innumerable events, large or small, known or unknown, which go to make up what we call history.

The literary tradition not only educates the writer but sets up certain expectations in the reader which must be fulfilled if the work is to be accepted. The enormous part which tradition plays is obscured for us by the value today placed on originality. Experiment in literature is, however, as dependent on tradition as attempts to fulfil expectations. It was only because definite expectations existed that experimental novelists could flout them; if the expectations had been different, the experiments would have to have taken another form.

Everyone is perfectly well aware that some of our attitudes are moulded, not by our own experiences, but by experiences which happened to other people a long time ago. Most political institutions in all countries were established at varying dates in the past and although they change with time they always retain something of their origin. The different emotional tone which the word 'revolution' carries in France and England is due to conditioning by historical tradition. The defeat of the Spanish 'Armada', or the defeat as seen by Englishmen at the time, still contributes something to the political thinking of the average citizen of this country. When the institutions are conspicuous, and the events known and taught at school, the individual can often escape from tradition so far as to rebel against it. It is, however, seldom possible to escape entirely. If the Armada had been successful, Elizabeth would not now be regarded as a great statesman, with all the subtle effects on attitudes to women, to the monarchy, Protestantism and many other things which this belief carries with it. Defeat instead of victory would have reversed these effects, so that while it is possible for an Englishman to argue that a defeat would have been more permanently beneficial, it is very difficult for him to escape from the diffused psychological results of victory.

The idea of a culture or a culture pattern may contain the influence of historical events; but it seems to give a much clearer picture, if a distinction is made between past and contemporary social conditions. While looked at from one angle, tradition and history may seem to limit a writer's range of choice, from another they widen it. The new has often grown from an attempt to copy the old, as the words 'renaissance' and 'revival', so often used in the history of art and literature, show. No idea of this phenomena can be gathered from the descriptions of the dominance of culture patterns.

There would be no difficulty in producing a sociological theory of the novel bringing in the influence of the past as well as that of the present. Such a theory would view literature as a result of the interaction of long-lasting phenomena, not only the literary traditions but also cultural patterns or attitudes deriving, for example, from Christian doctrine or from institutions as permanent as the monarchy in England, on the one hand, and, on the other, from the changing aspects of the social environment. This indeed is what most statements of the evolutionary theory of the novel amount to, and they might have seemed to provide a satisfactory explanation if, as was believed when such views were first put forward, nothing like it had appeared in any other society. Even the existence of Japanese literature was not suspected until the middle of the nineteenth century, and Chinese writings were only slightly known. Everyone is now aware that one book conforming to the descriptions and definitions intended to cover the novels of eighteenth- and nineteenth-century Europe, appeared in eleventh-century Japan, and a considerable number in China from the fifteenth century onwards.

The Far Eastern novel may provide some check on explanations of European fiction and suggest a different theory of the relation between fiction and society. It can act as a check on theories developed before its existence was realized because, if social forces produced a certain kind of literature, one must assume that similar forces or attitudes must have existed where this particular form occurred elsewhere. Any such forces in eighteenth-century England ought, therefore, to have some analogies or parallels in the Far East. It may appear foolish to expect that any theory can cover both Europe and the Far East, and if a really convincing sociological explanation had been produced for the European novel, it would no doubt be better to be content with it and to stress the differences rather than the resemblances between Far Eastern and European fiction. But no such explanation yet put forward can be accepted for the European novel, and if literature is moulded by sociological forces, there must have existed in all novel-producing countries conditions which were, in some essential way, similar. It is obvious that exactly the same phenomena cannot be expected; but things apparently, and indeed really, quite different may resemble each other in their social relations and their social functions. For example, a medieval baron and a Japanese damiyio had, as human beings, little in common but a fondness for fighting, a strong dislike of centralized government, and an ultimate dependence on agriculture. The reasons for which they could be made to fight, their conduct while fighting, their religion, their attitude to women, other classes and their sovereign, their taste in literature were wholly dissimilar. The structure of their society was, however, sufficiently like that of medieval Europe to allow historians and sociologists to talk of Japanese feudalism.

Cultural as well as sociological factors can be regarded in a similar light. A religion may seem extraordinary in its doctrines and exotic in its rituals, yet it might have the same effect which Protestantism is alleged to have had in stimulating an interest in psychological analysis.

THE JAPANESE NOVEL

The novel first appeared very early in Japan at the end of the tenth or beginning of the eleventh century, in a period of comparative peace and order, under what was, at least in theory, a centralized autocratic system. An attempt had been made to copy the whole Chinese Government apparatus, with a Civil Service and provincial governors appointed by the Emperor. It was, however, imposed on a social system composed of great nobles with their followers, and by the end of the eleventh century the Central Government had already lost much authority. This was not realized by the Court nobles, who were regarded and regarded themselves as far superior to the provincial nobility. There was, of course, nothing which could be called a middle class, and the lower classes were merely the despised tillers of the soil and the servants of the servants of the great.

The Court nobility was educated and cultivated, although in ways which Europeans might think frivolous. They were much occupied with caligraphy and Court ceremonial, as well as with writing poetry. Chinese language and literature had the same or a greater ascendency over Japanese as Latin had over the vernacular in the European Middle Ages; greater, because when they first came into contact with Chinese civilization the Japanese had no writing and adopted the Chinese script. Medieval Europe of course, also used the Roman alphabet, but the romance languages were descended from Latin. Japanese has nothing in common with Chinese, the Chinese script is not phonetic and is, according to linguistic authorities, markedly unsuitable for Japanese. A simpler form of phonetic writing was developed from it for the use of the less educated. All serious literature was written in Chinese, and although the original short Japanese verse form continued to be composed, men with literary ambitions attempted poems in Chinese. The language was, however, not considered suitable for women, who used the simplified script and thus escaped the dominance of Chinese models and the difficulties of Chinese script.

It is not surprising that fiction should have developed in this society, but its character is very unexpected to anyone who comes to it from European literature. All that survive are two not very interesting fairy stories and one great, elaborate, subtle book which, if we did not happen to know the facts, would have appeared to be the culmination of a long tradition. This, *The Tale of Genji*,[1] was written by Murasaki a Court lady, though one of not very exalted rank, and seems to depict a narrow and artificial society divorced from the main historic currents of the times, as was shown by the subsequent history of Japan. Isolated indeed from many of the elements which we in the West regard, and always have regarded, as an essential part of reality, yet even in translation it retains the power of inspiring not only interest, but, in some people at least, emotion as vivid as that produced by European novels. The names, but the names only, of some twenty other romances have been preserved, and it is open to anyone to say that in these we should find a steady progression towards the attitude and method of Murasaki in the *Tale of Genji*. Kroeber, the American anthropologist, in his essay on the Japanese and Chinese novel, assumes exactly this: 'Even as a novel, Genji does not stand alone, but occurs in the historic company of other wholly natural, non-fantastic fiction and narrative . . . together they evidence a pattern stylistic growth of which *Genji* constitutes merely the culmination.'[2]

The only 'wholly non-fantastic fiction' in early Japanese that still exist are short stories. The lost romances, as they are lost, can hardly be cited as evidence. The existing literary forms, when Murasaki started to write, were the short lyric, the fairy tale, the realistic anecdote and the diary. Keene, in his history of Japanese literature, derives the novel from a combination of two of these forms, the story frequently Indian in origin, which came with other influences from China, and the short prose introductions to poems.[3]

The prevailing form of verse in early Japan was so short and compressed as to lead to considerable obscurity; and as modern poets allow us notes to their work, Japanese poets provided a few introductory phrases in prose, which indicate the experience which inspired the poem, or the circumstances in which it was written. Verses lamenting the fading of the cherry blossom might be prefaced by a paragraph describing the death of a child or a mistress, linking the fading flowers with the transience of human

---

[1] Murasaki, Shikibu, *The Tale of Gengi*, translated by Arthur Waley, 1926–33.
[2] Kroeber, A. L., 'The Novel in Asia and Europe' in Kroeber, *The Nature of Culture*, Chicago, 1952.
[3] Keene, Donald, *Japanese Literature*, London, 1953.

life. In the *Ise Monogatari*, a work which is sometimes thought to have influenced Murasaki, a series of poems and anecdotes are grouped around one character, Narihiri, a famous courtier and poet of the ninth century. When, however, it is said that Murasaki was influenced by this work, it can only mean by the conception of the central figure and his preoccupation with love. The book is wholly unlike a novel; it consists of a series of detached stories and poems, in which Narihiri is not even mentioned by name. Each section begins instead with the phrase 'once there was a man' or 'once a great minister of the left', whereas *The Tale of Genji* is exactly what we mean by a novel.

Arthur Waley sees the feminine diaries of the period immediately before Murasaki, rather than any kind of story, as the germ of her book. The famous Chinese narrative poem called in English 'The Everlasting Wrong' has also been thought to have influenced her. The gap between the diary and a novel as elaborate as the *Tale of Genji* is very wide; it is wider still between a novel and a poem in another language, and one, moreover, which had none of the range of epic, but is short and concentrated.

The Japanese have always recognized *The Tale of Genji* as a great book apparently putting it into a different category to the lost romances. There is a discussion of the novel in *Genji* itself. Genji refers to the wildness and extravagance of the books, the word for which Waley has translated as romances, which seems to link them with fairy tales rather than with novels. But Genji goes on to say that he is 'amazed by the advances this art of fiction is now making', which suggests that there did exist something more like a novel, unless Murasaki was referring to her own work. Waley, however, separates the first chapter of *Genji* from the rest of the book by saying, 'Murasaki, still under the influence of her somewhat childish predecessors, writes in a manner which is a blend of the court chronicle with the conventional fairy tale.' If, when she started to write, there were books more like her own, it is not evident why this should be so. On the whole it appears there is a greater difference between Murasaki and her predecessors than there is between a great writer and earlier literature in any other language.

The Tale of Genji is too well known from Arthur Waley's translation to need any description. It is sufficient to say that there is nothing in it contrary to ordinary experience, nothing that could not have happened, although the incidents are sometimes explained in terms that we should not now accept; the idea, for example, that illness is caused through possession by some evil spirit.

There were some weak imitations of *The Tale of Genji* in the eleventh century, but then the novel seems to have disappeared until the beginning of the eighteenth century, although Murasaki's book was always regarded as a classic and was used, both by writers of the aristocratic Nō play and of the popular drama, as a source for plots. The same word, Monogatari, is used indeed both for Genji and for the works called in English 'military romances' or 'war tales'. It was, however, also used for historical as well as fictional narratives, and although it is now generally translated as 'tale', Ashton in his history of Japanese literature,[4] the first ever written in a European language, used 'narrative' as the equivalent.

The juxtaposition of feudalism and romance may seem to be a most striking confirmation of the view that a form of society creates its appropriate form of literature; but whether or not feudalism in Japan is really comparable to the society of the European Middle Ages, the Japanese war tales are not at all like medieval romances. Whether supposed to be straight history or supposed to be romance, they are always in the form of chronicles, and always deal with real events. There is no Arthur, no Holy Grail, no enchanted forests. Although the incidents are very different from those encountered in *The Tale of Genji*, one of the most striking things about them is the obvious influence of Murasaki's book. In *The Heike Monogatari*, which tells the story of the war between two great families, which resulted in the establishment of the Shogun as the real ruler of Japan, allusions and quotations from Genji are frequent, and some of the love episodes are obviously imitated from it. *The Heike Monogatari*[5] is a romance. *The Okagami Monogatari* is a chronicle, but it is told by two old men, and the opening scene between them is thought to be modelled on the scene in Genji in which the Prince and his friends discuss the women they have known.[6]

These romances are said to have been written to be sung or intoned, which makes the continuance of Heian literary techniques

[4] Aston, W. S., *History of Japanese Literature*, 1899.
[5] 'Heike Monogatari' (translated A. Sadler), *Transactions of the Asiatic Society of Japan*, 1918–19.
[6] See Sansom, George, *Japan—A Cultural History*, 1946.

and Heian sentiment all the more remarkable; one would have thought they would have been highly unsuitable for this medium.

When in the beginning of the eighteenth century a new merchant class grew up in the towns a new form of fiction was written for them; but is surprising to anyone familiar only with European literature that this took the form of the kind of short story which preceded the novel in Europe.

The tales of Saikaku,[7] the most famous of these writers, have been compared by an American scholar to the *Decameron*. Saikaku's books are generally collections of stories on a given theme, frequently erotic, such as *The Five Women Who Loved Love* and similar titles; but in one the theme is economic, how to get rich.[8] The stories are realistic in the sense that they deal with contemporary life, and that the supernatural plays only a minor part. But although Saikaku is considered to be one of the best writers of prose in Japanese, his stories are not, except as a picture of Japanese manners in the eighteenth century, very interesting in translation. There is little attempt at characterization; his object is to describe types, not individuals; the point of his stories lies in the anecdote and the contemporary background. Even in his tales, so different in every way from *The Tale of Genji*, the influence of Murasaki can be seen. His first book was an adaptation, some scholars say a parody, of the *Tale of Genji*, making the hero a contemporary merchant instead of a Heian prince.[9] Although some of Saikaku's books are long enough to be called novels, they did not inspire any school of realistic fiction during the century and a half that still remained before Japanese literature was transformed by European influences. Instead the realistic element tended to disappear, and to be replaced by fiction in which the incidents are so wild and unnatural that it approximates rather to fairy story than to romance, either of the Japanese or European Middle Ages.

Prose fiction in Japan seems to follow a course almost exactly contrary to its European counterpart. There are only a few short narrative poems, and immediately after the fairy or supernatural tale, and long before the drama, comes one long novel, with no element of the supernatural or of adventure. The next stage is

[7] Ihara Saikaku, *The Life of an Amourous Woman and Other Writings*, translated by Ivan Morris, 1963.

[8] *The Japanese Family Storehouse*, translated by G. W. Sargent, 1959.

[9] Saikaku and other writers of his time are discussed with translated examples in Howard Hibbett's *The Floating World In Japanese Fiction*, 1959.

romanticized history, and then the kind of short story often believed to be the start of realistic fiction in Europe; but which in Japan turned out to have no such sequel.

Japanese and European critics are agreed that *The Tale of Genji* is the greatest Japanese novel and probably the masterpiece of Japanese literature.

THE CHINESE NOVEL

The Tale of Genji is an aristocratic work in every sense. Chinese novels, on the other hand, at any rate in their earlier forms, were written by the people for the people. They were originally composed to be read aloud, and it is through this medium that they were known to the masses even in modern times.

Until the wholesale conversion of the Chinese to Western ideas, they did not regard novels as literature at all. They were not written about or discussed by recognized literary figures, and reading or writing them was regarded as rather disreputable. No one, therefore, knows more than the name, even if they know that, of the authors of the most famous of them. They appeared late in Chinese history, not until after the Mongol conquest; but once started they continued to be written in great numbers.

Among these it is agreed that five are outstanding:

The *San Kuo*[10] or *Romance of Three Kingdoms*; the *Shui Hu Chuan*[11] or 'bandit novel; the *Chin P'ing Mei*[12] a continuation of the adventures of one of the bandits in the *Shui Hu*; the *Hsi Yu Chi*, translated by Arthur Waley under the title *Monkey*, and the *Hung Lou Meng*[13] or *Dream of the Red Chamber*. Of these *Monkey* is a satirical fable rather than a novel. *The Romance of the Three Kingdoms*, as the

[10] *San Kuo*, translated by C. H. Brewitt-Taylor, Hong-Kong, 1929.

[11] *Shui Hu Chuan*, translated by Pearl Buck under the title *All Men Are Brothers*, London, 1937. This is not a translation of the Chinese title which is something more like 'The Tale of the Marshes'. It gives a somewhat misleading idea of the character of the book, which, although revolutionary, is hardly humanitarian. Pearl Buck's translation is based on the shortest edition of the last version, omitting the edifying end. It is discussed in Richard Gregg Irwin's *The Evolution of a Chinese Novel* (see overleaf). Franz Kuhn published a much-abridged German translation of the earlier version under the title *Die Räuber von Liang Schau Moor*, Leipzig, 1934, which Irwin considers retains more of the spirit of the original than *All Men Are Brothers*.

[12] *Chin P'ing Mei*, translated under the title *The Golden Lotus* by C. Egerton, 1939.

[13] *Dream of the Red Chamber*, translated from the abbreviated German version of Franz Kuhn by Florence and Isabel McHugh, 1958.

title given to the English translation shows, is a romance in the sense that its main characters are historical figures, and that their careers are interpreted with imaginative freedom.

It used to be thought that *The Romance of the Three Kingdoms* was the earliest, but it has now been decided that the 'bandit novel' was the first to appear. It also used to be said that *The Romance of the Three Kingdoms* at least, if not the 'bandit novel', was written under the Mongol dynasty; but this is now contradicted and their date has been moved to the Ming, the native Chinese dynasty, which replaced the Mongols.

The development of the first Chinese novel has been exhaustively studied, both by Chinese and by European scholars, and a book devoted to its rather complicated history, *The Evolution of a Chinese Novel*, by R. G. Irwin,[14] appeared in 1953. In this development there are two separate strands, the evolution of Chinese prose fiction and the evolution of the story of Sung Chiang, the leader of the bandits. Story-telling in China, as in other countries, appeared early; there are references to children being given money to go and listen to a story-teller when their elders wished to get rid of them in the literature of the Han dynasty (206 B.C.–A.D.220). The stories themselves are believed to have originated in tales told to illustrate Buddhist themes by missionaries or religious teachers. These soon developed into stories concerned with purely worldly affairs. Some of these were subsequently linked together in chains —tz'-u-hua. Among the tales were stories told about Sung Chiang and his thirty-six followers. He was the leader of an outlaw band in the closing years of the Sung dynasty, somewhere about A.D. 1114. Nothing is known of him but his name and the fact that he led a troop of outlaws or bandits.

The first stage in his saga is thought to have been the emergence of legends not connected with each other, but all about him and his band, and their fusion into story chains. Twenty-three surviving tz'-u-hua deal with incidents found in the novel; many have been lost, so there may have been others. The amalgamation of the separate episodes into a linked story is believed to have occurred in the last years of Mongol rule. Out of this material someone, about 1550, composed a novel. There were subsequently

[14] Irwin, Richard Gregg, *The Evolution of a Chinese Novel*, Cambridge, Mass., 1953. (See also Průsek, Jaroslav, 'Researches into the Beginnings of Chinese Popular Fiction', *Archiv Orientali*, 1939–40.)

127

at least three other versions. They all tell the story of Sung Chiang, the way each of his men came to join him, and the adventures and fate of the band itself. The latest version alters the end to soften the subversive impact of the book, which has been described as 'frankly revolutionary', has been banned in China at various periods, and is a great favourite with the present Chinese Government.

One of the episodes in this novel was expanded into another immense book, the *Chin P'ing Mei*. It is considered that 'judged on the basis of skilful portraiture, full-rounded emotion and power of language, *Chin P'ing Mei* surpassse the other Ming dynasty novels'. It is not an historical novel like the Shia-hua, but tells the story, particularly the love affairs, of a provincial merchant. It is always praised for its realistic atmosphere, but there seems to be a certain flaw in the realism: how on earth, in the known economic conditions of China, could an ordinary merchant have acquired the wealth which the leading character managed to amass? The novel had, for different reasons, as bad a reputation with the authorities as the bandit novel; they did not approve of the freedom with which it dealt with sex.

In spite of the traditional disdain of the educated for novels, they must have been widely read. Arthur Waley found in a book called *Advice to Wine Drinkers*, published about the end of the sixteenth or beginning of the seventeenth century, a list of books which a cultivated drinker should study; among them were the *Shui Hu* and the *Chin P'ing Mei*. 'A drinker who has not these at his finger tips is a mere soaker, and no true drinking companion.'[15]

The Chinese novel, unlike the Japanese, continued to live and develop, and the *Hung Lou Meng*, which in European languages is always called the *Dream of the Red Chamber*, although we are told the Chinese title does not mean this at all, was not written until the middle of the eighteenth century. This, the greatest of Chinese novels, was written by a Manchu, and is about the decline of a great Manchu family. That the family is Manchu and not Chinese was long conjectured, because of the absence of any reference to feet-binding in the story; and now seems to be confirmed, as the author has been identified.[16]

[15] Introduction to Bernard Miall's (much-abridged) translation of *Chin P'ing Mei*, 1939.
[16] See Wu-Shih Chang, *On the Dream of the Red Chamber*, 1961.

The length of the book and the profusion of subplots may make it confusing to readers used only to modern novels; but everyone must be struck by the subtlety of the characterization, especially of Pao Yu, the heir of the house. Sensitive, ineffective, dissipated and selfish, he is common in twentieth-century fiction, but as hero, at least, was quite unknown to the European novel in the eighteenth century.

Although there are fantastic episodes in the 'bandit novel', it is realistic in the sense that, although a story of adventure, the adventures arise from the lives and problems of ordinary people. The courage and strength of some of the outlaws may be impossibly great, but there is no attempt to create ideal characters. The realistic element is accentuated in *Ching P'ing Mei*, in which none of the main characters have any virtues at all, still less any heroic qualities. Even *The Romance of the Three Kingdoms* is hardly romantic in the European sense, but there is a soberness about the realism of *The Dream of the Red Chamber* which puts it into another category. Unlike the writer of *Ching P'ing Mei*, its author understood the economic foundations of the family fortune, and was as interested as Defoe in what everything cost, and how each festival or marriage was financed.

The plot undoubtedly describes the decline of a rich and aristocratic family, but although the main part of the plot is a comedy or perhaps a tragedy of manners, it is set in a supernatural framework and its real theme is still in dispute. The reader can choose between Fitzgerald, who in his cultural history of China, maintains that: 'The real aim of the book is a criticism of the rite-bound society of eighteenth-century China and of the Confucian philosophy which dominated it', and Franz Kuhn, who translated the book into German and suggested it could be given different interpretations but: 'from the Buddhist and Taoist point of view the answer might be: it is the story of the gradual awakening and the final transcendence of a soul originally sunk in the slime of temporal and material strivings'.

The book was obviously written to be read to oneself, and not to be read aloud, and in spite of the orthodox attitude to the novel it is clear that by the middle of the eighteenth century novels were meant for an educated audience. Like the earlier popular novels, *The Dream of the Red Chamber*, however, was written in ordinary everyday language, while all that was regarded as literature used classical Chinese, which by the fifteenth century was incomprehensible except to scholars.

When the first novels were thought to have been written under the Mongols, they used to be explained as the work of Chinese scholars who had lost their administrative jobs as a result of the conquest, and turned to Chinese history as a means of keeping the glorious past alive. The later date now chosen for the novels seems to rule out this explanation; but it is still employed to account for the drama which undoubtedly did arise under the Mongols; and if educated men had already turned to one form of popular literature, it may be natural that they should soon invent another.

It has also been suggested that the Mongols brought with them stories from Central Asia and the Near East, which stimulated imitations in Chinese.

The Far Eastern novel does not, of course, resemble the European novel exactly, and it differs more from the eighteenth-century than from the modern examples. There is nothing that corresponds to the kind of plot found in *Tom Jones, Pride and Prejudice and Waverley*. These novels, however much they differ in other ways, all deal with a limited series of incidents developed according to a logical scheme and leading to a definite conclusion: recognition and marriage in *Tom Jones*, marriage and reconciliation of the hero to real life in *Waverley*, recognition, in another sense, and marriage in *Pride and Prejudice*. The end can, of course, be death, as it is in Clarissa, but at this stage in the development of the novel, death brought about by the actions of the characters, not by the mere passing of time.

The Far Eastern novel has no such definite plot. *The Tale of Genji* is simply the life of a Japanese Prince. He is the hero as well as the subject of the book. We are obviously meant to find him both admirable and sympathetic. He dies, however, before the book is finished, and the last part is concerned with his supposed son, really the son of another man. 'The story', in Arthur Waley's words, 'fades out like a Chinese landscape.' The ending is so inconclusive that the uninstructed European reader might think that the work is not complete; this, indeed, has been suggested by Japanese critics. It appears, however, that the idea has now been rejected by most authoritative opinion.

There are many modern novels written on a plan similar to

that of the 'bandit novel': the adventures of a group of people all linked by some external event or factor. They are, however, modern and this was a form not used by the early European novelists, except where the link is as trivial as the passing of a coin or a dog from one person to another, which makes it a different kind of book to one in which the link is some significant event.

The decline of a family is also a subject often used by European writers, but again it is a modern theme. The eighteenth-century novel was concentrated on the life and adventures of one individual, not of a group.

In spite of these divergencies, the Far Eastern novel displays many of the characteristics held to distinguish the eighteenth-century novel from earlier forms of prose fiction. In a book published in 1957 these are said to be the invented plot dealing with ordinary life without miraculous or supernatural elements, the background of a definite time and place, the feel of 'authentic experience'. It is true that the Chinese novels have certain supernatural elements; at least, things happen in them which we believe to be impossible, and *The Dream of the Red Chamber* has a supernatural framework. This is, however, religious rather than merely supernatural, in the sense in which the supernatural appears in the Gothic novel. Even in *The Tale of Genji* there are certain concepts, such as possession, which in European civilization would be regarded as supernatural, but owing to the way they are treated they seem merely a part of Japanese life, which as ideas indeed they were.

In other respects the Far Eastern novel conforms to the specification drawn up from the early English novel. However, unusual the settings may seem to us, the writers were dealing with a life familiar to them. The background of Japanese palace or Chinese house is perfectly definite and described in detail, as is the seaside village to which Genji was banished.

Spengler, E. M. Forster and Northrop Fyre all regard a preoccupation with time as the particular mark of the novel, distinguishing it from all other forms of literature. A preoccupation with time is exactly what at least one historian of Japanese literature has found to be the main theme of Genji.

All those who have read the books in the original are agreed that they do give the illusion of authentic experience. Arthur Waley refers to 'the extraordinary reality, the almost historic character, with which she (Murasaki) invests her theme'. Fitz-gerald in his cultural history of China says of the 'bandit novel' that anyone familiar with the country, even today, will recognize the types and settings; and Pearl Buck, who translated the book, said the same. Both it and its successor *Chin P'ing Mei* retain some elements obviously drawn from folk tales; but *The Dream of the Red Chamber* has all the characteristics of the European novel except simplicity of narrative line.

No one would deny that the social background of the Far Eastern novel was wholly unlike that of eighteenth-century England. In spite of this, it might be possible to generalize the social factors usually put forward as having contributed to the rise of the English novel so that they would cover the Far East also, or alternatively to find some analogy between conditions in England, in China and in Japan. There does not, however, appear to be either obvious parallels or underlying similarities. None of the causes so familiar in histories of the European novel—the rise of the middle or commercial class, an increase in literacy, the appearance of a new reading public, itself depending on the increase in literacy—seem to exist in the same or even in disguised forms in China or Japan. Eberhard,[17] it is true, connects the rise of the Chinese novel with the growth of a middle class. Other experts, however, deny that a class comparable to the European middle class ever existed in China. In order to support his theory, Eberhard has to take a wholly different view of the meaning of the *Shui Hu*, the 'bandit novel', from that of other historians. He says that it 'held up ideals representative of the middle class in the guise of the gentleman-brigand'. This theory appears not to be shared by the present Chinese Government. Although it is now believed that none of the Chinese novels was written under the Mongols, Wittfogel still considers that the Chinese novel was primarily due to Mongol influence. The history of China is so different to that of Europe, and the position of merchants, trades-men and other middle class figures so dissimilar that, even if it is conceded that a middle class existed in China, there seems no reason why they should have produced a literary form which is more like its European counterpart than is the Chinese play or the Chinese poem.

The theory of class literature might be, and sometimes has

[17] Eberhard, Wolfram, *A History of China*, 1950.

been, generalized so that it becomes a theory that a new class creates a new form of literature; it is not necessary to insist on the new class being composed of merchants or businessmen, or that it should occupy a middle position between an aristocracy and peasants, serfs or labourers. In this form the idea, if accurate, could give a sociological explanation of the Far Eastern novel, and support the theory of the middle-class origin of the European novel. It seems a reasonable supposition that a new social group should find the existing literary forms inadequate and create fresh ones. But whether or not such a process can be found in other forms, it is not everywhere true of the novel. The invention of the novel in Japan was not in any way connected with the growth of a new class, but rather with the decay of an old one. There is no evidence that either the writers or the readers of the first Chinese novel belonged to a class that was in any sense 'new', and the author of the greatest of them, *The Dream of the Red Chamber*, belonged to a governing class which was losing its power and position.

China and Japan were literate, if literate are contrasted with illiterate societies, but there is no evidence that there was any sudden increase in literacy immediately before the novel appeared, or that the habit of reading spread to people who had not acquired it previously.

Another common idea about innovations in literature, as well as about masterpieces, is that they appear at a moment when the nation or the culture is at some kind of peak of achievement or period of expansion. This, if true, would be very important, because it would mean innovations in literature are linked to innovations in other fields. It is true of the medieval romance, of the English novel, of *La Princesse de Clèves*, and in a sense of *Don Quixote*; for although it was written after the defeat of the armada, Spain was still the greatest power in Europe and the greatest empire in the world. It is, however, not true of China. Although the 'bandit novel' is now considered as having appeared in the century when the Chinese had expelled a foreign and reinstated a Chinese dynasty, this was a mere interlude between two foreign conquests. China's greatest intellectual triumphs were already far in the past. The *Dream of the Red Chamber* was not only written in the eighteenth century, which no one would call a great period in Chinese history, but was written by a Manchu, a member of a decaying caste. While as to *The Tale of the Genji*, if imminent disappearance is a mark of decadence, then the Japan of Murasaki was decadent as, indeed, judged by this test, was the China of the Manchus.

Although the novel did not appear in China in the days of her greatest achievement, the impact of foreign ideas under the Mongols might be regarded as in some way parallel to the intellectual ferment of seventeenth-century Europe, and to have provided something of the same stimulus. China under the Mongols was more open to foreign influences than at any time in the past, or at any time in the future until the nineteenth century. This China is more familiar in Europe than any other, for it was the Cathay of Marco Polo. It was not only the extent of the Mongol Empire, which stretched from Korea to the Danube, but the good conditions and safety of the overland routes of Central Asia, which brought men of many nationalities and cultures to China. There was no restriction on entry as there was in some other periods, and there was more to attract foreigners than there ever had been before. The Mongol Emperors preferred foreigners as their officials; few of the Mongols themselves were sufficiently educated, and they did not trust the Chinese. Although the rulers favoured Buddhism, Christians and Moslems preached unhindered. The Chinese were never great travellers; but one Chinaman is known to have gone to France in the late thirteenth century, seen the King of England in Gascony, and Philip the Fair in Paris.

These contacts do not, it is true, seem to have produced much intellectual stimulus; at least the period has never been considered one of the great periods of Chinese philosophy. But Persian, Indian, even Byzantine influences have been detected in the visual arts and music of the period, so why not in literature as well? The first Chinese novelists might, it seems, have heard of the stories of almost any race, and been stimulated to imitation or rivalry. It must not be forgotten that stimulus may arise from repulsion as well as from attraction. Even the modern view that the *Shui Hu* and the *San Kuo* were really written under the Ming dynasty, would not necessarily be disastrous to the theory, because such cultural influences generally take some time to make themselves fully felt, and once experienced do not disappear; nor would the Mongol attempts to prevent the Chinese from learning

Mongol or other foreign languages, for these seem to have been intermittent only. Such an explanation would also provide a pleasing historical symmetry, because those scholars who see the beginning of the European novel in the medieval romance often explain the romance itself as the result of contact with stories from the same Near Eastern and Central Asian countries.

There was, however, neither a sudden inrush of foreign ideas in eleventh-century Japan nor any great native intellectual achievement. Indeed, historians have found that one of the most striking things about Japanese civilization in this period was its lack of any intellectual background at all. Waley, for example, says: 'It was a purely aesthetic and, above all, a literary civilisation. Never, among people of exquisite cultivation and lively intelligence, have purely intellectual pursuits played so small a part.[18] Sir George Sansom also refers to a society 'whose outlook on life was almost entirely aesthetic'.[19] Japan was, it is true, dominated by Chinese ideas in politics, art and philosophy, and men wrote in Chinese characters and, as far as they could, in Chinese itself. But the dominance of women in Heian literature is generally thought to have arisen just because they had escaped this alien sway. The first Japanese stories were perhaps written in imitation of the Chinese, but China herself had no novel at this date. Japan had little contact even with China at this particular moment and none with any other country; there were neither foreign merchants, missionaries nor adventurers.

The history of the Far Eastern novel provides a useful check on another theory of the rise of the European novel: the purely economic, or supply and demand explanation. It has often been pointed out that in the late seventeenth and early eighteenth century, in England works of fiction first became an economic commodity, for which a market or rather a series of markets existed. It is true that literature in Europe had usually been written for some kind of reward which was in the end economic, but the market had been differently organized. The 'remaniers' of the Middle Ages received voluntary gifts from patrons, not profits from sales. The transformation of the patron into the public has always been considered of great importance in the history of literature. It meant that, as under Elizabeth a man could

[18] Waley, Arthur, *The Pillow Book of Sei Shonagon*, 1928.
[19] Sansom, George, *Japan—a Cultural History*, revised edition, 1946.

live by writing plays, he could now live by writing novels. Economic demand for a certain kind of book is clearly one way in which social forces can act on literature, and it seems clear that it decides which genre shall be dominant, when dominance is taken to mean the relative numbers of each kind produced. It is easy enough to see how, once a particular form has been created, the interest of readers, expressed in terms of what they are prepared to pay for new examples, will stimulate its growth. So many blank-verse plays were written under Elizabeth and James I because people wanted to go to the theatre and see this kind of play, and because clever young men without wealth or influence could earn money by writing them.

The patron was still important in some forms of literature in the first half of the eighteenth century, but not for the novel, which was from the first written for a market. There was a demand for reading matter at all levels of society, and an organization to satisfy it; but this could only create the novel in the sense of giving the opportunity for such books to be written. It is not easy to see how there can be a defined and exact demand for something which does not yet exist. The publishers of Defoe and Richardson had not asked for a novel or even a story when they got *Robinson Crusoe* and *Pamela*, but for a biography and a series of edifying letters respectively. The nature of contemporary society can explain the wish to read either of these, but it does not tell us why Defoe and Richardson produced something so different.

Doubts thus occur even when thinking only about England, but if other novels and other countries are also considered, economic demand seems to lose much of its apparent influence. Madame de La Fayette did not write for money, nor did Murasaki. *La Princesse de Clèves* was distributed by the Parisian booksellers in the normal way. *The Tale of Genji* was obviously written for a small audience with whom the author was personally in touch, and there was, therefore, no need for another organization to distribute it. Both books might be called aristocratic novels. In contrast to these, if a popular novel is to exist, it is clear that some kind of distributive system is necessary. It is tempting to declare, as has often been done, that the English novel could not have developed without the particular kind of system which did in fact grow up. The Chinese novel, however, originated within a system so different that if the 'bandit novel' had never been written, everyone would have said that the story-teller with his audience gathered round him, would have prevented a long, connected story, as distinct from separate stories within a frame, from ever growing up. There was an organized book trade in China, and the market this provided may have contributed to the continuance and development of the Chinese novel.

No social factor can be discerned which links the European and the Far Eastern novel; but there are certain similarities in the origins of the Chinese novel and not the European novel, but the European romance. A fainter likeness can even be traced between novel, romance and *The Tale of Genji*. These resemblances suggest the kind of social conditions which allow the development of prose fiction.

Scholars tend to equate the 'bandit novel' and its successor, the *Ching P'ing Mei*, with the eighteenth-century European novel rather than with the European romance, because of their harsh realism; but they grew out of legends coalescing round an historical—or a pseudo-historical—figure in a way reminiscent of romance. In structure, too, their immense length and episodic character make them more like romance than novel. There is an analogy between the growth of the Chinese 'bandit novel', from the brief mention of a named but otherwise unknown character in an historical chronicle, and the development of the legend of Arthur. The analogy is not exact, because Arthur did not inspire one piece of fiction universally admitted to be a great work; but an innumerable collection of lays, stories and romances, creating a world in which the European imagination moved for centuries. Nor were the first romances written about Arthur as the first novel was written about Sung Chiang. There is also a parallel, less close indeed, but still perceptible, in the history of Japanese fiction. The *Ise Monogatari*, already mentioned as supposed to have influenced Murasaki, is believed to be a similar accretion of legend round the figure of Narihira, the famous courtier and poet. It was traditionally supposed to have been written by him, but in reality it consists, so we are told by the author of the latest English translation, of stories and poems (1) based on Narihira's life; (2) traditions about Narihira's life; (3) traditions and historical facts about other people which had somehow become attached to Narihira, and (4) folk stories.[20] This seems to resemble the process

[20] *Ise Monogatari*, edited with a translation by Fritz Vos, The Hague, 1957.

by which stories gathered round Arthur and Sung Chiang, and if Narihira is a very different kind of hero from either of these, Japan was a very different kind of society.

The Greek romances also seem to have originated in a collection of stories about an historical figure. The first romance or novel, as it is sometimes called, exists only in fragments, but from these it is plain that it is the story of Ninus, the founder of Ninevah, and the woman he loved. She, although not named, is taken to have been Semiramis, believed, at the time, to have been an historical figure, a belief shared by some modern scholars. As this tale was lost, and only discovered late in the nineteenth century, it is impossible to say whether it had any influence on subsequent fiction; unlike the famous romance about Alexander, known as the *Pseudo Callisthenes*, which inspired a whole cycle of romance in French.

A similar process, as has already been seen, is believed to have played some part in the genesis of the Spanish picaresque tale, although here the central figure is an anti-hero rather than a hero.

The collection of legends finally becomes, by what seems an inevitable sequence, a connected narrative; the model for other narratives about other figures, heroic, tragic or even comic. The type of hero chosen corresponds to the type of society, and to the position occupied within it by the audience for whom the stories are told. It is easy to see why the peasants, workmen and small tradesmen who made up the Chinese audience found Sung Chiang, the defiant outlaw, to their taste. It is also obvious why the medieval stories written primarily for an aristocratic audience, had a king or emperor, Arthur, Charlemagne or Alexander, as the central figure; although it remains a mystery why Arthur, the representative of a defeated race, should have been chosen to embody the ideals of the conquerors.

Social ideals largely dictate the character of the hero. The process through which stories, often originally belonging to some other figure, ancient folk tales, the myths of a discarded, even sometimes the legends of a living religion, are attracted to him, until in the end, they become the chronicle of his life, seem on the other hand to follow a universal pattern, irrespective of the social background.

A similar process presumably played some part in the creation of another form of literature—the epic; but as these poems date from remote centuries there is no such evidence as there is for the novel. Nor, as one might have thought from the influence which the epic idea had on the development of the European novel, have the same cultures always produced both epic and novel. There is no trace of the epic in China, although China is supposed to have had an 'heroic age', and no trace in Japan.

It is clear that an interest in the past is one of the impulses which stimulate the production of long, connected narratives, and this idea is supported by the way in which a renewed interest in history has from time to time invigorated it.

The unforgotten background of classical civilization meant that France in the eleventh century was deeply concerned with what had happened in the past. The core of history became overlaid with stories of magic weapons and incredible monsters; but the writers of the first prose romance seem to have taken considerable trouble to make their books appear to be authentic history. Chrétien had already cited the great book of the Bishop of Beauvais as authority for the story of *Cligès*, and a book belonging to the Count of Flanders as the source for *Percival*. The writers of the prose romances, however, made more elaborate explanations as to where they derived their knowledge. The prose *Lancelot* explains that the adventures of Arthur's knights were written down by learned clerks at the King's command, and that the papers dealing with Lancelot were discovered in the Royal Archives after Arthur's last battle on Salisbury Plain, and were translated out of the Latin for the love of Henry II of England. The statement seems to show considerable care to produce a plausible account of the sources. Henry II was known to have been particularly interested in Arthur and is said to have caused a search to be made for Arthur's tomb in Glastonbury.

The preface to *Perlevaus* similarly tells us that the book is a translation of a Latin work found in a holy house of religion in the Isle of Avalon. Nitze, indeed, thinks that this is merely part of the propaganda put out by Glastonbury in its claim to ecclesiastical supremacy; but it is strikingly like the information given about the source of *Lancelot*.

Both the *Morte d' Arthur* and *Petit Jehan de Saintré* are in a sense historical novels. The latter is clearly modelled on a chronicle, and the chronicle also had its influence on Caxton's editing of Malory's work. Caxton discusses the authenticity of the story of Arthur in his Preface in terms which might have been used at any date before the rise of scientific history:

> Whereto they answered, and one in specyal says, that hym that shold say or thynke that there was never suche a kyng callyd Arthur myght wel be aretted grete golye and blyndenesse, for he says that there were many evydences of the contrarye. Fyrst, ye may see his sepulture in the monasterye of Glastynburye; and also in Polycronycon, in the fifth book, the syxte chappytre, and in the seventh book, the twenty-thyrd chappytre, where his body was buryed, and after founden and translated into the sayd monasterye. Ye shal se also in th'ystorye of Bochas, in his book DE CASU PRINCIPUM parte of his noble actes, and also of his falle. Also Galfrydus, in his, Brutysshe book, recouteth his lyf. An in dyvers places of England many remembraunces ben yet of hym and shall remayne perpetuelly and also of his knyghtes: fyrst, in the abbey of Westmestre, at Saynt, Edwardes shryne, remayneth the prynte of his seal in reed waxe, closed in beryll, in whych is wryton PATRICIUS ARTHURUS BRITANNIE GALLIE GERMANIE DACIE IMPERATOR; item, in the castel of Dover ye may see Gauwayns skulle and mantel; at Wynchester, the Rounde Table; in other places Launcelottes swerde and many other thynges. Thenne, al these thynges consydered, there can no man reasonably gaysaye but there was a kyng of thys lande named Arthur.

The French heroic novel was historical and so was *La Princesse de Clèves*. Not only an interest in but a nostalgia for the past has often accompanied innovations in prose fiction. Such a sentiment has been attributed to Murasaki, Malory and La Sale, and may have been one of the principal stimulants of the author of the *San Kuo*. *Waverley* and *Middlemarch*, both of which introduced a new phase of the novel, were written about the period immediately preceding the author's lifetime.

It may be objected that the connection between history and the novel cannot be as close as is suggested, because all peoples are interested in their own past. This, however, is not universally true. History was not written in ancient India. This has been disputed on the grounds that historical works existed but have been lost. Most of the authorities who wrote the section on ancient India in *Historians of India, Pakistan and Ceylon*,[21] Indian as well as European, maintain that true history was absent except for

[21] *Historians of India, Pakistan and Ceylon*, edited C. H. Philips, 1961.

one writer in Kashmir. Even if it was written and subsequently lost, this in itself argues a certain lack of popular enthusiasm. Kashmir, in which the only book of true history was written, is also the only part of India in which books that have been called novels appeared.

There is the same lack of history in those countries of Southeast Asia much influenced by Hindoo culture. The first Siamese chronicle apparently dates from after A.D. 1362, although the first Thai kingdom in Siam was established somewhere about A.D. 870. The first Burmese chronicle was written between 1400 and 1422, and, we are told, simply reproduced scriptural traditions instead of recounting real events.

Another objection might be the absence of the novel in medieval Islam, where history was not only one of the main intellectual interests but perhaps the most original intellectual achievement, and yet there nothing like the novel was produced. The reason for this seems to be that the novel everywhere began as mere entertainment, and for historical figures to be used for this, the interest in history must be lively but not too serious. It must be the kind that delights in exciting incident and striking characters, not the kind that seeks for causes. European romance and Chinese novel bear the same relation to history that science fiction bears to science. Muslim historians were from the first concerned primarily to trace the dealings of God with man. It might also have been the intention of the medieval chroniclers of Europe, but history was not one of the subjects with which scholars in the tenth and eleventh centuries were much occupied and no historians who can be compared with Greek, Arabic or modern writers appeared in this period.

In China, history, although much cultivated, remained a mere catalogue of events set down without any attempt at narrative art. In any case, the people for whom the first novels were composed were not educated enough to read it.

Legends and stories about some historical or mythical figure can arise in any society; but a long connected narrative presupposes a number of people with sufficient leisure either to read or to be read to. As romance and novel are everywhere pure entertainment, the leisured audience must also be frivolous enough to want entertainment rather than instruction, and yet in some way important enough to induce men of talent to write for them. It might seem to follow that fiction will first be written for aristocrats, and this was true of Europe and Japan, but in China the audience was composed of the poorer sections. Male aristocrats are often extremely busy, and public opinion frequently expects them to have a taste in literature above mere fiction. Great ladies both have less to do than their husbands and brothers and are frequently, as in Europe and Japan, allowed mere amusement.

This combination of leisure and frivolity seems to explain the well-known connection between women and fiction in many periods. It is unnecessary to repeat the names of women novelists in many languages or to point out that they occupy a much higher position compared with men than in any other genre. Except in China, women appear to have been particularly important as an audience. The early romances were composed to glorify women and, it has been thought, especially for women.[22] Richardson's most enthusiastic admirers in England were women, and it has been suggested that the literacy of Englishwomen of all classes, and their demand for reading matter had something to do with the emergence of the eighteenth-century novel.

To write in Japanese, still more to write in the simplified script, was, in the eleventh century, considered beneath the dignity of serious scholars, and was left to women. The kind of people who listened to the first Chinese novels were not expected to be able to read the Chinese classics, and so public opinion did not prevent them enjoying popular tales. The leisure, which allowed them to listen to a story-teller, was probably due to the under-employment, which is endemic in pre-industrial societies.

There have been rich women in many civilizations, but few in which their status was high enough to allow them to write themselves, or to encourage others to write for them. In no Oriental society would a writer, who took himself as seriously as Chrétien de Troyes, have been likely to declare that both the matter and the *sens* of his book had been given to him by a woman.

Sociological factors are thus brought back into the history of the novel, but sociological factors of the most general kind. It is obvious that societies, different in every other way, could have a class with the required characteristics.

It is also obvious that the decisive moment in the development

[22] 'Le Roman médiéval, c'est un clerc et une dame qui l'ecoute', an often-quoted remark of Albert Thibaudet, the French medievalist.

of fiction comes when the connected narrative, whether in prose or verse, is first taken up and used by a writer of outstanding talent. The invention of a literary form is, however, so rare, and once invented it continues to be used over such long periods, that it is exceedingly difficult to be certain what contribution various social and sociological factors may have made to its appearance. The content of literature, particularly the content of the novel, shows the influence of society both more plainly, and in much greater detail, than the history of the novel as a literary form. If these influences are so evident and so all-pervading that any novel can be accurately described as a reflection or expression of the period in which it was written, the idea of the importance of sociological, as well as of social factors, would be strengthened and the idea of the importance of individual choice proportionately weakened. An examination of how far Defoe, Richardson and Fielding give an accurate picture of the life of their time can thus act as some sort of test of the idea that the individual contribution to the emergence of the novel was more important than is often admitted.

PART II

The Novel as a Reflection of Society

Introduction

The romance or novel takes a modern reader straight into another time, it shows how men and women (some of them, at any rate) thought and spoke, the problems of their world, the ideals they cherished; it illuminates and sometimes instructs. The technology of the age, or aspects of it, can generally be seen—especially transport and lighting.

From the *Tale of Genji*, as well as from the medieval romance and the eighteenth-century novel, it is clear how people got from place to place. Methods of lighting are even more evident; it is extraordinary how often the phrase 'she lit a candle or a lamp', 'he lifted the lantern', 'I turned on the light', occur in novels.

The word reflection, however, implies more than this. It must mean that the novel gives an accurate picture of the surface of life, and shows the dominant interests of the time, not only including everything, but relating everything to everything else in the exact proportions in which they existed. Any judgement it makes ought to be either valid or typical of the period. In addition to this it is often demanded that a novel should express the meaning or spirit of the time. Bound up with these ideas is the theory that a great writer somehow represents more than himself, is a spokesman for an age, a class, a country.

The concept of the *Zeitgeist* is an elusive one. Is it the spirit of the age as it appears to us, or as it appeared to those living in it? Dr. Johnson, for example, thought that no one would ever consider the eighteenth century as a great period of English civilization, but that subsequent ages would be struck by its great humanity to the poor. Today we take the opposite view. Another difficulty in the application of the theory is how to translate its manifestations in different phenomena into some common idiom. If the period is dominated by one idea or system of ideas; if, for example, the law is derived from some sacred book, the literature is liturgy and hymns, the visual arts concerned only with religious subjects, it is easy enough to see that all these activities are expressions of the same 'spirit'.

There are, however, few periods as integrated as this, and the eighteenth century in England was not one of them. Before discussing whether the novel of the time was inspired by the spirit or expressed the meaning of the age, it would be necessary to establish what this was. It, therefore, seems better to concentrate on its documentary value, on how far the picture it gives is accurate, and to what extent its authors can be regarded as representative of some particular section of opinion. The modern idea that *Robinson Crusoe* and *Clarissa* are allegories of social theories, as well, as stories about particular human beings reintroduces the spirit of the age in another, although a less all-pervading, form.

The picture of any society given in its literature does not always agree with the picture given by historians. It is, after all, from medieval literature that the recurring idea that life in the Middle Ages was really very jolly is largely derived. When the *Tale of Genji* was published in English most reviewers assumed that it presented an accurate map of the society of Heian Japan, experts, however, do not altogether agree. Murasaki also left a diary, a part of which has been translated. In this a rougher, coarser version of the life depicted in the novel is shown. Keene in his history of Japanese literature describes the contrast: 'The *Tale of Genji* is the novel of a society, the extremely civilised, perhaps even decadent, court of tenth century Japan. We should not, however, be misled into imagining that Lady Murasaki has given us a realistic portrait of contemporary conditions. Rather, her novel is the evocation of a world which never in fact existed. She tells us that the events she describes occurred at some indefinite period in the past, and hers was essentially a romantic view of a now faded golden world.'[1]

Sir George Sansom comes to a similar conclusion from a rather different point of view. 'The Chronicles', he says, 'and diaries of the time do not on thé whole confirm the impression of a frivolous, loose-living society of aristocrats which may be gained from too exclusive a study of the romantic literature of the 10th and 11th centuries. No doubt there were a great many gay young courtiers addicted to amorous adventures; but there seemed to

[1] Keene, Donald, *Japanese Literature*, 1953.

have been a compensating number of grave and industrious officials, men who were diligent in performing their ceremonial duties, scribbling their memoranda, issuing their orders and despatches, men steeped in the official routine.'[2]

In *The Tale of Genji* the provincial aristocrats are regarded in every way as inferior to the Court nobles, and appointment to a local governorship as almost a misfortune. Yet Sir George Sansom says, 'Provincial Governors on the expiry of their term of office would elect to remain in the country, there to found families living on large estates.' There is no hint of this in the book, any more than there is of the growing power of local magnates, also described by Sanson: 'By the middle of the Heian Era (say 950) the court could no longer keep the peace in the capital, nor could the aristocratic absentee-landlords, whether nobles or abbots, protect their own property without the assistance of armed forces maintained by local magnates.'[3] This does not appear in the novel either; the Emperor is depicted as all powerful.

The word 'reflection' gives the impression that the writer is an instrument for recording the life of his time, and a passive instrument like a mirror, not a selective one like a computer. Apart from any difference in ability or knowledge, novelists do not all start with the same intentions. They may try to paint an accurate picture of life as it is. On the other hand, their aim may be to produce an idealized version or, more rarely, a picture which is even darker than the reality. Sometimes one intention is fashionable, sometimes another. There is a corresponding tendency in readers both to want to read about people like themselves, in everyday scenes, and about the marvellous, the fantastic, the adventure that passes beyond the bounds of reality in time, place or psychology.

Literary conventions, as well as political, religious and moral ideas, set a limit to how far any novelist can go in either direction. These limits are, however, very wide in all periods, so that he is not forced to choose one or the other. *Le Lai de l'Ombre, La Chastelaine de Vergi* and *Fulke Fitzwarin* existed side by side with wild fairy tales. In 1751, in the midst of the triumphs of realistic fiction, *Peter Wilkins* was published, a book which, whether it is called science fiction or a fairy tale, is the antithesis of novels like *Tom Jones* or *Clarissa*.

[2] Sansom, George, *A Cultural History of Japan*, 1946.   [3] *Ibid.*

No one ever supposed that *La Princesse de Clèves* was an exact copy of contemporary manners, but only because of the diaries, letters and sermons of the period. If this novel had been the only piece of literature which survived what a misleading picture of France in the seventeenth century would have been derived from it.

The motive underlying the novel which idealizes rather than reflects is often considered to be a desire to hide the less pleasant aspects of reality; but it is just as often a desire to remove them by reforming manners. The difference between the France of *La Princesse de Clèves* and the France of St. Simon, or indeed of Mme de La Fayette herself, has been described by Ashton thus: 'La vie de Mme de La Fayette, c'est la vie de son temps, et . . . son oeuvre en est l'aidéal.'[4]

It has been suggested that those sombre minds who have alarmed the world with their dark visions had similar motives. A recent book on Ben Jonson said of him that he 'habitually used the devices of a small and somewhat misunderstood group of writers who celebrate their allegiance to an ideal world by creating the perversion of the real'. Other writers of this kind are said to be Swift, Poe and Baudelaire. This does not seem entirely adequate; but there is no doubt that writers do exist who paint a black picture, whatever their motives. Neither the dark nor the light, the literature of reconciliation nor of despair, gives an accurate picture of the society in which it was written, although, of course, it may reveal deeper trends or prophesy future developments.

Aesthetic as well as moral considerations may interfere with the photographic quality of any piece of literature. Jane Austen used to be reproached for not mentioning the distress of the agricultural labourer, or the long war. It is now more usual to say that the smaller gentry were so insulated from these realities that Jane Austen could not see them. We know that this sort of thing is nonsense, because we know that two of Jane Austen's brothers were naval officers, another a banker whose bank failed, and that her first cousin's husband was guillotined. Short of actually participating in the war (and, after all, Mrs. Admiral Croft was quite likely to have been at the Battle of Trafalgar), or of being in Paris during the Revolution, Jane Austen could hardly have been more involved in the main currents of history. A clergyman's daughter could not have avoided the sight of poverty and distress.

[4] Ashton, H., *Madame de la Fayette*, 1922.

The novels are obviously not intended to be an exact picture of the society of the day. Death as well as poverty, serious illness as well as sunken ships, are absent from her books because she was writing comedy, which is a kind of abstract art. This does not mean that they lack the seriousness which modern critics, as well as, Matthew Arnold, always demand, but merely that they show it in a different dimension from tragedy. Nor does it mean that she had no experience of suffering in her own life. Death, especially death in childbirth, is ever present in her letters; but its intrusion into her novels would have destroyed the atmosphere, as much as a scene showing the Duke in *Twelfth Night*, grappling with the problems of economic policy, would have devastated Illyria. The passage from *Emma*: 'In the present instance, it was sickness and poverty together which she came to visit; and after remaining there as long as she could give comfort or advice, she quitted the cottage with such an impression of the scene as made her say to Harriet, as they walked away: "These are the sights Harriet to do one good. How trifling they make everything else appear" ', shows that Jane Austen was well aware of this dark side of life but that she chose not to include it in her novels. Misery, especially sickness and poverty, do make ordinary love affairs seem trifling; but Jane Austen removes the impression, which might have been too strong for the tone of the book, by the irony of the subsequent conversation between Emma and Harriet.

Her advice to her niece suggesting that it would be better to postpone marriage 'by not beginning the business of mothering quite so early in life, you will be young in constitution, spirits, figure and countenance while Mrs. William Hammand is growing old by confinements and nursing' would be inconceivable in any of her novels.

Not even the surface of Regency life is exactly depicted. It is a solemn thought, but there is no doubt that all her heroes, except Edmund Bertrand and perhaps Henry Tilney, would on occasions have drunk too much. That there are no such incidents is not because she was unaware that men got drunk. In her letters she described a man who was more than a trifle disguised, without surprise or reprobation. 'Captain S.', she said, 'was certainly in liquor', at the party at her brother's house in Sloane Street. In her books she left out such incidents because this also would have broken their perfect pattern by suggesting a criticism of manners quite foreign to her purpose. She was indeed careful, as a letter to another niece, who was herself writing a novel, shows, not to allow anything unlikely to appear in her novels, because this, too, would have disturbed the reader's acceptance. There is a curious resemblance between the relation which her letters bear to her novels and the corresponding relation between Murasaki's diary and *The Tale of Genji*.

It is easy enough to make allowances for the author's intention, if sufficient is known about contemporary life from other sources, but not so easy if the only information is derived from literature. How difficult it may be is illustrated by the stimulating controversy as to whether the Robin Hood stories owe their origin to proletarian protest or knightly gaiety.[5]

This difficulty does not occur with the early eighteenth-century novelists, with the exception of Smollett. The strong element of caricature and practical joking in his books makes it hard to be certain when he was describing incidents that he thought might have happened and when he was deliberately exaggerating to make things funnier. The brutal jokes, so frequent in his novels, have generally been regarded as transcripts from eighteenth-century life. An American critic, however, regards them as mainly literary in inspiration: 'The enormous popularity of Cervantes' masterpiece was in a great measure responsible for the violent escapades, the sousings and beating that bulk so large in the comic picture of the eighteenth century.'[6]

On the other hand, Richardson, and Fielding in *Tom Jones* and *Amelia*, meant to give a plain, unvarnished picture, and although Defoe nowhere explicitly said so, it was probably his object, too. It is possible, of course, that fantasy or allegory are also 'reflections' of the society of their time; but to prove this would be much more difficult than to discover how far the realistic novelists achieved their aim. For the eighteenth century there is a wealth of data—including contemporary views on the books themselves —to provide material for judging them. Some of this indeed fails us for Defoe, because most of his novels are about people who have not left memoirs, diaries or letters. We remain in the dark

[5] Keen, Maurice, 'The Origins of Robin Hood', *Past and Present*, Nov. 1958; Holt, J. C., 'The Ballads of Robin Hood', *Past and Present*, Nov. 1960.

[6] Putney, R., *The Plan of Peregrine Pickle*, Publications of the Modern Languages Association of America, 1945.

about what a real Moll Flanders would have thought or said. The only authentic document are speeches before execution, a conventional form, and, moreover, the last words of the more spectacular criminals were alone preserved in the chap-books and news sheets. It might well be better not to discuss Defoe at all, but as he is often considered the realistic novelist *par excellence*, this would certainly be taken as evading the issue. While it is impossible to compare Defoe's characters with actual letters or memoires of the kind of people they are meant to represent, it is possible to examine the main characteristics of his work, and to discuss how far it was typical and representative of his period or class.

5

Defoe

Daniel Defoe certainly had one of the qualities necessary for a successful painter of the contemporary scene—a very wide knowledge of the society of his day. Although he was the son of a small tradesman, his political activities brought him into touch with the rich and powerful and also forced him to travel about England and even to go to Scotland, which was a rare journey for an Englishman of his day.

The odd thing about Defoe's novels is how little of his various interests and experience come into them. There are no politics in his books. Robinson Crusoe returned to England in 1687, but not a word is said of any political disturbances. Odder still is the absence of any kind of political background in *Colonel Jack*. One would have thought that a writer as interested in politics as we know Defoe to have been would have said something of the origin or the reasons for Colonel Jack's high Toryism. There may have been reasons for silence. The booksellers may have thought any serious treatment of politics would involve them with the law, or they may merely have felt that it would not interest the kind of reader the books were aimed at. But whatever the reasons it means that Defoe's novels do not give an accurate idea of this intensely political age. To make up for this they are full, or so it is always said, of the other two dominant interests of the period—religion and trade. Both are prominent in *Robinson Crusoe*, which is also considered by some critics to be an allegory of economic individualism.

It is often suggested that the plot of *Robinson Crusoe* is peculiarly characteristic of its age, and in one sense it is. People seem to have got themselves wrecked on desert islands in unusual numbers in the thirty years prior to its appearance. It is, as is well known, based on the story of one of these men, Alexander Selkirk. The fascination which the theme exercised is perhaps best shown by the way in which the simile or metaphor of the desert island was current before the publication of *Robinson Crusoe*. Anthony Henley, Member of Parliament and father of Lord Northington, used it in a letter to Swift in a way which, but for the date, 1708, would have made one think he had just read *Robinson Crusoe*: 'You are now cast on an inhospitable island; no mathematical figures on the sand, no vestiga hominum to be seen; perhaps at this very time reduced to one single barrel of damaged biscuit, and short allowance even of salt water. What is to be done? Another in your condition would look about; perhaps he might find some potatoes; or get an old piece of iron, and make a harpoon, and if he found Higgon sleeping on the shore, strike him and eat him.'[1]

It is, however, doubtful if the story is really so closely linked to its particular time. There are two main themes—the wreck and the man alone on the island. Stories of dangerous seas are common in many literatures. Even the desert island has appeared in societies remote both in time and place from eighteenth-century England. A famous example is an Arabic book said to have been written by Abu-Bakr-Ibn-Tufail about A.D. 1169.[2] This was three times translated during Defoe's lifetime—by George Keith, a Quaker, by Ashwell and by Simon Ockley. It is essentially a religious allegory, and is thought by some critics to have suggested the more serious elements in Crusoe's story. Its real theme is how the light of nature would reveal the existence of God even to a being solitary from birth. The child, however, had to live and learn about his environment, and the story might have suggested the theme of the solitary being and its allegorical potentialities. *Robinson Crusoe* is, however, in no way religious allegory. There is religion in the book, but it is a story, not of a revelation in solitude, but of physical survival under adverse conditions.

The kind of religion and the way in which it is used is indeed characteristic of the turn of the seventeenth century. There are various methods through which religion can be introduced into a piece of fiction; among them the use of allegory and symbolism, a plot which turns on a religious dilemma, and outright preaching.

[1] Swift, J., *Correspondence*, edited by L. Ball, 1910.
[2] Pastor, R., *The Idea of Robinson Crusoe*, 1930.

Although some critics have seen both symbolism and allegory in *Robinson Crusoe*, it is certain that Defoe did not intend to write a variant of the *Pilgrim's Progress*, but to produce an account of shipwreck and survival, alone on an island, which would be taken as authentic.

The religion is introduced through the reflections of Crusoe himself and through the attempt to teach Friday, which make them a kind of sermon. This is connected with a definite aspect of contemporary culture—the appetite for sermons. Strange as it may seem to us, people of the time enjoyed listening to and reading sermons. It may have been a duty, but it was an agreeable duty. On the other hand, this was by no means limited to the early seventeen hundreds; it began with the rise of Protestantism itself and extended over the first half of the nineteenth century—indeed, by 1719 it was losing its hold on sophisticated people. In the seventeenth century some of the most important pieces of English prose are sermons. Although there are eighteenth-century sermons which are mentioned in detailed textbooks of English literature, there is nothing that can be compared with Donne or Jeremy Taylor.

The fusing of religion with stories of adventure and crime was, however, new. In the stories of crime and criminals which prepared the way for *Moll Flanders*, *Colonel Jack* and *Roxana*, references to religion are so brief and conventional that they cannot be connected with any particular doctrine or persuasion. That they occur at all does indeed distinguish them from the modern crime story, as well as from the Spanish picaresque novel, and so might be held to be characteristic of their period. On the other hand, there is a religious element in a great many earlier stories about wickedness which must weaken the link between this element and eighteenth-century society.

In Defoe religion appears to be both stronger and more sincere than in the other writers who dealt with the same kind of subject. This is so plain that his novels have been described as an expression of Puritanism. One of the most influential of the books which spread this view is Beljambe's *Men of Letters and the English Public in the Eighteenth Century*.[3] The translators of this work said they were frequently puzzled as to what Beljambe meant by 'Puritan',

[3] Beljambe, A., *Men of Letters and the English Public in the Eighteenth Century*, translated by E. D. Lorimer, 1948.

as well they might be, because he used it indifferently for Dissenters and members of the Established Church. That Defoe thought of himself as Puritan is unlikely, because the word in his lifetime was still mainly abusive or at least critical. He was a Presbyterian, a persuasion on the extreme 'right' wing of dissent. The minister under which his father sat was Samual Annesley, a nephew of the Earl of Anglesey, who had been educated at Oxford. Although he finally resigned his living, St. Giles Cripplegate, he had accepted a re-presentation from Charles II at the Restoration, and was accused by his enemies of having been originally ordained in the Church of England by a bishop. All this made him an unusual dissenting minister, even for a Presbyterian.

Defoe's religious convictions must have been genuine, because it would have been, one must suppose, greatly to his advantage to join the Established Church. He never showed the slightest signs of doing so; although Sutherland points out, in his life of Defoe, that he once applied for a place in the Audit Office which, if he had secured it, would have meant that he would occasionally have had to attend his parish church. Considering everything, there can be no doubt that he must have felt either a sincere attachment to the Presbyterian faith or a sincere revulsion from the Church of England. But although there is an element in his novels which can be described as Puritan, there are also many other strands of thought of quite a different kind. Harley said that he was a 'formal fellow', so there may have been something in his bearing of the gravity, if not the sanctimoniousness, of the Commonwealth Puritan. But Presbyterians are Calvinists and hold the doctrine of predestination. This is the theory that, in every generation, God selects a number of human beings to save and that all the rest are damned. *The Family Instructor* is an exposition of Calvinism; but although anyone knowing the facts may detect its traces in the novels, it is doubtful if it could be found if they were all we knew of their author. When debating whether to settle down in England after his first wreck, Crusoe does indeed refer to 'a secret overruling decree that hurries us on to be the instrument of our own destruction'. This might imply the doctrine of predestination, but the suggestion is in no way worked out.

When he considers whether he should attack and kill the cannibals he comes very near to a theory of the relativity of moral judgements. 'How do I know what God himself judges in this particular case? It is certain that these people do not commit this as a crime; it is not against their own consciences reproving or their light reproaching them . . . They think it no more a crime to kill a captive taken in war, than we do to kill an ox; nor to eat human flesh, than we do to eat mutton.'

Defoe believed in the value of 'secret hints or pressings of the mind'; what we should call presentiments or precognition. Robinson Crusoe is twice guided by such feelings, and Defoe declared his belief in them in many of his other writings. This has been taken to be characteristic of Puritanism; but Defoe did not think they came directly from God. He attributed them 'to the converse of spirits, and the secret communications between those bodied and those unembodied'—another curious anticipation of a modern doctrine.

In other respects the religious doctrines of Robinson Crusoe seem to be ones to which any Protestant Christian could subscribe, Protestant because of Crusoe's belief in the all sufficiency of the Bible. One of the most remarkable things about Crusoe is his tolerance of other sects, even of Roman Catholics—a most un-Puritan attitude. Surely no Puritan would have allowed Crusoe to conform to the Roman Catholic Church whilst in Brazil, and surely no Puritan would have said: 'There we shall see there have been other flocks than those in our own fold, other paths to Heaven from those we elect men from. . . .

'How many actions of men which we, seeing only from outside, have now censured, shall we find there by that penetration that cannot err, be accepted from their inside sincerity? How many an opinion we condemn here shall we there see to be orthodox? In a word, how many contradicting notions and principles which we thought inconsistent with true religion shall we then find to be reconcilable to themselves, to one another and to the fountains of truth?' This remarkable tolerance led one critic to suggest that Defoe had been influenced by the deism which was a main intellectual current of the time. This, however, seems to be a mistake, as he speaks in the *Serious Reflections of Robinson Crusoe* of 'natural religion' in a way which shows he was familiar with deist arguments but he refers to them with some scorn: 'A sort of people who will acknowledge a God, but he must be such a one as they please to make him, a fine, well-bred, good-natured, gentleman-like deity that cannot have the heart to damn any of his creatures to an eternal punishment.' Although Defoe may consciously have rejected the change in doctrine which accompanied the growing tolerance, Robinson Crusoe's sentiments seem to have been influenced by Locke rather than by any Puritan writer. In this he was representative of Presbyterian opinion in general, on which the influence of Locke is well known. Locke's influence drew Presbyterianism away from what we usually consider 'Puritan' towards the position of Latitudinarian bishops such as Hoadley, who, although a Whig, was certainly no Puritan. He said in one of his sermons: 'Christian moderation will dispose men not to be hard upon their brothers of different parties or different denominations.' Halifax, too, remarked in *Advice to a Daughter*, 'It is not true devotion to put on an angry zeal against those who may be of different denominations.'

Defoe's charity was not confined to differences of opinion in religion, at times he extended it to sinners as well. *Moll Flanders* and *Colonel Jack* were in the line of previous novels about criminals; but if they are compared with earlier works it can be seen that Moll and Jack are treated with much greater imaginative sympathy and this does not only seem to be due to Defoe's greater skill as a writer.

In *The Serious Reflections of Robinson Crusoe*, a work in which one would think that his true opinions were likely to appear, if anywhere, because he wrote it after the enormous success of *Robinson Crusoe* focused public attention on him as it had hardly been attracted before, he put forward views about the effect of circumstances on a man's honesty which in some ways anticipate the more advanced thought of today: 'I am of the opinion that I could state a circumstance in which there is not one man alive that would be honest. Necessity is above the power of human nature, and for Providence to suffer a man to fall into that necessity is to suppose him to sin, because nature is not furnished with power to defend itself, nor grace itself able to fortify the mind against it.'

This, with its element of excuse, is the very antithesis of Puritanism. It may seem to resemble the doctrine of predestination, and indeed the idea of predetermined fate in one context may predispose anyone to accept it in another; but the step from God's choice of the saved and the damned to society's responsibility for making criminals is a large one. A typical Puritan might have said with Defoe, 'He that is dishonest in your eyes, by a causal or other crime which he commits, may rise from that disaster by a sincere repentance, and be tomorrow an honester man than thyself in the eyes of his Maker.' But he would never have denied the efficacy of grace even in the most adverse circumstances, or have said as Defoe does later in *The Reflections*, 'Necessity makes an honest man; and if the world was to be the judge according to the common received notion, there would not be an honest poor man alive.' Baxter's 'There but for the Grace of God go I' sounds not unlike it at first, but on reflection clearly reveals a different spirit.

Defoe returned to the theme in *Colonel Jack*. The Colonel asks his clerk who had been transported for stealing, but who was repentant; 'Suppose you to be under the same necessity, in the same starving condition, should you not take the same course?'

He replied very sharply. 'That shows us the need we have of the petition in the Lord's prayer "Lead us not into temptation. . . ." I should even beg of God not to be let into such snares as human nature cannot resist.'

All this seems to approximate to Lillio's remark about the hero of his tragedy, who murdered the uncle who had befriended him to get money for his mistress: 'Perhaps, had we like him been tryed, like him we had fallen too.' Lillio's attitude to his criminal is generally taken to be an example of sensibility rather than of Puritanism.

When Defoe went to a country dominated by a Puritan Church, he seems to have disliked the Church. He paid some high compliments to the Scottish character in his poem *Caledonia*, but even here he remarked that if their religion had a fault it was 'too much of zeal'. Writing to Harley from Scotland in one of his secret reports he said: 'I find there bigotry without popery and God's priests ride upon God's people as well as the superior clergy of less pure churches. Certainly the clergy have more to account for than in other places, where the customary slavery of other nations is inverted but is every jot as fatal as there. The priests lead silly women, these silly women more silly men; the women are the instructors, and the men are mere machines wound up fast as the spring goes at home.'[4] It is true that this refers mainly to the opposition to the Union, a project which Defoe was not only paid to defend but seems to have wholeheartedly supported. On the other hand, one would have thought a Presbyterian, whose

[4] Historical MSS. Commission, Portland MSS., Vol. IV.

religion placed various civil disabilities on him in England, would have found in Scotland something of a promised land. Although he sent his son to the University of Glasgow and proposed the setting up of a sort of hostel with tutorial supervision for English Nonconformist youths in Scottish university towns, he does not seem to have thought the country either a paradise, or a model for the rest of the world.

Another un-Puritan quality is the importance which he attached to love—one could almost call it romantic love—in his book *A Treatise Concerning The Uses And Abuses Of The Marriage Bed.* It has been said that love meant nothing to Defoe and sex very little. Indeed, love is not a subject much treated in his novels. But a more forthright declaration than his, that mutual love is the only basis for marriage, could hardly be found in the literature of the time: 'How little is regarded of that one essential and absolutely necessary part of the composition called love, without which the matrimonial state is, I think, hardly lawful, I am sure is not rational and, I think, can never be happy.' Now, this is not a specifically Puritan attitude, as Defoe himself shows in criticizing the religious as well as the ungodly: 'Not virtue, not fidelity to the marriage bed, not conscience of the conjugal duty, not religion, will do it; no not RELIGION.

'How miserably do the pious and devout, the religious and conscientious live together! The husbands here, the wives there, by jarring tempers, discording affections, and in short, mere want of love and friendship, grow scandals to the married life.'

He distinguishes, of course, between love and mere sexual desire or lust as he calls it, but this attitude was not confined to Puritans. It is strange how little of the high value he placed on love appears in his novels—the novel being a form of literature which most writers find peculiarly suitable to the illustration of problems of love and marriage.

Such evidence as exists seems to show that, while it is clear that Defoe was a Puritan in the sense of being a Dissenter and accepting many Puritan doctrines and some Puritan views, he was very far from being typical or representative. The Puritan elements, even in his religion, were heavily diluted by others, but this, of course, makes him not less but more a man of his time. All the ideas comprised in the term had by the time Defoe wrote his first novel, decisively failed in England. They were to be revived to some extent indeed by Wesley, but without any of the political radicalism of the seventeenth-century Puritans. This failure is obscured for many people by the theory of the connection between the extremer forms of Protestantism and the beginning of capitalism. This frequently leads to an exaggerated idea of the influence of Puritanism on the middle classes. Most Dissenters were tradesmen. This, however, does not allow the reversal of the statement that most tradesmen were Dissenters, a reversal which often seems to be tacitly if not explicitly made. Ashton points out in his economic history of the eighteenth century that 'Many, perhaps most, of the leaders of trade and commerce were Episcopalians.'[5] A little reflection will show that Dissenters must have been in a minority among businessmen because, if the whole trade of the nation had been in their hands, how could any government have continued the laws which forbade anyone but a member of the Church of England to vote at Parliamentary elections, to stand as a candidate either for Parliament or municipal office, or to go to a university? It is true that all these prohibitions were not rigidly enforced on Protestant Dissenters after the accession of George I, but the attempt to repeal them in 1717 was defeated.

It can, of course, be said that the ideas or ideals of the Puritans had a great influence on some members of the Church of England. When this statement is made, and it often is, it is generally views about sexual morality which are in mind but all forms of Christianity place a high value on chastity, George Herbert as much as Baxter, Dr. Johnson as determinedly as Richardson.

The late seventeenth and early eighteenth century was a time of commercial expansion and of innovation in banking and commercial organization. This brought with it an outburst of theories on the meaning and proper way to conduct economic affairs. Defoe, as we know from his other writings, was deeply interested in all this, and most critics have found the author of *The Complete English Tradesman* and the *Essay upon Projects* in the novels, particularly in *Robinson Crusoe*. Their strangest characteristic, however, is that there is much less of this than one would expect, and what there is does not seem to have greatly inspired Defoe. Only one book, *Robinson Crusoe*, is about a merchant or trader. His commercial activities are, however, in the first part only a means of getting

[5] Ashton, T. H., *An Economic History of England, the Eighteenth Century*, 1955.

him on to the island. While in the second, which is concerned with his activities as a merchant, the inspiration has clearly failed. It is indeed impossible to understand the first chapters of *Colonel Jack* without knowing what a commercial bill is, and Colonel Jack himself finally secured a plantation in America by trading. But he left it to enter the French Army and make an abortive attempt to take part in the Jacobite revolt of 1715. Both he and Robinson Crusoe were, moreover, merchants not producers (except of the agricultural products on Colonel Jack's plantation). Industry as distinct from commerce plays no part in any novel of Defoe. He does indeed give details of prices and earnings, both legitimate and illegitimate, much more frequently than most novelists, but this seems to be characteristic rather of Defoe himself than of any social class or widespread attitude. If it was typical of the period, surely it would be found in subsequent novels. Nothing like it appears either in those which are forgotten or those which are remembered. His characters consider money the most important thing in the world and, as has often been said, they view even death, birth and love mainly from the economic aspect. This pre-occupation is generally thought to be characteristic of the middle class. But in reality it is not, and never has been, the mark of any class which has a surplus of income above its immediate needs, whether the class is the English eighteenth-century tradesman or the modern English working class. It is on the contrary the very poor who tend to view everything from the economic angle. There is no doubt that this emphasis in Defoe's novels comes mainly from his own interest in such problems, but it may also be related to his audience, if indeed, as experts say, they were the lower rather than the middle classes.

Robinson Crusoe is supposed to show most plainly the new respect for trade and the new individualistic approach to economic affairs, although it is doubtful if anyone would have thought this if he had not read *The Complete English Tradesman* as well. The books on economics and the other journalistic works of Defoe are essential to understanding his personality, but they prove nothing about the relation between the novel and society.

Robinson Crusoe is indeed a merchant, and in the latter part of the book his trading activities seem to be regarded as praise-worthy, but anyone who seeks to find in the book a reflection of the prevailing ideas about trading activities is faced with a difficulty at the beginning. If there were nothing left but *Robinson Crusoe* as a source for the contemporary view one would suppose that public opinion regarded trade, at least trade carried on in ships, as somehow wicked or unlawful. Robinson Crusoe attributes 'the life of misery which afterwards befell him' to his disregard of his father's wishes that he should become a lawyer. On first meeting a storm at sea he says: 'I now began to reflect seriously upon what I had done and how justly I was overtaken by the judgement of heaven and for my wicked leaving on my father's house, and abandoning my duty; all the good council of my parents, my father's tears and my mother's entreaties came now fresh into my mind . . . reproached me with the contempt of advice and the breach of my duty to God and my father.' But what was this breach of duty? There seemed three possibilities: that it was a sin to forsake a calling marked out for him by Providence, or that it was a sin to forsake the middle station so eloquently described by his father 'as the best state in the world, the most suited to human beings', or thirdly, it might be the sin of disobedience to his father. The odd thing is, however, that none of these things were believed to be wrong by Defoe himself, or by anyone else. A contemporary journalist, Gildon, raised this very objection when the book first appeared. His attack did not show any sensibility to literary quality, but when he asked why Crusoe's father thought a Yorkshire attorney to be a better man than a sailor it was he rather than Defoe who was reflecting contemporary opinion: 'I dare believe there are few men who consider justly, that would think the profession of a Yorkshire attorney of more benefit to mankind than that of a sea-man, or would judge that Robinson Crusoe was very criminal in rejecting the former, and choosing the latter as to provoke Divine Providence to raise two storms—and in the last of them to destroy many ships and men, purely to deter him from that course of life.'[6] Gildon was equally emphatic about the lack of sin in a grown-up son's persisting in his own choice of a profession: 'I would by no means be thought to encourage disobedience to parents; but the honouring of our father and mother does not include a duty of blindly submitting to all their commands, whether good or bad, rational or irrational, to the entire exclusion of all manner of free agency from the

[6] Gildon, Charles, *Life and Strange, Surprising Adventures of D . . . . . . D . . . . . .*, 1719.

children, which would in fact to make the children of free men absolute slaves.'

It may be true that these remarks are impregnated with the spirit of the age of reason and Defoe's attitude already belonged to the past, but if it is, Defoe can hardly at the same time be regarded as the representative of the new capitalism.

To make Crusoe's sin his wish to leave 'that state of life to which it had pleased God to call him' (apart from being a mis-quotation from the Catechism of that Church from which Defoe so vigorously dissented) meets with equal difficulties. The pursuit of wealth and the raising of oneself from a lower to a higher station, far from being regarded as sinful in 1719, was considered positively meritorious. Of course, any religious believer, from the Catholic to the Quaker, would have thought it sinful to be so immersed in the cares of this world as to forget the next. Anyone at the time would have been able to quote the text about the treasure of this world and the treasure in heaven. But this is not a prominent motif in Defoe's novels.

The difficulty about the nature of Crusoe's sin only arises if it is believed that anything in a famous novel must be representative of the society in which it was written. In reality this part of the book need not be taken too seriously. As Sutherland says, it is almost certain that Defoe himself thought his novels were a decline from his previous books, and that this view was also taken by the public opinion of his time. It was as if some modern publicist, used to discussing the problems of mass culture or industrial productivity, had sunk to the writing of science fiction for the American pulp magazines. From all we know of Defoe, it is unlikely that he would have written anything which he thought positively harmful, and he always put in 'the word in season'. Anyone buying *Roxana* would find a reminder of God and a future life as well as the story of a courtesan; but to suppose Defoe carefully weighed every word at the beginning of a book composed in the circumstances surrounding *Robinson Crusoe* is surely a mistake. Crusoe had to be got to the island and the idea that ill conduct brings an immediate punishment in this world had been prominent in many kinds of literature for many centuries. It is not to be supposed that Defoe, writing for 'honest Dick and Moll', would be careful in choosing the kind of ill conduct or strictly logical in showing its effects. He had, after all, no idea that his book would be read by Pope and Swift, by Coleridge and Karl Marx.

There is a school of modern critics which approaches *Robinson Crusoe* from another angle, regarding it as an exposition or an allegory of economic individualism. This theory seems originally to have been derived from Marx, although Leslie Stephen took a rather similar view, considering the book as an allegory of British overseas expansion. The idea has been revived and most carefully worked out by Ian Watt.[7]

It cannot possibly be true on the conscious level. No one in his senses would choose the story of a man cast alone on an uninhabited island to illustrate a theory which only applies to the exchange of goods and services. The essence of economic individualism is the view that a better result will be attained by leaving economic decisions to individuals than by any kind of centralized plan or government intervention. It is not at all easy to be sure what Defoe thought about this. Sir Dudley North had, in his *Discourses On Trade*, stated, rather than argued, that 'the whole world is to trade, but as one nation or people, and therein nations are as persons', and that 'no laws can set prices in trade, the rates of which must and will make themselves. When such laws do happen to take hold, it is so much impediment to trade and therefore prejudicial.'[8] In spite of Sir Dudley and even earlier examples of arguments for free enterprise and free trade, a rigorous intellectual treatment of the subject did not appear until the publication of Adam Smith's *Wealth of Nations* in 1776.

Defoe made suggestions about economic policy, but these were confined to particular aspects. As far as can be seen, he had no original general theory. At various times he advocated that the responsibility for roads should be centralized, that a kind of social insurance should be established and that the 'King', by which he meant the State, should insure the whole of Great Britain's overseas transactions. He supported the prohibition of imports of printed silk from India, China and Persia, and rejected the idea that competition in the Indian trade would be more efficient than the monopoly of the East India Company. His pamphlet, *A Brief Statement Of The Question Between the Printed and Painted Callicoes and the Woollen and Silk Manufacture*, is an

---

[7] Watt, Ian, *op. cit.*
[8] North, Dudley, *Discourses on Trade*, 1691.

exposition of mercantilism, an economic doctrine the very opposite of *laisser-faire*. In the same pamphlet he expresses admiration for the economic policy of France. This attitude, if based on any economic philosophy, would appear to be one of interventism.

If it is not possible to attribute to Defoe a conscious intention of writing an allegory of capitalism, can one read into Robinson Crusoe an unconscious allegory of capitalism, free enterprise, or economic individualism? Confusion seems to have been produced by some writers of economic textbooks who have used the situation of Crusoe to illustrate economic activities. Ian Watt, for example, believes that Robinson Crusoe has been 'very appropriately used by many economic theorists as their illustration of homo economicus'.[9] No economist has regarded Robinson Crusoe as any more concerned with economics than every human being must be, they have only used his activities to illustrate the nature of some economic behaviour, for example saving, which would, in their simpler forms, be much the same for a solitary individual as for an individual in society.

When obliged to admit that the story of Robinson Crusoe was not so completely true as he had claimed in the Preface, Defoe himself said that it was an allegory not of the economic system but of his own life. What he meant is not obvious from his career as we know it; but it may be that he was first attracted by the desert-island theme because he felt himself to be isolated. It must be remembered that Defoe's contemporaries did not regard him as a great or even as an honest man. By 1719 he had acquired an exceedingly evil reputation, and this is not all: failure in itself tends to a feeling of isolation and Defoe seems to have been isolated by temperament as well as by experience. Some aspects of this have often been noticed: his unusual attitude to criminals, and to marriage, his advocacy of education for women and some of his suggestions about economic policy. Ian Watt and Arnold Kettle prefer to explain this loneliness as a result of the isolation of the individual involved in the growth of the modern world. Ian Watt quotes Oliver Goldsmith's *Deserted Village* in support of this thesis. But as this poem appeared in 1770 it hardly seems to be good evidence for the state of affairs in 1719. People, or some people, feel this isolation in large towns at the present day.

⁹ Watt, Ian, *op. cit.*

It is, however, an anachronism to attribute anything similar to the early part of the eighteenth century. Towns were too small to comprise a 'crowd' in the modern sense; the population of London in 1700 was estimated at 670,000, and it is unlikely that Defoe, who was born and brought up in London, felt himself to be lost in a crowd. The family, moreover, still remained the fundamental economic unit. There are other and more likely reasons for Defoe's feelings of isolation.

He was not only unfortunate in his personal affairs, it must have seemed to him that the currents of history were flowing away from his hopes. As far as he was a Puritan, Puritanism had not only been defeated by the restoration of Charles II, but there had been a steady decline in the influence and numbers of Dissenters. In 1717 there was a move to remove their civil disabilities, and the bishops who argued against the proposal adduced this decline as a reason against the Bill. Plumb says that by 1717 there was no dissenting peer,[10] and although there were important merchants in the City who were Dissenters, these were fewer than they had been, and as yet there were no signs of the revival of much that was Puritan in Wesley's teaching. Defoe must have been relieved by the accession of George I with its removal of the threat of a Stuart restoration at Queen Anne's death; but he surely would have thought that public affairs were falling into the hands of the cynical and frivolous.

In reality, *Robinson Crusoe* is neither an allegory of capitalism nor of Defoe's own life. Fundamentally, it is a story of man against nature; a theme which was later to become common but as the basis of a prose story it was then new in literature. This theme always has a fascination, even if it is not superlatively well done as it is in *Crusoe*, presumably because it appeals to the most fundamental of all instincts, the instinct of survival. Sutherland's comment seems to be much more illuminating than the theories of allegory or symbolism: 'To read *Robinson Crusoe* is to be compelled to face up to all sorts of physical problems that civilised man has long since forgotten. It is in some sense to retrace the history of the human race; it is certainly to look again with the unspoiled eyes of childhood on many things that one has long since ceased to notice at all.'[11] This is surely what still attracts so many people to the book.

[10] Plumb, J. H., *op. cit.*   [11] Sutherland, J., *Life of Defoe*, 1937.

Tillyard can indeed describe it as 'a version of the story of the Prodigal Son—in terms not unlike the progression from Do Well to Do Better, to Do Best in *Piers Plowman*'.[12] There is more truth in this than in the idea that it is a study of free enterprise anticipating not the subsequent arguments for this kind of economic system but modern misconceptions about it. On the other hand, were anyone's religious emotions ever aroused either by Crusoe's story or by his meditations? Even on the crudest level, the reader is much more interested in Crusoe's own efforts than in incidents such as the way in which tools float rather than sink which might be regarded as due to the intervention of God'. The book is firmly anchored in the material world, and survival in such a world is not only its ostensible but also its real theme. A survival not merely physical but also of mental integrity and of self-respect. Crusoe remains a man although he is without any of the supports of society. This is surely what Malraux meant when he said that *Robinson Crusoe* was one of the few books which seemed to him to remain true after the experience of concentration camps, gas chambers and torture.[13] This core of the book comes, as far as we are able to see, from Defoe himself rather than from the society, either in which he grew up or in which he wrote the book. Of course, if one compares his treatment of the story with anything that might be written on such a theme today, certain differences stand out. Instead of Crusoe's reflections on religion, we should have pages about his sexual difficulties, and nostalgic memories of his childhood.

The impression that *Robinson Crusoe* is the product of a mind not only original, but almost eccentric, is supported by what we know about Defoe's own life and other writings, and by the peculiarities of his style. The clarity of this is always noticed in any study, and it is usual to regard it as a mark of the time and to connect it with the well-known views of Sprat of the Royal Society, which are alluded to by Defoe himself: 'Who can behold, without indignation, how many mists and uncertainties, these specious tropes and figures have brought on our knowledge? . . . And in a few words, I dare say, that of all the studies of men, nothing may be sooner obtained, than this vicious abundance of phrase, this trick of metaphors, this volubility of tongue, which makes so great a

---

[12] Tillyard, E. M., *The Epic Strain in the English Novel*, 1958.
[13] Malraux, André, *The Walnut Trees of Altenburg*, 1952.

noise in the world. . . . It will suffice my present purpose, to point out, what has been done by the Royal Society, towards the correcting of its excesses in natural philosophy; to which it is, of all others, a most professed enemy.'[14]

There is no doubt that there was a general tendency for a plainer, simpler prose at the time; but in a careful study of Defoe's language published by the University of Uppsala in 1910 Lannert has shown that there is a considerable difference between Defoe's style and that of his contemporaries. Both in *Robinson Crusoe* and in his other works there is a much smaller proportion of words of foreign extraction, especially of Latin derivatives, than there are in the writings of his contemporaries. He shares this characteristic with Bunyan, and no doubt it is partly due to their lack of a classical education. For Defoe it was in part also a deliberate preference. He said of his schoolmaster that 'he taught his pupils to write a masculine and manly style, to write the most polite English and at the same time to know how to suit their manner as well to the subject they were to write upon as to the persons and degrees they were to write to; and all equally free and plain, without foolish flourishes and ridiculous flights of jingling bombast in style, or dull meanness of expression below the dignity of the subject or the character of the writer'.

It was the fashion of the time to quote extensively both from classical authors and English poets. This, too, is absent in Defoe and may to some extent be due to a Puritan upbringing. It may come partly from the hostility, often felt by men who have not received what the world of their day considers the best education, towards the orthodox tradition. Something of this kind pervades the remarks about 'foolish flourishes' and 'ridiculous flights of jingling bombast'.

Can one really say of Defoe, with the *Oxford History of English Literature*, 'embodying as he does the essence of the new middle class', or regard him as embodying the essence of any other collective noun? He did not represent middle-class opinions, at least as far as these were expressed in their attitude towards criminals, Roman Catholics or Government policy. He wanted to shut the theatres, greatly frequented by the middle class of London. The *Oxford History* says: 'In advocating education of women Defoe was expressing the determination of the new class to cultivate its

[14] Portland MSS., *op. cit.*

brains.' As has already been argued, the term 'middle class' is hardly applicable to the early eighteenth century, and people in a middle station of life did not really have a common attitude to politics or anything else. What information there is does not suggest that they placed any particular value on education, and certainly not on education for women.

Defoe was a Whig, apparently a sincere although certainly not a representative Whig, and yet he wrote to Harley: 'I had before now tendered you a scheme of general intelligence . . . I had a design to propose or settle a private office for the conducting matters of this nature, so directed as neither in general to be suspected of what it should act, and yet be as publicly known as any other. That in this office, and with the help of Mr. St. John's backstairs, a correspondence may be effectually settled with every part of England and all the world besides, and yet the very clerks know not what they are doing.'[15] It would be absurd to imagine that this would sound in the ears of his contemporaries as it does in ours, since we know only too much about systems of intelligence in which the very clerks do not know what they are doing. But it would be equally absurd to think that the average man, whether Whig or Tory, would not have regarded the establishment of such a system as an outrage.

Sometimes it seems, at least in his later years, as if Defoe had no opinions of his own at all. In *The Trueborn Englishman* he had written, ''Tis personal virtue only makes us great.' Yet in *The Complete English Gentleman* he rejects the already ancient platitude that the term 'gentleman' signifies 'a man of generous principles, of a great generous soul', in favour of the view that 'our modern acceptance of a gentleman is . . . a person born of some known ancient family'. As the design of the book was to reform the education of the children of the great, these sentences may merely have been inserted to persuade their parents to read it. But a little later on he displays a hostility, surely at that date quite unnecessary, to those economic activities he is always supposed, and apparently rightly supposed, to have regarded so highly: 'You see I am willing to give up the first money-getting wretch, who amassed the estate, though he rode in his coach and four and perhaps coach and six, wore a sword (the latter I think our laws should restrain); in short perhaps he had all the ensigns of

---

[15] Portland MSS., *op. cit.*

grandeur that a true-bred gentleman is distinguished by, yet the stock jobber, the 'change alley broker, the projector or whatever low-prized thing he was, may be allowed to hang about him too much for the first age to give him so much as the shadow of a gentleman. Purse-proud, insolent, without manners, and too often without sense, he discovers his mechanic qualifications on all occasions; the dialect of the alley hangs like a brogue upon his tingue.' This is indeed connected with Defoe's hostility to stock-jobbers in which he agreed, if in nothing else, with the Jacobite Sir Dudley North, but he does not in this book contrast the honest tradesman with the dishonest financier.

In *The Complete English Tradesman*, Defoe had referred with approbation to the number of marriages between the nobility and the City, while in *Treatise Concerning The Uses And Abuses Of The Marriage Bed* he says of inequality of blood: 'This is an article in matrimony which they, who would be thought to expect any felicity in married life, ought very carefully to avoid', and goes on to illustrate this view by stories of unhappy marriages between aristocrats and the sons and daughters of businessmen.

These contradictions may be the shifting reflections of social change; but they make it difficult to regard Defoe as representative of any class, sect or opinion. His isolation as a writer further illustrates this. In spite of the popularity of *Robinson Crusoe*, no novelist attempted to imitate Defoe's literary technique, as distinct from copying the plot of *Robinson Crusoe*, until the twentieth century.

6

Richardson

There is no difficulty in checking the picture given in Richardson's novels either against real-life documents or against accounts given by other novelists, because all his characters, except Pamela, belong to the country gentry or to the aristocracy who left abundant records in the shape of letters, memoirs, account-books and wills. These were the kind of people described also in the novels of Fielding, Smollett and, later, Fanny Burney. Contemporaries also gave their view as to the accuracy of his delineation. Lady Mary Wortley Montague,[1] Chesterfield,[2] Walpole[3] and Fulke Greville[4] all declared that the manners in his books were not the manners of the people he was supposed to be writing about. This judgement is confirmed by their own letters and memoirs. To take only a few instances: Lovelace, supposed to be the model of a fine gentleman, swore at his servants. 'Good-humoured as he is thought to be in the main to other people's servants, . . . he is apt sometimes to break out into a passion with his own, an oath or a curse follows'—behaviour which Chesterfield told his son a gentleman never indulged in. It is not to be supposed that no one ever swore at servants, but from all the records we have, the convention against it, at least in the presence of other people, seems to have been as strong in the eighteenth as in the nineteenth century. The memoirs of John Macdonald,[5] a footman, bear this out. That is, if we can believe him. He declared that nearly all his mistresses were in love with him. According to his own account,

[1] Wortley-Montague, Lady Mary, *Letters*, edited by Lord Wharncliffe, 1887.
[2] Chesterfield, *op. cit.*
[3] Walpole, Horace, *Letters*, edited by P. Toynbee, 1903-25.
[4] Greville, Fulke, *Maxime and Characters*, 1756.
[5] Macdonald, John, *Memoirs of an Eighteenth-Century Footman*, 1934.

conduct which even today would ensure instant dismissal was met with the mildest of rebukes. Lovelace is also said to have knocked two of his groom's teeth out, and from all we know of eighteenth-century menservants it would be extremely improbable that the man would have stayed with him. When Nightingale, in *Tom Jones*, struck his footman after great provocation, the footman fought back and was in process of strangling him when Tom intervened.

Lady Mary Montague said that 'she had been brought up to consider no one beneath her and to regard poverty as almost a merit in itself'.[6] When she wrote this she had come to think it nonsense, which may be an instance of the 'hardening of caste' referred to by J. H. Plumb.[7] It seems, however, to be connected with Pope's behaviour to her, which might indeed lead anyone to feel it unsafe to mix with people outside her own class. Fielding's Sophia called the chambermaid who waited on her at the inn nothing but 'Child', 'My dear' and 'Sweetheart'. Fielding frequently pointed out that he, unlike some other authors, was familiar with the manners of the great.

Lord M., Lovelace's uncle, a peer with a vast property, including five boroughs which returned Members of Parliament, never opened his mouth without producing a proverb. Lady Mary Montague said how unlike a man of his rank this was. Anyone born to such possessions received the most careful education in the ceremonious manners of the time. Would Mr. Greville have tried to force Sir Charles Grandison to fight him without seconds or witnesses? Although duels at the time seemed to have occasionally been fought without seconds, if he had killed his antagonist it would have exposed him to a prosecution for murder and, considering Grandison's position in the county, he would almost certainly have been convicted.

Even from the distance of two hundred years it can be seen that the quarrels between Clarissa and her sister are the quarrels of kitchenmaids, not of young ladies. Only Mme du Deffand praised the details and minuteness of Richardson's description, and she had never been in England.

In *Pamela*, indeed, he was writing of the kind of people he was familiar with, and Pamela herself seems to be a more correct

[6] Quoted in Halsband, R., *The Life of Lady Wortley-Montague*, 1956.
[7] *Op. cit.*

picture of an eighteenth-century maidservant than any of the numerous abigails who appear in Fielding or Smollett. Everyone will remember the misspelling and inappropriate wording of their letters. We have the letters of an eighteenth-century maidservant, Elizabeth Woollat, who married Jedediah Strutt, the inventor, and although her spelling is erratic, her use of words is perfectly correct. She was in service with a dissenting minister, and therefore probably came from a lower station of society than the girls who waited on Fielding's ladies; service with the great was in those days an occupation with comparatively great rewards and of comparatively high status. No doubt Elizabeth Woollat was a remarkable girl, but her letters recall Pamela's rather than Honor's in *Tom Jones*:

Elizabeth Woollat to Jedediah Strutt

A bilit so soon Jerry I fancy won't a little surprise you but I was so a greably surpris'd when I came hom this morning to find every thing just as I left them, the House was in a profound sylanse and not one person got up. John I believe lay an hour after; they had not the least suspission of my ever being out of my Room, my over fear of being wanted at hom made me quite rude to John for I believe I did not speak when we parted but pray give my servis to him and tell him yt a pleasant Gardin an open Alcove a bowl of punch an a new sweet hart is not all Equvelant to his Good Companny.

I shou'd like much to know wheather your Tyranical Master has made anny discoverry about your erly adventer last night, you need never be at a los for to send for if you give my Brother a Letter anny time it will Com as from him, as you say I have no reason to suspect your sincerity. I have wrote without the least reserve and depend upon your Goodness not to expose my Nonsense this from your Friend and Wellwisher

E: Woolat

Elizabeth Woollat to Jedediah Strutt

Derby March the 3: 1768

My Friend

I rec'd your letter of Friendship Jany ye 16th but what shall I say to it, surprise & pleasure taken place by turns ever since. You cou'd not pay me a greater compliment than by ranking mee amongst ye number of your friends, which I hope I shall allways endeavour to deserve and as such shall look upon my self as a sharer in your misery. But shall I believe you to be, in jest, or are you sincear, I cant but say it a pears to me a little romantick, (tho theres not a Juba, a portius, a Marcus, yt stir ye passions in a more elegant manner.) When I compare your Letters they are some what inconsisttant; in ye first you say you are a vers to writeing, in your next, that you have done all you can by Letters, that She is at ye distance of near forty miles, is verry young, and yet your Findern. But I will Judg favourably and immagine it to be ye effect of a mind disordered, but I hope this fit of Frensy will soone a bate, you will much obloige me if youl tell me who this cruel charmer is, this incensable fair, who lets you sigh and languish, mourn and while away your pressious moments, which mights be rendred by her so so easy in ye injoyment of em . . . But you desire to know where I live. I am still at Dr Lathams and I believe I allways shall be here, ye place for what I know may be enchanted for I cant get away.

But youl think I shall never have don, I will assure you I trouble you with my Letters out of interest, if not kindness; since mine to you will procure yours to me: so yt I write to you more for my own sake then yours; less to make you think I write well, then to learn from you to write better, There you see interest in my kindness, which is like ye friendship of the world rather to make a friend then to be a friend: but I am yours, as a true plain dealer &c:

E: Woolat[8]

Richardson himself, no doubt, had some influence on the second letter, but this in itself seems to show a certain level of education.

In his two other novels Richardson failed to give an accurate picture of the surface of eighteenth-century life, because he had never mixed with the kind of people he was describing. This has no bearing on the value of the books as literature, but it has considerable bearing on how far they give an accurate picture of the age.

It is not only lack of knowledge which makes Richardson an untrustworthy guide. The nature of his books also tend to distortion. *Clarissa*, his greatest novel, in some ways anticipates a modern form of literature, the thriller, and even *Pamela* has something of it. Just as anyone who took John Buchan's books as a source for what was likely to happen in Scotland between the wars would fall into serious error, so anyone who assumes from Richardson that people could behave like Lovelace or even like Mr. B. with impunity would be mistaken.

[8] Fitton, A. P., and Wadsworth, R. R. S., *The Strutts and the Arkwrights,* 1958.

Clarissa's dilemma—that of a girl whose parents were urging her to marry a man she disliked—was a perfectly real one. But neither the motives of her parents nor the course of the story have the same basis in contemporary life.

Many critics have pointed out that, while no doubt very odd things could happen in the depths of Wales or Cumberland, in London all Clarissa had to do to escape from Lovelace was to go to a magistrate. This objection to the probability of Clarissa's behaviour was raised soon after the book was published, and has often been repeated since, by Sir Walter Scott, among others. As a criticism of the book it is beside the point, but if one wants to read it not as a piece of literature but as a source of social history, it is worth remembering that rape was a capital crime. Richardson himself seems to feel some faint misgivings about this, as Lovelace more than once says that, of course, shame would prevent a woman giving evidence in such a case. It is true that among the characters who have been considered prototypes of Lovelace, neither Lord Baltimore nor Colonel Charteris were hanged. Lord Baltimore, who was indicted for the rape of a Quaker girl, was acquitted by his peers, so we must assume that he was innocent—but he left the country. Colonel Charteris, who was found guilty of the rape of a maidservant, was only imprisoned for a few years, and then pardoned by the King. This immunity from punishment, however, does not show any tenderness on the part of public opinion for this particular crime. Eighteenth-century justice, although in theory extremely harsh, was also extremely capricious. Even late in the century Beckford complained that of the twenty people sentenced to death at one assize, only the homosexual was actually hanged. The victims of both Charteris and Baltimore were girls of humble station. Lovelace's abduction and rape of a daughter of a rich and landed family would have been proportionately more dangerous.

Smollett's Emilia in a somewhat similar situation, remarking that 'I confide too much in my innocence and the authority of the law to permit one thought of fear . . . opened the door, and walking downstairs with surprising resolution, committed herself to the care of a watch-man, who accommodated her with a hackney chair, in which she was safely conveyed to her uncle's house.' It is true that she had not quarrelled with her family. Although Clarissa was alone in London, such a well-educated and prudent girl, as we are constantly told she was, must have known that she only had to go to a magistrate, or even to any respectable citizen, to be perfectly safe.

There is another element in both *Pamela* and *Clarissa* which, while it undoubtedly increased their popularity and still gives them a perennial attraction, diminishes their contemporary flavour: this is the ageless nature of their basic story. *Pamela* is a variation of Cinderella, and *Clarissa* of the story of the persecuted maiden. In this framework they are fundamentally about one of the most permanent elements in human life—sex. In both, although more strongly in *Clarissa*, sex with a flavour of abnormality. There is nothing unique to the eighteenth century in this. The relations between Pamela and her master may indeed be, in a way, special to their own time. Richardson, after all, said he got the idea from a real case. Before the eighteenth century Pamela would either have been of a higher class or else would not have been educated enough to write letters. After the eighteenth century, although individual country squires may still have tried to seduce their maidservants, no one would have dared to behave like Mr. B. When the novel was dramatized by Goldoni, Pamela ceased to be a servant, because, it was said, 'an Italian gentleman could not marry a servant', and to this extent the book reflects the comparative fluidity of class distinctions in England.

Clarissa might have been set in almost any period of human history except the present, and some of the incidents would seem to belong to the Middle Ages rather than the eighteenth century. This, of course, is exactly contrary to the view put forward by some modern critics, who hold *Clarissa* to be an attack on 'property marriage' (marriage based on financial considerations), or as dealing with the main social problem of the eighteenth century, rather surprisingly said to be the reconciliation of the manners of the rising middle class with the manners of the aristocracy.

The first idea has been elaborately worked out by Christopher Hill,[9] who maintains that *Clarissa* 'represents the supreme criticism of property marriage' and this criticism is alleged to be a middle-class reaction to aristocratic manners. There is no evidence for this latter interpretation and some evidence against it. Ian Watt,[10] who enthusiastically follows Christopher Hill as to the

[9] Hill, Christopher, *Clarissa Harlowe and her Times*, Essays in Criticism, 1955.
[10] Watt, Ian, *op. cit.*

meaning of *Clarissa*, himself quotes Sir William Temple as deploring the prevalence of financial considerations in the choice of a husband or wife. In Curll's *Miscellanea*, published 1726, there is *An Essay on the Mischief of giving Fortunes with Women in Marriage*, which has been attributed to Lady Mary Montague. She certainly advocated legislation to prohibit dowries in a conversation in 1736.[11]

Defoe, in his book on marriage, said tradesmen were more interested in the financial aspect of marriage than the nobility. This is probably not true, and it is doubtful how much Defoe knew about the nobility; but the remark at least suggests that the middle class themselves were not averse to 'property marriage'. Between Defoe's book and *Clarissa* there is a space of twenty years; but it seems unlikely that any fundamental changes in middle-class attitudes to marriage should have occurred in this period. This dislike of marrying for money or rank was probably an individual rather than a class reaction. The period is full of peers who married actresses, their own housekeepers and their penniless mistresses.

Richardson himself said that one of his objects in writing the book was 'to caution parents against the undue exercise of their natural authority over their children in the great article of marriage', but this was only one of his aims. The others, which he clearly thought as, if not more important, were 'to warn the considerate and thoughtless of one sex against the base arts and designs of the other . . . to warn children against preferring a man of pleasure to a man of probity . . . but above all to investigate the highest and most important doctrines not only of morality but of Christianity'. Richardson undoubtedly thought it wrong to marry for money alone without affection or esteem. So did everyone else, at least in theory, which distinguished the eighteenth century from the Middle Ages. It is, however, most unlikely that he thought it wrong to take financial considerations into account. After all, the virtuous Clarissa is ready to delay her marriage with Lovelace so that proper settlements may be made.

He never made any forthright declaration, as did both Fielding and Defoe, that mutual affection was the only basis for marriage, and that parents had no right to interfere with their daughter's choice. Defoe, in *The Treatise Concerning Uses and Abuses Of The Marriage Bed* had been perfectly definite. If the parent

[11] Quoted in Halsband, *op. cit.*

commands his child to marry such a person, and the child either cannot love the person, or at the same time declares he or she is engaged in effection to another, the command of the parent cannot be lawfully obeyed, because it is unlawful for the child to marry any person he or she cannot love.'

It is true that enormous claims were still made for parental authority, as by Dr. Delaney in a sermon, but in many ways clergymen seem to have been more out of touch with the realities of life in the eighteenth century than at any other time. They were not only telling children, but the lower orders, that their only duty was to obey. This, in a period in which the lower orders, in towns at any rate, were not only accustomed to make their views plain by throwing rotten eggs and dead cats, even if they did not go as far as actual violence, but in which the current political theories conceded them the right to do so.

In more sophisticated circles it appears that the ordinary view was that 'a Parent can no more force a child to marry against her consent, than a child is permitted to act contrary to the Parent'.

McKillop, in his biography of Richardson, quotes Fanny Burney, when wishing to refuse a young man despite her father's doubts, as saying in her diary: 'I was terrified to death. I felt the utter impossibility of resisting not merely my father's persuasion but even his advice.' But is not Fanny dramatizing her situation here? It seems most unlikely from all we know of Dr. Burney and his relations with his children that he would have tried to persuade her to marry anyone she did not like. At any rate, there was a widely held opinion that daughters were entitled to refuse anyone repugnant to them, even against their parents' wishes, although they were not justified in marrying against them. This doctrine, which would have justified Clarissa, Richardson nowhere clearly states.

It is not easy to discover what Richardson really thought about marriage. If we may take Sir Charles Grandison as representing his creator's opinion, he indeed more than once protests against parents urging their daughters to marry men they did not love, and stigmatized it as cruelty. But when asked his considered opinion as to whether girls should be allowed complete freedom to choose their own husbands, he said, 'Love at first sight may be only fancy. Such a young love may be easily given up, and ought, to a parent's judgement.' He arranged a marriage between a lady of 'not more than three or four and thirty' and his old and dissipated uncle before they had ever seen each other. It is true that the lady's family was extremely poor and, in the conditions of the period, common sense would have undoubtedly dictated her consent, but the large settlements provided by the bridegroom and the help he might give to her family in a lawsuit about their property were admittedly her main motive. It is certain that no hero of Fielding's would have acted thus, and Richardson could not have made his Christian hero take such a step if he had really objected either to arranged marriage or to marrying for financial considerations. Perhaps Sir Charles showed even less value for love when he thought that he was going to marry Clementina, and wrote of Harriet Byron, who if he did not absolutely know must have strongly suspected was in love with him, 'If the noble Clementina is to be mine, my heart will be greatly gratified, if, before she received my vows, I could know, that Miss Byron had given her hand, in compliance with the entreaties of all her friends, to the deserving Earl of D.' He certainly knew she was not in love with the Earl of D.

Mrs. Selby, Harriet Byron's supremely virtuous grandmother, had seen the husband with whom she was to be so happy only 'in company two or three times', and looked on him merely as 'a good sort of man'. She was at first unwilling to accept him, but yielded to the arguments of a friend. In spite of the long discussions which take place, it is impossible to discover from *Sir Charles Grandison* exactly what Richardson really thought should be the basis for marriage. He had tried to portray a perfect marriage based on love in Sir Charles Grandison's union with Harriet. But it seems almost as if he was alarmed by his own attitude, and hastily introduced into the later part of the book a series of successful marriages based merely on esteem. In Charlotte Grandison's case hardly even on esteem, but on something more like indifference mixed with contempt. It must not be forgotten that Richardson strongly disapproved of the conduct of Sophia Weston in *Tom Jones*—'the runaway, the inn-frequenting Sophia', as he called her.

If *Clarissa* is not meant as a tract against financial considerations in marriage, it is still more unlikely that Richardson intended it to be 'a damning indictment' of his society. Of course, a writer can damn his society without meaning to; but *Clarissa* could never have been effective as social criticism, because the Harlowe family are so extraordinary. It is not only that they are not living characters, but that their actions contradict the motives which Richardson gives them. We are told that they are a rich and rising family, and that their ultimate aim is to secure a peerage for the son James. In order to forward this purpose the two uncles have remained unmarried, and also with this object they forced Clarissa to reject the rich and well-born Lovelace, the heir to his uncle's vast estates and likely also, in some unexplained way, to become a peer himself, and try to force her to marry Solmes, old, low-born, boorish and practically illiterate. Anyone in James Harlow's position would have realized that he was far more likely to be made a peer if his brother-in-law was one already, and Lovelace, moreover, was going to inherit the patronage of five Parliamentary boroughs, which would certainly have clinched the matter. Why was he, then, so determined against Lovelace? They had quarrelled at the university, and this is reasonable. But the main reason given by Richardson, and the one seized on by critics who are determined to see a photographic representation of eighteenth-century life in the book, is that as the grandfather had left the bulk of his estate to Clarissa, James is afraid that if she marries Lovelace the uncles will leave her their property to support the dignity of her husband's peerage. Surely this is a complete misunderstanding of the psychology of landowners. Family pride was tied up with the family name. This is what the proverb means which was quoted by James Harlowe, 'In daughters men bring up chickens for another man's table.' Only if the male line failed would any one ambitious for his family have left money to his niece's husband in preference to his own nephew. What satisfaction would it have given to the family pride of the Harlowe uncles to see their property absorbed in the vast possessions of Lord M., or perhaps made the provision for a younger son? Richardson was probably less familiar with country gentlemen, either new or old, than with fashionable society. He had had some business connection with the Duke of Wharton, he had dined with the Speaker of the House of Commons even before *Pamela* had made him famous; afterwards he had met many of the more cultivated and respectable of the great, but there is no reason to think he ever came in contact with people like the Harlowes, who stayed in the country, busily adding acre to acre. His unfamiliarity with the countryside is illustrated by his description of Lovelace as a good landlord because he did not rack-rent his tenants, and if they fell into arrears not only forgave them the debt but gave them money to buy clothes to come to church. In reality there was far more in a landlord's duties, even from the point of view of the tenants, than this capricious kind of charity. We are told indeed that he improved his estate, but not that he encouraged experiments in cultivation or saw that none of his tenants was unjustly treated by magistrates. The idea that Richardson did not know much about life in the country is supported by Sir Charles Grandison's remark, when someone suggested he should become a magistrate, 'Would persons of sense and distinction . . . more frequently than they do, undertake the task, it would be lighter to everyone, and would keep the great power vested in this class of magistrates . . . out of mean and mercenery hands.' This could only apply to London, where the work was so heavy and continuous that men of standing neither could nor would undertake it; but all considerable landowners were magistrates in their counties, except those who had annoyed the Government sufficiently to cause it either not to appoint them or to remove them from the quorum.

The conduct of everyone in the first part of *Clarissa* is highly improbable from start to finish, beginning with the grandfather who left his property to his youngest granddaughter, entirely passing over his eldest son, this son's son and his elder granddaughter. We are told that he thought they were rich enough already, and modern critics seem to think that this is plausible and rather creditable. If they know families in which such a will, even today, would not cause an embittered family quarrel, one can only envy them. And we are told furthermore that he left Clarissa the family pictures and the family jewels. Although no one ever seems to think so, James Harlowe, odious as he is, had really been hardly done by.

The validity of the idea that the book is about the relations between classes, and not about the relations between a man and a woman, depends upon the exact status of the Harlowe family. It is often said that they are a new family, typical of the rising middle class. Indeed, their status continually declines; one writer lately describes them as 'London tradesmen', whereas, in fact, the uncles, at least, were East India merchants. What we are told about their class position could not be more muddled and confusing. Lovelace at moments seems to think that they are beneath him and says that they were unknown to the county a hundred years ago. But Clarissa, and as the heroine surely she who should be attended to, declares that her family was 'no inconsiderable or upstart one on either side'. Her mother, indeed, was the only daughter of a viscount. There are, of course, viscounts and viscounts, but there is no indication that this one was either disreputable or poor. The behaviour of this lady is another anomaly: from all we know of eighteenth-century women, it is most unlikely that a peer's daughter would have accepted so meekly the decision to marry her own extremely beautiful and rich daughter to a man like Solmes.

Lovelace had originally been introduced to the Harlowes because his uncle, Lord M., a rich earl, had suggested a marriage between his nephew and Clarissa's elder sister. This is also inconsistent with any great disparity between the two families. If there really had been such a difference in rank, Lovelace would not have been obliged to accept the challenge of Clarissa's uncle (Colonel Mordaunt) to the duel in which he was killed. He might have waived the privileges of his rank because he was conscious of his sin towards Clarissa; but there is no suggestion of this in the book, or that he thought the colonel in any way beneath him.

Another question that must suggest itself to anyone who really takes this part of the book seriously is why it never occurred to the Harlowes that Clarissa might leave Solmes for Lovelace after she was married? Such incidents were not unknown any more than was divorce. The settlements which Solmes promised to make on Clarissa and her own money would then have been as much lost to the family as if she had married Lovelace. Or, alternatively, how were they going to prevent her marrying anyone she chose if, as seemed likely from their respective ages, she outlived her husband? Of course, Richardson knew, and we know, that Clarissa was too good to elope, but did her brother believe it?

Christopher Hill thinks there was something peculiar to the period about the importance attached to material considerations in marriage. Professor Habbakuk has deduced, from a study of marriage settlements in the eighteenth century, that from the middle of the seventeenth century marriage among the upper classes was 'bent more systematically to the accumulation of landed wealth'.[12] Whether this is so or not, no one would deny that financial considerations and the question of estates played a large part in marriage arrangements. But none of the more famous quarrels over marriage between children and parents turned on this point in either the seventeenth or eighteenth centuries. In the case of Dorothy Osborne and William Temple the two families had taken different sides in the Civil War and Temple had the reputation of being an atheist. It is obvious from her letters that the opposition of Dorothy Osborne's brother was caused not by any financial considerations but by his jealousy of her love for Temple.

Edward Montague had an intense dislike of entails and refused to settle his property on his eldest son, which so enraged the Duke of Kingston, Lady Mary Montague's father, that he forbade the match. As the marriage turned out to be a failure, the Duke's real reason may have been that he thought Montague would not make his daughter happy. It is not known whether the Duke of Richmond objected to his daughter's marriage with Henry Fox, the first Lord Holland, because of his age—he was only four years younger than the Duke—because his family was new, because he was poor or because of his somewhat dubious reputation. The marriage of Mary Granville, afterwards Mrs. Delaney, to her first husband, Pendarvis, seems more like the case of Clarissa than any other. Pendarvis was old, rich, physically unprepossessing, and given to drink, but he was well-born and came from an ancient Cornish family. The marriage was arranged by her uncle, not by her father; Mrs. Delaney definitely says that her parents would never have consented had they realized how much she disliked it. Her father was not only poor and dependent on his elder brother, but was more or less a Jacobite, and thus in a peculiarly vulnerable position. Money hardly seems to have come into this case either, except that, of course, everyone was pleased to have secured such a match for a penniless girl. But Lord Lansdowne, Mary's uncle did not trouble himself to get a proper settlement, so that when Mr. Pendarvis died she was left with a very small income, not with her husband's whole estate, as he had promised. It appears to have been not so much money as political influence in Cornwall, that

[12] Habbakuk, H. J., 'Marriage Settlements in the Eighteenth Century', *Transactions of the Royal Historical Society*, 1950.

most priceless eighteenth century asset, which attracted Lord Lansdowne to the match.[13]

Whatever Richardson's conscious intentions may have been, *Clarissa* is not really either about liberty of choice in marriage or about the relations between classes; he was not a writer who could deal with social problems. In *Sir Charles Grandison* he attempts to deal with a real social problem: what a Christian gentleman should do if forced into a position in which public opinion would think he should fight a duel. He evades the issue by the fairy-tale solution of making his hero such a good swordsman that he could disarm his antagonist without in any way harming him. Contemporaries seem, even during the publication of the book, to have pointed out that this made the story useless as a tract against duelling, since Richardson tried to reply to this objection in a concluding note: 'It has been objected by some persons, that a man less able by strength or skill to repell an affront, could not with such honour have extricated himself out of difficulties on refusing a challenge, and goes on to protest against the current idea of honour. This, however, does not dispose of the argument that the case of Sir Charles Grandison gave no hint of a solution to the ordinary man.

The story of the Harlowes could never have been a fable for the times, because, even in the eighteenth century, few parents would have wished their daughters to marry a man with Solmes's disadvantages. And as far as preaching went, parents were more likely to say, 'I should never behave like that', than regard their behaviour as a lesson for themselves.

The Harlowes' behaviour comes from quite another source than indignation at the prevailing view of marriage. As Robinson Crusoe had to be got to the desert island, so must Clarissa be raped. The most serious of all Richardson's intentions, that of showing virtue triumphant in the most adverse circumstances, demanded it. But in the eighteenth century it was difficult to invent incidents which would put a virtuous young lady sufficiently into Lovelace's power. Pamela was a servant in her master's house when faced with a somewhat similar threat. Ladies of position, however, did not go about alone; they were attended by maids, manservants, and generally by some of their relations as well. Moreover, Richardson was determined that Clarissa

13 Quoted in Halsband, *op. cit.*

should not be so passionately in love that she was prepared to risk everything. And even if she had been, no such self-respecting young woman would have eloped, and in the ordinary way no one as virtuous as Clarissa would have met Lovelace alone. She had to be so persecuted by her family that the abduction by Lovelace should appear probable. And a further difficulty then arose: why should parents persecute a daughter as good, as affectionate as Clarissa? Some reason had to be invented, and this was not an aspect of his art in which Richardson had much talent or in which he seems to have been much interested. The audience for whom he was writing would almost certainly have considered that if the suitor produced for her had been reasonably young, well-born and sensible, Clarissa should have obliged her parents. Solmes had therefore to be made in every way repulsive, and the whole story of the legacy invented. There may, in the first part of the book, be a movement towards stressing a difference in class between Clarissa and Lovelace, but it soon fades away. One has to remember that Lovelace had not only to be extremely attractive but also to have glamour. Glamour would be enhanced by his uncle, the Earl, and by his rather vague background of wealth and position. Although Richardson was undoubtedly middle class, in his books he seems little conscious of any antagonism between men of his station and the aristocracy. Almost the only instance is in *Sir Charles Grandison*, when Harriet rebukes Charlotte Grandison for referring to some acquaintances as 'cits'.

Clarissa has nothing to do with the social structure. The real theme is love, or rather sex, and the two main characters are isolated from the rest of the world as men and women are in the sexual act. The theme of isolation has indeed been attributed to the social circumstances of the time which isolated the individual and left him a prey to loneliness. But, as has already been pointed out when the same explanation for *Robinson Crusoe* was discussed, there is not a shred of evidence for this. Political and social ideas stressed the social tie; in theory, at least, the different classes were bound to each other by reciprocal obligations. The control which landlords exercised over the votes of their tenants is an example of this; shocking to later opinion, it was at the time considered not only perfectly legitimate but rather admirable, because the tie between landlord and tenant was supposed to transcend the merely economic.

The isolation of Clarissa and Lovelace is the isolation of sexual infatuation, and the reason why none of the machinery of contemporary justice is introduced is not only that it would have been fatal to the plot, but also that the drama lies in the minds of the two chief characters. Richardson was quite capable of cheating in other parts of his work, but not in the analysis of emotion. Here, in spite of his prejudices, he is completely honest. As in *Pamela*, while Richardson was praising his heroine's virtue he depicted her as a clever and calculating rather than a high-principled girl, so in *Clarissa* we are told a great deal about her 'prudence', whereas she is really remarkably silly, and the way she falls into fits, faints or weeps when the circumstances call for coolness and common-sense is not calculated to attract a modern reader. But as the book proceeds even the most up-to-date reader must be more and more caught up, and her behaviour after the rape is really moving, in spite of the archaic conventions within which she exists. Although not the paragon which Richardson, and indeed her contemporaries, thought her, she is a real character, a girl abandoned by her family (the improbability of the Harlowes' behaviour does not in the least matter to the book, as a piece of literature, and not as a source for social history) and in love with a man whom her education, and indeed her instincts, tell her is bad. For Richardson finally admitted, when questioned by correspondents, that Clarissa was in love: 'As to Clarissa's being in downright love, I must acknowledge that I rather choose to have it imputed to her . . . by her penetrating friend, and then a reader will be ready enough to believe it, the more ready for not owning it, or being blind to it herself, than to think herself that she is.' That Richardson manages to convey the ambivalence of her attitude, the genuine revulsion as well as the genuine attraction she feels towards Lovelace in the day of a purely rationalistic psychology, is one of the aspects of the book in which he shows his genius.

In a way this genius is shown in the delineation of Lovelace, too; but while Clarissa is a possible character—and there are women who resemble her today, although their peculiar qualities are shown in other aspects of life—Lovelace is quite unreal. For some male readers he seems to occupy a position as a fantasy figure, somewhat similar to the Cinderella-Jane Eyre type for women—at least to judge by the comments of some critics. There was, of course, never a man like Lovelace, so talented and yet so completely occupied with the seduction of unwilling females. Sir Walter Scott said long ago, 'The gallants of our age are content to give up at the first resistance', and this is probably true of the gallants of all ages, much as it may pain a woman to admit it.

Since Johnson, in his *Life of Rowe*, said that Richardson 'expanded' the character of Lotherio in Rowe's *Fair Penitant* into Lovelace, many attempts have been made to find prototypes for him. Richardson himself said that he had actually known a similar character in his youth. Some critics have thought that this might have been the second Duke of Wharton, but, although he was a rake, he was a very different kind of rake from Lovelace. There seems to be not much point in fixing on any particular model, either in life or literature, for Lovelace is the hero of Restoration comedy removed from the conventions that made him credible, and with a streak of abnormality added. Richardson can manage the wit and the intelligence; it is when he tries to give his hero reality by adding some sort of social background that he fails. This is partly because of Richardson's ignorance of the world in which Lovelace moves, and partly because of the romanticism with which he is treated throughout. The remark, 'he troubles not his head with politics, though nobody knows the interest of princes and courts better than he is said to do,' is rather absurd in connection with an eighteenth-century squire, even a rich squire, who was neither in Parliament nor in the Diplomatic Service.

Yet this figure of fantasy captured Richardson's own time and has entranced many readers since. This is not because he is skilfully transferred from contemporary society to a book but because of the intense conviction of his creator. It has often been said that Richardson was more sympathetic with Lovelace than he realized, or that he was subconsciously attracted by the idea of the rake, but this is surely not the explanation. Is it not rather that Richardson was intensely interested in sex, particularly in sex streaked with cruelty or violence, in an age which provided no scientific or psychological justification for such an interest? Richardson in real life seems to have been a good, if sometimes a silly man, and we do not know what exactly it was about rape which so fascinated him. He surely was fascinated by it. Two of his books are about the situation of a woman in the power of a man violently in love and yet unwilling to marry her, and even in *Sir Charles Grandison* there is an attempt at abduction. It may be that cruelty in love was one of Richardson's temptations, or that Lovelace represented to him the glamour of the wickedness he renounced when he renounced 'the pomps and vanities of this wicked world', or, on the contrary, that he identified himself with the trembling victim rather than with the triumphant violator, or his attitude may really have been a puzzled, scientific curiosity. The latter supposition gains support because, though not a real man, Lovelace is a real psychological case. As a landlord, a fine gentleman, or even as a lover, he has little contact with any kind of reality, but as a sadist, with a touch of paranoia, he is perfectly real. Some of the sexual fantasies into which his letters occasionally sink, besides being quite revolting, verge on madness, as when he suggests the kidnapping and rape of Miss Howe, her mother and her maid. Not that Richardson consciously thought he was mad; quite the contrary. But he here shows an insight into psychopathology which, although common in great writers, was unusual in Richardson's time. When Fulke Greville, who might be regarded as a real life counterpart of the kind of man Lovelace was meant to be, said Richardson's rakes were 'strange debauchees', this touch of madness is perhaps what he meant.

To seek in Richardson accurate information about the contemporary scene, or to treat his books as social allegories, is clearly a mistake. In order to read *Clarissa* as a study in class relations it is, moreover, necessary to ignore its religious background. The book is often discussed as if Clarissa's 'sure and certain hope' of life after death was delusive or irrelevant. Whether modern critics believe in it or not, is neither here nor there, it is an integral part of the main theme which, as Sir Walter Scott said, is 'chastity of the soul'. His remarks bring us much nearer to the spirit of the book than any modern criticism, which is not surprising, as he was born only ten years after Richardson's death. 'There is another pride amid the sorrow with which we contemplate the distresses of such a being as Clarissa, rising even over that personal dishonour, which, when it has once taken place, under what circumstances soever, is generally understood to imply degradation. It was reserved for Richardson to show that there is a chastity of the soul, which can beam out spotless and unsullied, even after that of the person has been violated.' Scott's remarks show how original Richardson's attitude was, not only in his time, but for many subsequent generations.

To a modern taste Clarissa's behaviour would be more moving if she had not the assurance of heaven. But to disregard the religious framework is wholly to misinterpret the book. If problems of class and property shrink before the intense and complicated emotions of the characters, they grow even smaller before the great drama of redemption and salvation. This Christian background has some bearing even on Richardson's literary technique. The minute detail in which he relates every thought and feeling and describes every incident may not only derive from his interest in psychology but may also stem from the idea that on slight episodes and hidden feelings Clarissa's eternal destiny, as well as her temporal fate, will be decided.

This preoccupation is by no means peculiar to the eighteenth century, and although it forms one strand in the life of the time it is not what is usually meant when reference is made to eighteenth-century attitudes and opinions. In *Clarissa* it is expressed in the terms and by the symbols sanctioned by the conventions of the period. The insistence on personal salvation, and the whole apparatus of the edifying death-bed is not in tune with modern sentiment; but they had appeared before the seventeen-forties and were to exist long afterwards. As the religion of Europe is, or was until recently, Christianity, this framework tends to recur in many periods and is, indeed, not wholly absent from modern fiction. However, it makes no appearance in *Pamela*, nor in emotional, as distinct from conventional terms, in *Sir Charles Grandison*, and may not have been in accordance with Richardson's own daily life.

The religion in *Clarissa* is generally called middle-class Puritanism. Richardson was undoubtedly of the middle station or, to be more exact, he was a London tradesman and his books depict the manners with which he was familiar—but it is doubtful how far he was a Puritan. He was a member of the Church of England, and does not seem to have felt any sympathy for religious activities which might be regarded as revivals of Puritanism. When asked if there were anyone who represented Sir Charles Grandison among the contemporary great, he is said to have replied, 'Lord Dartmouth might have if he had not been a Methodist.' One of the minor wicked characters in *Sir Charles Grandison* is allowed to be converted by a Methodist, and credit is given to them for being able to instil some religion into 'such people as tanners and colliers'. These references are, however, patronizing rather than approving. Richardson's only connection with the Puritan tradition is the story that his father had been concerned in Monmouth's rebellion. There is no evidence for this, and even if it were true Monmouth's followers were not necessarily Puritans, any more than the Duke himself or Grey, his first lieutenant.

Richardson's books are not Puritan in any possible sense of the word, except for the high value they place on sexual chastity, especially in women. However, it cannot be too often repeated that this is not confined to Puritans. Richardson strongly reprobated the conduct of Tom Jones, but so did the High Church Tory, Johnson. Richardson's books are full of quotations, many of them from playwrights no Puritan could approve, and it is evident from Lovelace's letters that Richardson was as familiar with Restoration comedy as Restoration tragedy. Richardson nowhere gives the slightest hint of any objection to the stage, which was a characteristic Puritan tenet. The admiration he everywhere expresses for Shakespeare was far from being at the time, or indeed for long afterwards, a Puritan or a 'serious' attitude to our national playwright.

Clarissa's preparation for death, the design of a broken lily at the head of her will, and the keeping of her coffin and shroud in her bedroom, seem baroque rather than Puritan. The coffin, indeed, is reminiscent of no Puritan divine, but of Donne. There is, certainly, a sharp contrast between Tom Jones's and Sir Charles Grandison's attitude to sex. Does this reflect a class distinction or is it, on the contrary, the personal opinion of the two writers which we see in the books? There is no doubt that *Tom Jones* reflects the common opinion on these matters more closely than *Sir Charles Grandison*, and indeed continued to do so even in the Victorian age, when no novelist could admit it, although the Victorians were, of course, sincerely shocked by Tom Jones's taking money from Lady Bellaston. The novels of Smollett and Sterne, Hogarth's *Rake's Progress*, contemporary sermons, and the details of life in York, closely studied because of the interest in Sterne himself, all suggest that the ordinary middle-class man was as lax as any of the great. Richardson, in the person of Sir Charles Grandison, said, 'There were too many examples of vice among the great, as well as among the middling', which hardly sounds as if he thought there were any superior virtue in the middle class. In theory, as apart from practice, the aristocracy may have taken a more lighthearted or enlightened view of these matters than their inferiors. Lyttleton, to whom *Tom Jones* was dedicated, was an eminently 'serious' character. He was subsequently known as the 'good' Lord Lyttleton, yet he seems to have found nothing objectionable in a novel which profoundly shocked Dr. Johnson as well as Richardson. He wrote to a girl who had been in service at his country house and been seduced by his brother: 'I always believed you had a very good heart and were a woman of virtue. Your weakness for my brother will not, in my opinion, take that character from you, if you act discreetly and honestly in other respects.' He indeed reproached his brother for not telling him about the affair, but mainly because his ignorance had prevented him from doing anything to help the girl when she had a child.

It is a mistake, however, to exaggerate the austerity of Richardson's attitude. His disapproval of Tom Jones's conduct was undoubtedly sharpened by his jealousy of Fielding. That pattern of virtue, Sir Charles Grandison, thought he had obligations to his father's mistress, rebuked his sister's haughty attitude to her and subsequently invited her and her sons, both legitimate and illegitimate, to pay him social visits. He preached to her, of course, and his favour was conditional on her leading a virtuous life; but how differently Thackeray would have treated a similar situation.

Richardson was, of course, in the language of his time, 'serious', which meant he had a conscience, both social and individual, and was interested in problems of conduct and morality. To attribute 'seriousness' to all those of a middle station is to take an extremely optimistic view of them.

The world of fashion is indeed credited with greater licence in the novels as well as in much of the serious literature of the period. This is partly because the amours of a peer were news and the affaires of a grocer were not, and partly because, as far as these things cost money, most peers had more of it. Brown's *Estimate of the Manners and the Principles of the Times* is sometimes quoted as evidence of the greater freedom of manners in fashionable society, though why anyone should pay any attention to a writer who believed the main character of his time to be 'effeminacy', is hard to see. In any case, he appears to have included the prosperous middle class in his strictures, for he states, 'The principles of the common people will scarce find a place in the account. For though the sum total of a nation's immediate happiness must arise and be estimated from the manners and principles of the whole; the principles of those who lead, not of those who are led; of those who govern, not of those who are governed; all those, in short, who make the laws and execute them will ever determine the strength or weakness . . . of such.' He must surely have included lawyers and clergymen among those who, if they did not make the laws, at least helped to execute them.

The serious were fairly certainly a minority in the middle station of life as elsewhere. Indeed, it seems to be a mistake to divide classes in this as in other matters, as Cowper remarked at a somewhat later date,

> We boast some rich ones whom the Gospel sways
> And one who wears a coronet and prays.

And he was underestimating, for not only the second Earl of Dartmouth, here referred to, but the twenty-third Earl of Buchan, was a Methodist. The Countess of Huntingdon's connection was a Methodist sect which continued to exist until the end of the nineteenth century. Horace Walpole told Mann in 1747, 'Methodism in the metropolis is more fashionable than anything but Brag. The women play very deep at both', and in 1749, 'If you ever think of returning to England . . . you must prepare yourself with Methodism . . . Lady Fanny Shirley has chosen that way of conferring the dregs of her beauty upon Jesus Christ; and Mr. Lyttleton is very near making the same sacrifice of the dregs of all those various characters which he has worn.'[14] This may be exaggerated, but Walpole himself, as an undergraduate, had visited the Cambridge Gaol and prayed with the criminals. Sir Charles Hanbury Williams, in a letter to his son-in-law to be, the young Earl of Essex, after urging him to read Tillotson for the style, added, 'The beauty of our religion shows nowhere so strong as in those works . . . I am convinced that there is nothing can purify the mind and open the way to all happiness more than the faith and practice of Christianity. With shame I confess to you that I did not always think so: nay I laughed at those things. But I freely own to you at that time I had very little knowledge of them.'

Mrs. Delaney, before her second marriage, when she still

14 Walpole, Horace, *op. cit.*

moved in fashionable society, had a flirtation with John Wesley, if not with Methodism. Lady Huntingdon used to give parties in which religion played the same part as music might have done in Edwardian days, and all the town went to them. Even Chesterfield —under protest, it is true—once gave her twenty guineas towards the building of a chapel. It must be remembered not only that England was, in a modern phrase, a mobile society, but also that it was a very small one, and in these conditions ideas and attitudes, as well as men, will circulate freely among different sections of the population.

If there were more interest in religion among the great than is often suggested, Richardson's own attitude to sexual morality is not as forthright and simple as is sometimes assumed. There is a curious ambivalence in all his judgements—an ambivalence to be found also in all his interesting characters. He proclaimed Pamela to be a pattern of virtuous conduct, and yet he makes it plain to the reader, if not to himself, that she was both attracted by Mr. B. and determined to be the Squire's lady, and that her behaviour was calculated not only to protect her own virtue but also not to unduly restrain Mr. B.'s ardour. Richardson was plainly fascinated by his own imagination in Lovelace, and many critics have complained of a devious, almost deceptive, strain in Clarissa herself.

Even Sir Charles Grandison said he had been perplexed by 'what some would call a double love'. In the last part of *Sir Charles*, a situation develops which Richardson either did not dare to exploit or was by that time too tired to attempt. Emily Jervois is the hero's ward and both in love with him and devoted to Harriet, now his wife. She confesses her love to Harriet and a home is hastily found for her elsewhere. It is obvious that this contains the germ of a novel very unlike the book in which it is found, and must somehow have attracted Richardson, because it serves no purpose in the story, not even that of showing once again the hero's superhuman virtue, because he never knows of it.

Richardson indeed expressed his religious convictions in middle-class terms, if a great want of taste is what critics mean by this phrase, but in spite of this it is as hard to see him as the spokesman of a class as to see Defoe in the role. His books, at least *Pamela* and *Clarissa*, enjoyed a vast popularity both in England and abroad; that they were as much read and as greatly admired on the Continent as at home is perhaps some indication that they are not primarily concerned with English problems. It seems likely, moreover, that Richardson's popularity is similar to that of those folk stories noted by Bartlett in which a motive is preferred because it is absent from real life. There were few house-maids who could in reality aspire to marry the Squire, and although there was plenty of violence in eighteenth-century life, it was not the kind of violence encountered in *Clarissa*.

The different views of Richardson's work taken by his con-temporaries show that Richardson was not reflecting the general mood either of average or of any section of opinion. The Reverend Benjamin Slocock recommended *Pamela* from his pulpit, which impressed contemporary opinion. Modern research has, however, revealed that this was a form of advertisement, paid for by Richardson assuming responsibility for a bad debt, owed to Slocock. Another clergyman, however, wrote a set of verses celebrating the book, and there is no reason to think that his admiration was not spontaneous. Pope is reported to have said that 'the book would do more good than many of the new ser-mons'. Other reactions were, however, different. The details and what the period called the 'warmth' of the descriptions of Mr. B.'s attempt to seduce Pamela, the behaviour of Pamela herself, obviously calculated not wholly to discourage him, and the just objection that Richardson seemed to think that everything scandalous in Mr. B.'s conduct was obliterated by marriage, forcibly struck some critics. While others complained that the story would encourage maidservants to try to attract the admira-tion of the sons of the families for whom they worked with the idea of marriage. What Fielding thought can be seen not only from *Joseph Andrews* but also from *Shamela*, about which his nineteenth-century biographers are mostly silent, but which modern critics are convinced was written by Fielding. In it both 'the warmth' and Pamela's determination to secure a wedding ring are satirized; this might be called the reaction of a man of the world. The Puritan objections were voiced by Dr. Watts, a friend of Richardson's, who said: 'The ladies are forced to blush when they say they have read it.' More ordinary opinions were put forward in various pamphlets, one entitled *Anti-Pamela or Feigned Innocence*.

There was no more unanimity of opinion about *Clarissa*. Fielding praised it highly not only for its literacy but for its moral qualities. Lady Mary Montague, on the other hand, said it was likely 'to do more general harm than all the works of Lord Rochester'. The majority of its readers, including Fielding, who wrote to Richardson while the book was coming out in volumes, separated by several months, begged him to give it a happy ending, which could only mean a marriage between Clarissa and Lovelace. This would have destroyed the whole purpose, both moral and artistic, of the work, and the demand for it showed a total misunderstanding of the author's purpose. If his audience is unable to understand an author, is he still to be regarded as representative or typical of those who misunderstood him?

If it is impossible to regard Richardson as the spokesman of any particular section of opinion, it is, on the other hand, fairly easy to see where sociological pressures moulded his work. The conventions of the time permitted him to describe Mr. B.'s and Lovelace's attempts at seduction in much greater detail than would have been allowed in the nineteenth century, although not so minutely as prescribed today. They confined him, on the other hand, to love between men and women. There is no reason to think that Richardson was in any way interested in homosexuality, but he could not have written a book in which even the villain was a homosexual. There are homosexual incidents in Smollett, but they are slight. The only abnormality which Richardson could analyse in detail was sadism, and this had to be limited to mental cruelty: Lovelace could not beat up Clarissa, as a similar character might do in a modern novel. It is to this limitation that Lovelace's use of drugs to stupefy his victim is possibly due, because it certainly seems to be inconsistent with his own statements as to his motives.

The choice of a rich landowner as a model hero in *Sir Charles Grandison*, a baronet and not a peer, is typical of eighteenth-century opinion. It was considered that a large landowner had, of all men, the most extended opportunities for benevolence, as well as the heaviest responsibilities if he neglected to use them. Sir Charles is a baronet because a title conferred an added glamour. He is not a peer, because such a rank carried with it privileges and responsibilities with which Richardson probably felt he could not cope.

These examples show that the part played by sociological factors in Richardson's work was a minor one. Both his themes and his techniques were dictated by his temperament, which led him both to exaggerate and to distort certain elements in contemporary life, and wholly to neglect others. Both the neglect and the distortion may be partly due to his education and to his experiences, both reflections of his 'station', but no one who reads the books can doubt that it is mainly Richardson's own personality which is expressed in them.

7

Fielding

Most readers probably feel that the picture given in *Tom Jones* and *Amelia* is more like eighteenth-century life than that found in other books of the period, simply because it is more like life in general. Young men like Tom Jones are more plentiful than young men like Lovelace. The situation in both books is quite alien to any modern experience, but there are elements in Squire Western recognizable in some fathers today, whereas there are absolutely none in Mr. Harlowe. There is no doubt that this impression is to some extent correct. Fielding was well equipped both by temperament and experience to portray the contemporary scene; but it also derives from the quality of his genius, and from his enormous influence on the nineteenth-century English novel. Nothing seems more real than what we already know, and most people come to Fielding having read Scott, Dickens and Thackeray, as well as a host of minor novelists. Fielding's influence is perceptible everywhere; but is perhaps most easily seen in the continuance and transformation of characters introduced into the novel by him. Of these one of the most famous is Squire Western.

He is so vivid a figure that critics from Hazlitt to Empson have taken him as a transcript from life. On the other hand, Ketton-Cremer,[1] in his introduction to the letters of St. Clair of Sustead, remarked how unlike the squires and parsons revealed in them were to those in the novels of the period. Mingay's study *English Landed Society in the Eighteenth Century* bears this out.[2] One of the reasons why we believe in the Squire is that he is presented in a comic convention that was often used afterwards, and which is

[1] Ketton-Cremer, R. W., *Country Neighbourhoods*, 1951.
[2] Mingay, G. E., *English Landed Society in the Eighteenth Century*, 1963.

even still sometimes employed. Just after he has declared that he loves his daughter better than his own soul, he hears from her aunt that she is in love, and immediately exclaims 'How in love . . . in love without acquainting me! I'll disinherit her, I'll turn her out of doors stark naked without a penny. Is all kindness vor o'ur and vondness to o'ur come to this, to fall in love without asking me leave?' He here foreshadows Sir Anthony Absolute and many fathers in later comedy and farce. In his other aspects one can see the germ of Squire Osbaldestone in *Rob Roy*, as well as of Sir Pitt Crawley.

He had literary ancestors as well as descendants. Fielding himself had already used a slighter version in his first play, *Love in Several Masques*. The Squire has something in him of the uncouth country gentleman of Restoration comedy, and perhaps of Justice Shallow, as well as of a more universal figure, the rough countryman as seen by the polished townsman. A type which amused so many generations must, of course, have had some examples in real life. If he is a caricature, he must have been a caricature which could be easily recognized as mockery of something real.

In Fielding's portrait of him there may be, as well as comic exaggeration, an element of political propaganda. Western was a Tory. Fielding was a strong Whig, and *Tom Jones* was published in 1749, only four years after the last Jacobite rising. Fielding may be insinuating that this is what Jacobites and Tories are like—ignorant, tyrannical in their own countryside, prepared to deliver Great Britain over to an absolute monarch, and yet unwilling to pay the proper deference to their own superiors in rank. For although when he says 'I hate all lords; they are a parcel of courtiers and Hanoverians and I shall have nothing to do with them', a modern reader may think he is showing a manly independence, Fielding probably meant it, not only as a joke, but as a mark of Jacobite ignorance and uncouth stupidity. Fielding was a barrister and, when he wrote *Tom Jones*, a full-time London magistrate; and the portrait of the squire as magistrate is a professional's view of the amateur. It is quite likely that the tenants and labourers in Wiltshire felt that what they lost in the Squire's disregard of the letter of the law in such matters as poaching, they gained in his view of other misdemeanours.

It is through his conversation that Western becomes more real than Harlowe. It is not only Fielding's humour, but his ability to reproduce the idiom of the period which gives his readers the illusion of authenticity. This aspect of his writing was commented on in his day and can be recognized if the novels are compared with other documents.

Francis Coventry, in his introduction to his novel *Pompey the Little*, said, 'I once heard a very fine lady condemning some highly finished conversations in one of your (Fielding's) works, Sir, for this curious reason—"because," said she, "t'is such stuff as passes every day between me and my maid".' Whether this story is true or not, it indicates what was thought at the time. Although Fielding prided himself on his knowledge of the world of fashion, the dialogue of the great is not reproduced with such fidelity as the speech of the lower orders, partly because of the convention that the virtuous upper classes should speak in standard English. In reality, Allworthy, Tom and Sophy as well as the Squire would have had a Somersetshire accent.

We have specimens of the speech of the lower orders in the reports of cases in Fielding's court, supplied by his clerk, and published in the *Covent Garden Journal*. In the issue of May 19th, 1752, a woman complained of her husband in the following words:

'Sir, he has mortified me all over, and I goes in danger of my life, night and day . . . I would not make my afferdavy to anything that was false for the whole world; but I can safely take my afferdavy that he has mortified me from head to foot, and he has my child too. Whereof I could shew your worship if your worship was a woman; but to be sure our sexe's modesty can't go as far as that before men, to be sure. Your worship however understands me very well; and I hope you will do me justice and send him to gaol.'

On January 21st of the same year a man complained of his wife in words which, if encountered in a novel, would certainly have been set down to the influence of Shakespeare. 'May it please your worship, this woman my wife is a very sober, discreet and intemperate woman as can live, for the matter of that as for sober, I mean when she does not take a cup or so; for indeed when she does she is the veriest balragger upon the face of the earth, and whenever that is, which to be sure is oftener than it should be, she flies upon me like any dragoness.' It is unnecessary to point out how this sort of thing is echoed in the novels.

Fielding's knowledge of the English world was very wide, wider even than Defoe's. He had mixed with the great, not as a paid agent, but as a relation and a guest. He had known depths as low as those to which Defoe had ever sunk, and as a magistrate he had learnt more about crime and criminals than any other novelist of his time. In addition, both his temperament and his opinions allowed him to paint the social scene with a certain detachment.

He was not emotionally involved with his characters as was Richardson; we are not meant to identify ourselves with Tom Jones, Sophia, Captain Booth or Amelia, but to view them with detached sympathy. Fielding said in *Amelia*, 'Life may as properly be called an art as any other', and the interest of his novels is to show how the characters conducted this difficult art. To regard life as an art in itself induces a certain distance, and when joined with a strongly ironic temperament tends to repel some readers. Richardson asked, 'Who can care for any of his people?' and although he objected to them mainly because they were 'low', it was probably also the highly intellectual nature of Fielding's work which baffled him. This results in a perfectly deliberate concentration on comedy. A modern authority on Fielding, much as he admires his work, has pointed to this as a limitation of his art: 'At crucial moments he avoids, even shirks, one might say—emotional scenes . . . In scenes of emotional elevation he is seldom implicitly or unconsciously present. In scenes of comedy tinged with acid, he does have the sense of presence.'[3]

A writer who regards life as an art will be more aware of his minor and less engrossed with his central characters, than one who looks on it as a search for personal salvation or personal happiness. Fielding was interested not only in people, but also in the relationship between people; the social tie was artistically as well as ethically important to him.

It may seem odd to make such a distinction between novelists, as, of course, all novelists must be concerned with relations between people. Some of them, however, of whom Madame de La Fayette, Defoe and Richardson are examples, like to concentrate on two or three, while others prefer to develop their theme through the complexity of large numbers. There is no connection between the quality of any book and this choice between few or

[3] Sherburn, George, 'Fielding's Social Outlook', *Philological Quarterly*, 1956.

many. Indeed, the many-charactered novel may lose in intensity what it gains in realism, but it is clear that it is likely to give the more accurate picture of society. Lovelace and Clarissa exist in a sort of social void; we are told something of Lovelace's relations with his tenants, but we never see him dealing with any of a landlord's problems or involved in any relation with another human being unconnected with his pursuit of women. The minor characters only exist through their reactions to him and to Clarissa. Lord M. is a shadow, not at all solidified by his fondness for proverbs. The tarts in the house in which Clarissa is imprisoned in London are stereotypes, although stereotypes depicted with a certain grisly impressiveness. We are never told anything of Clarissa's poor; they remain a collective noun, the proper appendage of a good woman. Tom Jones, on the other hand, becames real through his relations with other people. Fielding meant his readers to feel that he deserved Sophia in the end because of his magnanimity to Black George, his forgiveness of the highwayman, and his intervention to persuade Nightingale to marry the girl he had seduced. Clarissa's maid is a name only; Sophia's Mrs. Honour is a character and an important one.

Fielding's approach was, as far as we can see, fundamentally a result of his temperament, but it was reinforced by his religious opinions. He believed our duty to our neighbour to be the most important part of the Christian life. This was the root of his dislike of those Methodists who emphasized 'grace' at the expense of 'works'—the 'hellish doctrine', as he called it. This, too, is the paradox of *Tom Jones*, that the hero, because of his generosity and kindliness, in spite of his habit of slipping into bed with any woman who was willing, was a better Christian than many of those whose sexual conduct was more correct.

This type of Christianity is characteristic both of the eighteenth and of the twentieth century. In the seventeenth men had fought over points of doctrine until in England believing Christians, sensible men, and political philosophers were sickened and disgusted. They sought in Christian charity a solution to political as well as religious difficulties:

> For modes of faith let graceless zealots fight,
> He can't be wrong whose life is in the right:
> In faith and hope the world will disagree,
> But all mankind's concern is charity.

The creed was formulated in the eighteenth century; but the ordinary Anglo-Saxon Christian today would heartily endorse it, even if he would prefer it to be stated in prose.

This form of Christianity was one of the motives which inspired Fielding to attempt not only the reform of manners, at which many other writers had previously aimed, but also the reform of institutions. As Sherburn said in his well-known essay on Fielding's social outlook, 'He shows a curiosity as to the organisation of society as well as the to conduct of private lives.'[4] The dedication of *Amelia* to Ralph Allen begins, 'The following book is sincerely designed to promote the cause of virtue, and to expose some of the most glaring evils, as well public as private, which at present infest the country,' which makes it the first social reform novel. The opening chapters of *Colonel Jack*, it is true, give a picture of child criminals, but it soon wanders away into a mere tale of adventure. It is absurd to regard Richardson's books as either pictures or criticism of society. The only suggestion anywhere made for social action is in *Sir Charles Grandison*, where there is a proposal for 'Protestant nunneries' as a solution to the problem of the poor, unmarried gentlewoman. Sir Charles also thought it would be a good thing to revive the sumptuary laws, which had attempted to lay down the dress appropriate to each class. Defoe might be held to suggest the necessity of reform by implication; but *Amelia* is the first novel in which social evils are laid out for the consideration of those who thought in terms, not of touching the individual heart, but of Acts of Parliament.

The social problems in the book are, of course, those with which Fielding himself, as the Magistrate for Westminster and Middlesex, had to deal—the administration of the criminal law, the state of the prisons, the condition of the poor. He also glances at the abuses to which the prevailing system of appointment to posts under Government might lead. The reforming element in the book, although prominent, is far from being the only one. Among other things it is meant to be a modern version of the *Aeneid*. It seems to be true that the portrait of Amelia herself is, in part, a memorial to his own wife; while there is, as in his other novels—even the light-hearted *Joseph Andrews*—an abundance of comment social, moral, aesthetic and religious.

Fielding leaves us in no doubt when he intends a criticism of

4 *Ibid.*

social arrangements; in accordance with his own temperament and the literary technique of the period, he does not argue by implication. Where he believes it would be possible to find a remedy in legislation he says so. This type of comment, although it appears in all his books, is more frequent and also more serious in *Amelia*. Mr. Thrasher, ignorant, corrupt and incompetent, was meant as an indictment of the system of justic in London, as is shown by the remark with which he is introduced: 'I own, I have been sometimes inclined to think that this office of a justice of the peace requires some knowledge of the law'. This is heavily reinforced by a footnote which draws the reader's attention to the evils of the practice of charging people guilty of abusive language —then no offence against the law—with a riot. An example of social comment in *Tom Jones* is Allworthy's protest against parents attempting to compel their daughters to marry against their will: 'To force a woman into a marriage contrary to her consent or approbation is an act of such injustice and oppression that I wish the laws of our country could restrain it.' Many writers had expressed similar views as to the wickedness of such parents, but only Fielding suggested recourse to legislation. This is almost certainly a result of his experience, and is perhaps also in some degree a reflection of his station. He came of the class which was concerned with legislation.

The wicked peers in *Tom Jones* and *Amelia* are, on the other hand, bad men, not evil institutions. Here Fielding is not attacking the power of the House of Lords or the privileges of peers, or even insinuating that such privileges corrupt; but showing, by example, what a Christian, or indeed a gentleman, must avoid.

Other remarks have a timeless reference. 'His Lordship, who was strictly a man of honour, and would by no means have been guilty of an action which the world in general would have condemned', describes a type of character which exists in all societies and will continue in any imaginable future. The sentences 'The great are deceived if they imagine they have appropriated ambition and vanity to themselves. These noble qualities flourish as notably in a country church . . . as in the drawing-room' are, with a change of locale, as true today as they were then. It is easy to mistake one type of comment for another. For example, the remark, 'Those members of society, who are born to furnish the blessings of life, now began to light their candles, in order to pursue their daily labours, for the use of those born to enjoy those blessings', would in a modern, or even in a nineteenth-century context, imply a desire for some social reorganization. But no one at this date, least of all Fielding, as we know from the proposals he made for reforming the Poor Law, supposed this to be possible. It must be taken as a comment on a sad but inevitable state of affairs, a criticism of life rather than of society.

It may or may not be significant that Fielding's social purpose is much more evident in *Amelia* than in *Tom Jones*, and *Amelia*, although not all critics have agreed, is generally taken to be a less perfect work of art. But for those who read fiction for information about the life of its time *Amelia*, just because of its didactic intention, is, within limits, extraordinarily informative. It is not only Fielding's accurate descriptions of London justice, of prisons and of such things as the law relating to debtors, but the wide range of the book, which takes in, as well as the manners of the time, something of the legal and political structure.

Prisons and masquerades, the opinions of a cultivated and devout clergyman, and of an equally devout but eccentric soldier are depicted. The crimes for which a warrant was necessary for arrest and the crimes for which any citizen could take a man into custody, together with the knowledge which the London mob possessed of this distinction, are all to be found: 'Murphy who knew well the temper of the mob, cried out, "If you are a bailiff, shew me your writ. Gentlemen, he pretends to arrest me without a writ." Upon this, one of the sturdiest and forwardest of the mob, and who by a superior strength of body and of lungs presided in this assembly, declared he would suffer no such thing. "D—n me," he says, ". . . shew me your writ or let the gentleman go— you shall not arrest a man contrary to law." '

The whole system of 'obliging' by which politics were largely carried on, and many minor offices filled, is part of the fabric of this book. This system is indeed viewed entirely from the side of the 'obligee' or perhaps it would be more accurate to say of the original 'obligee'. For Colonel James, if he had succeeded in obtaining an appointment for Captain Booth, which would have exiled him from the country, would also have been 'obliged' and have had to repay the Minister with votes, speeches or some other form of support.

Dr. Harrison, the good clergyman: 'happened to be in the

neighbourhood of a nobleman of his acquaintance, and whom he knew to have very considerable interest with the Ministers at that time. The doctor, who was very well known to this nobleman, took this opportunity of paying him a visit in order to recommend poor Booth to his favour. Nor did he much doubt of his success, the favour he was to ask being a very small one, and to which he thought the service of Booth gave so just a title.' Every question, however, has two sides; how it appeared to the nobleman can be gleaned from a letter of Lord Chesterfield to Lord Huntingdom, written the year after the publication of *Amelia*. 'Mr. Hastings, your kinsman, has a mind to what he calls a small place, and like all candidates for small places thinks there is nothing so easy as to get one, and is persuaded *one word from your Lordship* would do the business. The contrary of this is exactly true, for everybody being equally fit for these places, everybody asks for them and those who have the disposal of them, always say that they are, and indeed commonly are engaged ten deep.'[5]

Amelia itself, although it was far from Fielding's intention, must rouse some sympathy for the 'great', who were obviously pestered from morning till night by people who, at least according to modern ideas, had no claim on them. Their porters, too, who had to sort out the innumerable applicants, hardly seem as much to blame as Fielding appears to have thought, even if they did accept bribes.

Fielding had heard eighteenth-century politicians talk and we have not, but the cynicism displayed by the nobleman in the interview with Dr. Harrison is not at all like the views of contemporary politicians, even when expressed in private letters. Indeed, it is altogether unlikely that any politicians anywhere ever said things such as: 'Do you not know, doctor, that this is as corrupt a nation as ever existed under the sun? And would you think of governing such people by the strict principles of honesty and morality?' Speeches of this kind seem reminiscences of the propaganda Fielding wrote for Pitt, Chesterfield and Lyttleton, when they were opposing Walpole, rather than a recollection of anyone's words. This despair of the commonwealth is more the cliché of patriots out of office than a likely characteristic of the views of a nobleman, who 'possessed great influence with Ministers'.

Of the factual accuracy of *Amelia* there is no doubt, in the sense,

[5] Chesterfield, Philip, Dormer Stanhope Earl of, *Letters to Lord Huntingdon*, 1923.

that these things could happen. The 'trading' magistrates of London were notorious, the prisons were as described, officers could get appointments for reasons quite unconnected with their ability or their fitness for the job. One character, Colonel Bath is so rooted in social reality as to be practically incomprehensible to modern readers. He is so infatuated with 'the point of honour' as to insist on fighting Captain Booth because Booth refuses to challenge Bath's brother-in-law, his own intimate friend.

The book's accuracy in a wider sense is another question. If *Amelia* was the only salvage from some forgotten civilization, most readers would surely think it depicted a country in an advanced state of decay. In reality the Army, whose officers were largely appointed by the extraordinary methods outlined, was found adequate to any task it was asked to perform—except the impossible one of defeating the American colonists. Fielding, himself universally admitted to be one of the best, if not the best, London magistrate of the century, had been appointed through interest, and it is doubtful if a really conscientious nineteenth-century administration would have selected him.

Fielding combined veneration for the principles of the Constitution with the view that any actual administration was corrupt; at least, this is the impression to be derived from the novels. Fielding was no mere member of the public. He had been closely connected with the opposition to Walpole, in his later years he was a magistrate in touch with the Government, and had prepared a memorandum on crime in London for the Duke of Newcastle. Yet the novels seem to reflect the gossip of the time rather than the facts. Modern inquiry has considerably changed the old picture of eighteenth-century politics. However odd the system may seem to us, it was neither so corrupt nor so incompetent as was once supposed. Hughes has shown that although patronage may have been important in nominating men to what we should now call the Civil Service, they were rarely appointed without some test of their fitness; indeed, for some departments there was a qualifying examination as early as 1740.[6] If some of the occupants of the senior offices did not do the work for which their positions were originally established, many of them did other things. J. H. Plumb, for instance, says of those targets of nineteenth-century satire, the clerks of the Board of

[6] Hughes, E., *Studies in Administration and Finance*, 1934.

Green Cloth: 'These men played the part of junior ministers. Although they lacked administrative responsibility in the narrow sense, in all other ways they may be regarded as hard-working members of the government, fully deserving their £500 a year.'[7] The idea of the wholesale bribery of Members of Parliament by Walpole and George III has also been considerably modified. Some men went into Parliament as a career and, in a few cases, received direct financial rewards. Fielding and Smollett would no doubt have been surprised by the verdict of a modern historian that 'The distribution of patronage savoured more of jobbery, even of charity, than of Parliamentary corruption',[8] and astounded to hear how hard men like Sandwich and Newcastle worked.

Fielding's very sanity led him to ignore the abnormal and neurotic, as evident in his time as in ours. He was well aware of the kind of sexual deviation which engaged so much of Richardson's attention, as is shown by his comment on Blifil's determination to marry Sophia whether she liked him or not.

. . . Now the agonies which affected the mind of Sophia rather augmented than impaired her beauty; for her tears added brightness to her eyes, and her breasts rose higher with her sighs. Indeed no one hath seen beauty in its highest lustre, who hath never seen it in distress. Blifil therefore looked on this human ortolan with greater desire than when he had viewed her last; nor was his desire at all lessened by the aversion which he discovered in her to himself. On the contrary, this served rather to heighten the pleasure he proposed in rifling her charms, as it added triumph to lust; nay, he had some further views, from obtaining the absolute possession of her person, which we detest too much even to mention; and revenge itself was not without its share in the gratifications which he promised himself. The rivalling poor Jones, and supplanting him in her affections, added another spur to his pursuit, and promised another additional rapture to his enjoyment.

Although Fielding probably wrote the pamphlet called *The Female Husband* which describes a case of female homosexuality, he probably did it to earn some money, rather than out of interest in the subject. There is no reason to suppose he quarrelled with the literary conventions of the time. These only allowed the slightest allusion to such subjects in any but pornographic fiction, although

[7] Plumb, J. H., *op. cit.*
[8] Owen, J. B., *The Rise of the Pelhams*, 1957.

they permitted charges of unnatural passions to be freely bandied about in political controversy—the exact opposite of what is dictated by our present conventions.

Nor are the extravagancies of conduct and character which the times permitted to be found in Fielding. The omission of the abnormal and eccentric give the impression of a more sober and orderly world than is found in the diaries and letters of the time. The roughness of life is clearly shown; but there is little of the wildness which, a sign of vitality and a signal of freedom, transforms the country of *Amelia* into the country which conquered India, discovered Australia, defeated Napoleon and initiated the Industrial Revolution.

Although the experience of the twentieth century has amply justified the eighteenth-century distrust of enthusiasm, one cannot but feel that Fielding was rather unjust to the Methodists. This may indeed be a reflection of educated opinion at the time; but his hostility to science, especially for some reason to natural history, seemed to have been a more personal eccentricity. He objected to science not on the grounds, for which some prophetic insight might be claimed, that it was dangerous, but that it was 'trifling'. This indeed is not a prominent motif in the novels, it requires fairly close study to detect it; but it is certainly there, and is confirmed by Fielding's writings in periodicals. In *The Journey from this World to the Next* an unfortunate spirit who had devoted his life to the 'study of butterflies' is given a poor reception. Momus, on receiving his reply, 'made him no answer but with great scorn pushed him back'. In *Tom Jones* we are told that one of the amusements of the age was 'natural philosophy, or rather unnatural philosophy, which deals in the wonderful, and knows nothing of nature, except her monsters and imperfections'. This may be a legacy from Swift or even Pope in some moods; but if it is, it shows how dangerous it is to treat writers as spokesmen or representatives, for hostility to science has often been regarded as a characteristic of the pessimistic High Church satirists. Fielding's attitude may on the other hand, have been derived not from the literary tradition but from his religious opinions. Too minute an inquiry into nature was held by some latitudinarian divines, as well as by ministers of more austere sects, to savour of presumption, and to distract men from their duty to their neighbour. In this sense Fielding may be said to be reflecting a section of public opinion. But the emergence of natural history was one of the most important intellectual trends in the eighteenth century, considering its subsequent development, as important as the technological innovations, and of this Fielding gave a highly misleading impression.

There is one attitude very characteristic of the eighteenth century which differs markedly from that prevalent in some periods and it plays a vital part in *Tom Jones*; indeed, the famous plot could not have been the same without it. This is the attitude to illegitimacy. Once that it is known that Tom is the son of Allworthy's sister, everyone thinks it right and natural that he should inherit his uncle's property, although his parents were never married. This is the view of an aristocratic society, because it is the blood that counts and not a ceremony, either civil or religious. It was, of course, not confined to the eighteenth century, as witness William the Bastard, Duke of Normandy. It was not, however, shared by the nobility of other countries in the eighteenth century, as Chesterfield found, when he tried to secure diplomatic posts for his son. Although in origin a class attitude it was undoubtedly strengthened by rationalism, and by the Protestant refusal to follow the Catholic Church in regarding marriage as a sacrament. No one in *Tom Jones* argues the case for the illegitimate child, the only hint that there might be another view is Allworthy's remark, 'I am not ashamed to own him.' He makes no declaration about the injustice of the law or the self-righteousness of society. This lack of argument shows how widely diffused the attitude must have been. Fielding's unquestioning acceptance of it links him both to his time and to the class in which he was born. This, however, is the only specifically aristocratic sentiment which can be attributed to him, and even this, although deriving from an aristocratic outlook, was certainly also adopted by some men of a middle station.

In spite of these examples, it is not easy to regard Fielding as the mouthpiece of any class. Indeed if his own life, as well as his novels, is taken into account, it is difficult to define his class in eighteenth-century terms. But, unlike Defoe and Richardson, he did represent an intellectual position—that of Latitudinarian Christianity. At least the labours of scholars over the past thirty years seem to have established this. That labours were needed might be thought to indicate that Fielding's religion did not play a vital part in his books; but *Tom Jones*, with the same incidents, would have been a different book without this background.

But if Fielding was thus representative of a school of Christian doctrine, it became in his hands a highly personal faith. He went farther in charity towards sexual sins, at least in *Tom Jones*, than most of those who shared his religious views. This was exaggerated by nineteenth-century critics; all Fielding ever implied was that the lapses of an unmarried man, if not accompanied by deceit or cruelty, were forgivable and perhaps inevitable. In *Amelia*, however, he seriously discussed whether adultery ought not to be made a crime. A good woman would, of course, forgive a repentant husband, but Captain Booth is not presented as a 'hero', while Tom Jones, in a sense, is. In his *Inquiry into the causes of the Late Increase of Robbers* Fielding took a much graver view of drunkenness than he did even in *Amelia*, itself a more 'serious' book, in the eighteenth-century sense of the word, than *Tom Jones*. A comparison of the views expressed in Fielding's pamphlets, and those implied in the novels, suggests a doubt as to how far the latter were meant to apply to life. For example, there is no doubt that Fielding approved, and meant the reader to approve, of Tom Jones's forgiveness of the highwayman. Yet nothing made him more angry, when he was a magistrate and men refused or failed to prosecute. It is true that it was the fictional highwayman's first attempt, only undertaken in despair at the misery of his wife and children, and that it was Fielding's duty as a magistrate to get the real robbers apprehended and convicted; but if we did not have the details of his career we might gravely misunderstand his attitude to crime and criminals.

No sociological, historical or even social factors appear to have determined that the most influential English novelist of the century, in his own country, although not on the Continent, should have been a Latitudinarian Christian. Methodism or even the religion of extreme High-Churchmen may have led men to write hymns rather than novels—although Methodism did enter the English novel in Brooke's *The Fool of Quality*. There seems, however, no reason, sociological or intellectual, why the great novelist should not have been a deist or a sceptic. Perhaps a real sceptic would have the same difficulties in publishing a novel as a Jacobite might have done; but Deism was almost respectable, if not enthusiastically approved. Possibly Fielding's ideas approximated more closely to those of the average educated man than either of these alternatives. This idea gains support from the fact that the social problems in *Amelia* are the problems that worried his contemporaries. He did not discuss unnoticed evils. Laments over the state of the prisons, over political corruption, and over the abuses of the Poor Law were platitudes of the time. Where Fielding differed was in going farther than platitudes, in describing what was wrong with greater sharpness and in proposing remedies, some of which ran as much counter to the public opinion of his day as to that of ours.

8

Contemporary Events, Ideas and Institutions in the Eighteenth Century Novel

The picture of eighteenth-century life drawn by Defoe, Richardson and Fielding does not, when considered as a whole, seem so accurate or so comprehensive as to deserve the name of 'reflection'. On the other hand, parts of the sociological landscape in which the stories are set are clearly 'reflections' in the sense that they do not represent a choice by the writer, but rather a passive acceptance of what was there. These comprise, as well as the mechanism of daily life and the surface manners of the age, some contemporary events, some common assumptions and something of the institutional framework. If any of these cease to be background and become significant elements in the plot, then they also cease to be 'reflections'. For example, the English class system, as it appears in the eighteenth-century novel, has, if one likes thinking in metaphors, some of the attributes of an image in a mirror. Once novelists become concerned with attacking or defending it, it loses some of these attributes, and becomes less a 'reflection' and more a deliberate construction.

If we know nothing or very little of the age in which the book was written, all 'reflections' are equally interesting. In a period as well documented as the eighteenth century most people are interested only in those reflections which reveal something peculiar to the period, or first appearing in it. For example, it could be discovered from the novels that England was a monarchy, and that marriage was monogamous. Neither of these pieces of information are of any interest, because England has always, except during the Commonwealth been a monarchy, and because monogamy is characteristic not of England in the eighteenth century but of European civilization.

Contemporary events, such as wars, famines or earthquakes, are true 'reflections' in the sense that they are both peculiar to the period and that they cannot be put into a novel before they have happened. An element of choice does exist, however, as to whether they are introduced or not. In the eighteenth-century novel events occur in so capricious a manner that their appearance is clearly due to the personal choice of the writer. This is, of course, a reflection of the life of the time. No event was of such an overwhelming kind that it had to be put into any contemporary novel or, at least, into any that aimed at realism. This, although in striking contrast to the twentieth century, is not unique to the eighteenth; in some earlier periods, as well as in some later, history was also of this unobtrusive character.

One event indeed dominates Fielding's whole social landscape —the 'Glorious Revolution' of 1688. But when he wrote his first novel the Revolution was already nearly fifty years in the past, a fact of history, if of recent history. Some consciousness of it can be discerned in Richardson. But it had no impact—at least it makes no appearance in the work of Defoe, the novelist who actually lived through it.

Robinson Crusoe was wrecked on his island in pursuit of negroes to work his own and his neighbours' plantations, obviously as slaves, although the word is not used when the expedition is discussed. This is, however, not related to anything else in the book. He might just as well have been engaged in any other kind of activity which involved a sea voyage. The rebellion of 1715 is part of the story of *Colonel Jack* but it is merely an excuse for adventure. The similar episode of 1745 appears in *Tom Jones*, but only as background; it has no significance for the plot and no particular meaning for any of the characters. It allows Fielding to give a satirical picture of the public reaction, but that is all. One might have thought that it was so startling and important that any book, published such a short time afterwards, must have included it, were it not completely absent from the work of Richardson.

Fielding's view of the '45 was, of course, strikingly different from that of the other major novelist who dealt with it. It was the contemporary view of an English Whig, not the retrospective view of a Scottish Tory. It is an impressive example of the effect of a literary tradition that every novelist, English as well as Scots, who wrote after Scott adopted the Scottish view.

It is more important for the sociology of literature that the Jacobite High Anglican school of thought makes no appearance in a novel, except as an object of satire, until it had ceased to have any practical importance. Smollett indeed in *Peregrine Pickle* alludes to Jacobites as 'exiled from their native home, in consequence of their adherence to an unfortunate and ruined cause', with sympathy and respect. 'Though our young gentlemen differed widely from them in political principles . . . he could easily comprehend how a man of the most unblemished morals might, by the prejudice of education, or indispensable attachments, be engaged in such a blameworthy and pernicious undertaking.'

This has a gentleness and gravity unlike Smollett's usual utterances. The meeting with the exiles is, however, a very minor incident, and Mr. Jolter, the High Tory Divine, is caricatured as much as the republican Doctor. Smollett's feelings about the '45 are more plainly expressed in the poem *The Tears of Scotland*, than in any of his novels.

There are indeed both political and sociological reasons for the predominantly Whig tone of the early novel. Although there was no censorship, booksellers and authors were prosecuted for sedition as well as obscenity, and it would, no doubt, have been difficult to get a Jacobite novel published. There were also certain advantages in putting forward sound Whig principles. All patronage was in Whig hands and a substantial part of the economic rewards of writing might be 'a place under government'. Neither fear nor hope, however, seems to have played any part in inspiring the novelist's political views; Defoe, Richardson and Fielding were Whigs by genuine conviction, and even Smollett, although he supported Bute, accepted the principles of 1688.

To be a Whig in the age of Fielding meant to be a supporter of the dominant party and the established order. In the age of Defoe it was a very different matter; for most of his life Defoe was a member of a party still struggling for existence, and which more than once, seemed to have been decisively defeated.

A society in which those novelists most highly regarded, both in their own time and by subsequent generations, are convinced supporters of the established order clearly has a different atmosphere from one in which they are rebels. But what the exact consequences were for the novel is by no means easy to see. It did not in any way prohibit criticism, even harsh criticism, of some aspects of society, as a similar dominance of eighteenth-century Toryism might have done.

The fundamental assumption of the Whig creed, the supreme value of liberty, in the sense of freedom from coercion by the State, is frequently alluded to by Fielding, and to a minor degree by Richardson. The way in which this conception was spreading from the political to other spheres can also be detected. When Miss Western constantly declares that 'this is a land of liberty' and women are as much entitled to freedom as men, Fielding no doubt meant it as satire; but it is some indication of the effect which political theory was having on other aspects of life.

In Richardson similar remarks are more in the nature of universally accepted platitudes. When Clarissa says to Lovelace, 'Is it your intention to permit me to quit? To permit the freedom which is the birthright of an English subject?' the remark is so inappropriate to the situation that it is plain that 'freedom' was to Richardson merely a conditioned response to the word 'English subject'. Nor are the references in *Sir Charles Grandison* any less conventional.

The social pressure which impelled Fielding, in *Tom Jones*, after praising the autocratic rule of the King of the Gypsies, to add a long paragraph explaining that he was in no way advocating 'arbitrary government' is obvious.

Political theory was not only extremely important at the time, but was to be one of the legacies of the eighteenth century to the future. As far as the novels indicate its nature, and the weight attached to it by public opinion, they are accurate mirrors. On the other hand, liberty, apart from freedom of choice in marriage, is not a major theme in any novel. Fielding, in *Amelia*, contrasted theory with what might happen in practice; but no one wrote a book which explored the nature and meaning of liberty. The whole conception remains part of the background only.

The outline of the English class system can be clearly seen in Richardson and Fielding, and with it something of the other aspect of the political theory of the time, the necessity of 'subordination'.

It is, however, perhaps because the novelists were Whigs, much less clearly expressed, and appears much less important than the theme of liberty.

It is indeed taken for granted that different classes have different rights and duties. This has, of course, been disputed both by Marxists anxious to fit the writers into the theory of the class war, and by critics anxious to make the books more sympathetic to modern readers. They forget, however, the background both of political and of cosmological theory. The idea of the mixed constitution, as well as the idea of the great chain of being, makes it unlikely that the early eighteenth-century novelists would advance views either of class antagonism or of social democracy. That they did not do so can be clearly seen in Richardson. If he had held any nineteenth-century ideas he would have expressed them through Sir Charles Grandison. Sir Charles gives no hint of any such views. Clarissa points out that Lovelace's 'birth and fortune' entitle him to a civil reception from her family three times in her first seven letters.

The general attitude towards aristocratic predominance was not, however, among educated men, a mere acceptance of existing institutions. They were well aware that there had been 'levelling' doctrines in the Civil War and, in its political aspect, aristocracy was continuously challenged by the absolute monarchies of the Continent. The English nobility was highly conscious of this and had the habit of referring to its European counterparts as 'gilded appendages to a throne'.

It is fairly clear that in this atmosphere the abolition or modification of class privileges would not be made a major theme in any novel. It is also obvious that the power of the aristocracy would make wicked and silly peers and landowners a worth-while target, both for the moralist and the satirist, and this is exactly what we find in novels: criticism of those who fell below the standard their responsibilities demanded—no attacks on institutions.

Among these figures the local magistrate is presented in much greater detail, indeed looms larger than any other, even than the peers. This is because he was more immediately important to the average person, and his shortcomings were likely to have a more disastrous effect than the misdeeds of the wickedest lord.

One of the consequences of the social structure, and a consesequence which had great significance for the novelist, was the importance attached to the family. It is prominent in the novels because it is the basis of the conflict between parent and child over marriage. To a modern eye the attitude of the fathers in eighteenth-century fiction is incomprehensible. In the eighteenth century the desire to extend the possessions and aggrandize the fortunes of the family was a motive, which although no doubt aristocratic in origin, was present in all classes, except the poorest. This attitude is not snobbery but a wish for real wealth and power. The conflict thus has much deeper roots than in the nineteenth-century novel, in which it also appears in an attenuated form.

The importance of the family explains much of the weight attached to financial considerations in marriage, but not all. Even the virtuous characters are more aware of the necessity of some money than people are in modern or in nineteenth-century novels. This is a reflection of the whole society. Fundamentally it arose from economic conditions. The economic foundation was agriculture, and agriculture organized on a basis of large estates, entailed on the eldest male heir. Industry and commerce were mainly organized on a family basis, which meant that there were far fewer opportunities for earning a living than in the modern world. The hangers-on of the 'great', a feature in all novels, are symptoms of this. There was a prevalent idea that there were certain standards of living appropriate to each station, and that there was a level below which it was not only a misfortune but a disgrace for a gentleman to fall.

If the subordination of class to class is implied rather than stated, the necessity of the subordination of women to men, although nowhere alluded to by Defoe, is evident everywhere in Richardson, and is expressly stated by Fielding in that pattern of virtue, Allworthy. He says of Sophia: 'Whenever I have seen her in the company of men, she hath been all attention, with the modesty of a learner, not the forwardness of a teacher. . . . Indeed she always shewed the highest deference to the understandings of men; a quality absolutely essential to the making of a good wife. I shall only add, that as she is most apparently void of all affectation, this deference must be certainly real.' This attitude sharply distinguishes the eighteenth-century novel from not only the modern but also the nineteenth-century novel as well as from the medieval romance. The deference, as far as lovers were concerned, was in romance due from the man to the woman; the revival of much of the medieval literary convention coloured the nineteenth-century novel.

In literature the eighteenth-century attitude to women was rather odious, and the law supported it; but in the aristocratic society, of which we know so much more than of any other, it seems to have been considerably less unpleasant. This is, of course, the exact opposite of what is conjectured, rather than exactly known, of the relations between life and literature in the Middle Ages.

The doctrine of liberty, the class structure and the attitude to women seem to be the main reflections of contemporary society to be found in the novels. The fact that the common assumptions were political and social, and not religious or scientific is, of course, itself a sociological phenomenon, and one very important to the understanding of the period.

Many other reflections of the life of the time have been discovered by various critics. Their existence is, however, doubtful. Firstly, because different writers have formed the most diverse impressions of eighteenth-century England from its novels. Secondly, most of these impressions have been derived from interpreting certain passages, rather than from finding unequivocal statements.

It would not be difficult to relate some of the characteristics of the novel to their sociological background. For instance, the absence of the 'domestic novel', that is the novel without any kind of adventure or startling incident, might be connected with the contempt expressed for female understanding. It is indeed much more an invention of women than of men; but even Fanny Burney in *Evelina* incorporated something of adventure taken from the male novelists. This, however, may be, as well as a result of the literary tradition, a reflection of the general life of the time.

If life is as rough as it was in the eighteenth century it may be as difficult to write a novel like *Emma* or *The Tale of Genji*, as would be for reasons similar, although not the same today.

Le Lai de l'Ombre must, however, not be forgotten. It is, although a poem, a 'domestic' story, and was written in a period much rougher than the eighteenth century.

A connection might also be postulated between the social system and one of the more formal elements in the novels—the convention that prohibited the use of idiomatic and familiar speech among members of the upper classes, unless the character was meant to be comic. This convention is nowhere more evident than in Richardson. Yet when Clarissa's maid reports a conversation she makes the Harlowes say: ' "They have got me down" as Hannah overheard them say'. This particular phrase may belong more to Richardson's own circle than to the Harlowes. Conversations reported in Walpole's letters are not so stilted as they are in novels; nor is the dialogue in *Fanny Hill*, a frankly pornographic book, which did not observe this convention, any more than others.

One might suppose that the convention itself arose from ideas of dignity and decorum which must form a part of an aristocratic social atmosphere. Decorum was due to the dignity of literature no less than to the dignity of rank. A certain pompousness was expected of any piece of literature, even fiction, which was meant to be taken really seriously. The more hierarchical the society the more attention will be paid to ceremony, and that the word 'pompous' has come to have an increasingly derogatory meaning, clearly has some connection with political and social changes. Yet although we relish the utmost laxity, both in grammar and dialogue in plays or novels, we, too, expect a certain pompousness, in the most serious works we know—scientific and philosophical treatises.

Another correlation might be made between the optimistic tone of the novels and the political convictions of their authors. To be in tune with majority opinion and to believe that the existing political system is the best so far invented, and is moreover unique to one's own country, would no doubt tend to make one cheerful. The only piece of fiction written by a High Church Tory is extremely gloomy. There seems, however, no way of testing any of these hypotheses, and they thus lose any interest they might otherwise have had.

There is indeed one aspect of the century fully discernible in its fiction. This is the general softening of manners which occurred during its course. The contrast between Smollett's *Peregrine Pickle* published in 1751 and *The Vicar of Wakefield* which appeared in 1766 is astonishing. Still more the contrast between *Peregrine Pickle* and *A Sentimental Journey* (1768). The change has not been unanimously approved by modern critics, some of whom talk of the sentimentality and weakness of Goldsmith. If, however, it is a real reflection, no one could fail to rejoice. But is it a reflection or a programme? From what is known of the life of the period it seemed to have been in the 1760s the reaction of exceptional men, and it was not until the end of the century that it can be regarded as characteristic of, at least, the educated classes. This is still more true of those traces which appear in Richardson and Fielding. In both it is connected with the cult of sensibility rather than with humanitarian sentiment, although Sir Charles Grandison refused to allow his horses' tails to be docked, and a regard for animals was one of the most fundamental, as well as one of the most striking developments of humanitarian thought.

Ridiculous as some of the literary manifestations of sensibility may have been, it was not the mere fashion it has frequently been considered; it was rather foam on the deeper current of feeling, which at least showed which way the stream was flowing. *Clarissa*, in its aspect of sympathy with suffering, was one of the sources of sensibility. If Clarissa's misfortunes were exceptional—and considered in cold blood may look rather contrived—the tears shed over her probably contributed something to the increasing awareness of the cruelty in everyday life.

There are signs of some of the other aspects of sensibility in Fielding, the last place most people would look for it. Fielding was not indeed at all 'sentimental' as both Richardson and Sterne undoubtedly were, but his virtuous characters, men as well as women, weep at the spectacle of good actions no less than at sad scenes, as when 'a torrent of tears gushed' from Captain Booth's eyes when recounting Amelia's behaviour after she broke her nose. 'Such tears are apt to flow from a truly noble heart, at the hearing of anything surprisingly great and glorious'. Amelia is in danger of fainting, and has to be revived with a glass of water when she hears, many years after it happened, how Mrs. Bennett's mother fell down a well and was drowned.

The marks of sensibility also appear in angelic children, later so horribly developed by Dickens. Little Betsy, for example, in *Tom Jones*, who, when she thinks her sister is dying, says: 'I am resolved I won't be left behind.' 'Are you not afraid to die, my little Betsy?' said Jones. 'Yes,' answered she, 'I was always afraid to die; but I am not afraid of going anywhere with those I love.'

This kind of thing is not the mere sentimentality it afterwards became, since it was based on a solid philosophic foundation. Fielding and the other eighteenth-century novelists, except Defoe, believed in the fundamental goodness of human nature. Defoe, who whatever else he believed, certainly did not believe this, invented no such little prattlers. It was the experience of the French Revolution, no less than the evangelical insistence on human depravity, which made the children in *The Fairchild Family* so remarkably different.

The importance given to these or any other sociological elements that may be found must inevitably be largely a matter of personal judgement. One possible way of attempting to find a rational basis for such a judgement is to ask oneself how far a knowledge of the sociological and cultural background helps to an understanding of the books. It seems to be of little assistance in reading Defoe or Richardson. It might even, for some people, be a hindrance to the enjoyment if not the comprehension of *Clarissa*. The one book which a knowledge of eighteenth-century thought has helped to elucidate is *Tom Jones*. In one sense this may appear to have been superfluous, because it has been, at least since the beginning of the nineteenth century (except perhaps for *Robinson Crusoe*), the most popular of the early novels. How much has been gained by an understanding of Fielding's religious position can, however, be seen if any modern essay on the book is compared with what was written before 1914.

Just as there are some novels which seem to be curiously independent of the society in which they were written, and others which appear to have arisen from it, so there are some novels to the understanding of which a knowledge of their sociological background is, if not essential, at least helpful, and others which hardly seem to require this knowledge at all.

If it is asked what sort of information about the society of their time is given by these novels, the answer can best be expressed in a science-fiction metaphor. Reading old books is a kind of travelling in time, but the kind in which a man from another time comes to the present, not the kind in which we go back to the past. What he tells us is true, important and authentic, but it is coloured by his own temperament, experience and interests. The account he gives is not necessarily accurate nor are his criticisms necessarily valid. The relation between a novelist and the social background of his novels thus confirms the impression, derived from the history of fiction, that the writer and the writer's experience, solitary as well as social, play a decisive role.

This conclusion may appear to carry the argument no further, because if sociological forces and cultural patterns do not directly determine the nature of the work, they do so indirectly by their influence in moulding the personality of the writer. There is, however, some evidence for non-social factors in literature, both for factors which are non-social in origin and for factors which are impervious to social influences.

PART III

Towards a Theory of the Novel and Society

9

The Writer and Society

Any theory of the social determination of art and literature depends on two assumptions: (1) that the fundamental impulses to these activities are themselves social, and (2) that those aspects of human personality significant for them are the creation of society. The first idea is often expressed in the form that art is essentially communication and thus a response to other people, if not to social 'facts' or cultural 'patterns'. Whether or not this is actually stated in the older theories, it was present in them all. It is now supported by the view that character and ability are the creation of society or culture. The basic similarity of all human beings, the 'human nature' so much insisted on in the eighteenth century, has declined with a wider experience of alien cultures, which has revealed ideas and behaviour most extraordinary to European eyes.

ART AS COMMUNICATION

Up to a short time ago it seemed undeniable that any kind of art was a specifically human activity and essentially a form of communication. This idea has, however, been considerably weakened, if not destroyed, by the discovery that apes and even some monkeys like to draw and paint. Ape art is purely individual and has no social basis or correlatives. Apes do not work for any kind of reward, neither the interest of their fellows nor prizes held out by human beings. Desmond Morris, who has studied their artistic efforts, tells us that when one of them was engrossed with pencil or paint brush he would resent any other ape coming near.[1]

Most human artists are not unlike apes in this; few writers,

[1] Morris, Desmond, *The Biology of Art*, 1962.

composers or painters want or even tolerate an audience while they are working. The higher faculties of man appear when the work is finished, whereas the ape loses all interest in his painting once it is completed, indeed, seems unable to 'see' it in the sense in which a human sees it. Most, although not absolutely all, artists wish to show their work to other people.

Apes are not taught to paint, it is not a circus trick. When the creature is given a pencil it starts moving it across the paper in a way which Morris suggests is related to the anatomical structure of the animal, indeed he has called his book *The Biology of Art*. When the ape has discovered that it can make patterns on a piece of paper, it continues for what appears to be sheer enjoyment; this Morris has named a 'self-rewarding activity', one performed for 'its own sake rather than to attain any basic biological goal'. 'Self-rewarding' activities in the form of 'play' have, of course long been known in all animals, as well as more sophisticated types, in man, often called 'curiosity' or 'self-expression'. If Morris offered a reward, it destroyed the value of the work, because the ape lost interest in his painting, wanting only to finish and get the titbit. It may seem strange to talk of the 'value' of this sort of painting, but some human beings seem to take pleasure in these pictures.

Although this sort of play is not social in the sense of being shared with its fellows or encouraged by their applause, it depends on a social situation between man and ape. Indeed, Morris has conjectured that art has never developed or been observed even in a rudimentary form among wild apes, because it is only while their parents provide for their needs that any animal can afford to spend much time in self-rewarding activities. The simplest human society lifts, to some degree, the burden of self-preservation from its members' shoulders and allows them to give some attention to these pursuits. In this sense art is indeed a social product, although it seems to start from the solitary and not from the social aspects of a living creature's experience.

The idea that the basic impulse towards the visual arts is biological rather than social is strengthened because children, like apes, draw and scribble, and these scribbles, in all countries, go through the same phases before developing any kind of cultural or individual characteristics. The first stage, after basic scribbles, is what those who have studied these things call 'diagrams', that is the Greek cross, the square, the diagonal cross, the circle, the triangle and the odd-shaped diagonal. Desmond Morris says of them: 'The interesting point about the growth of the diagrams is that they appear to rely for their sources almost entirely on the previous scribbles, rather than on any external influences. The child's aesthetic growth appears from the Kellog's study, to be a remarkably independent and private association between the paper, the pencil and the brain. Even at a later stage, when the early pictorial images are appearing for the first time, there appears to be only a minimum of reference to the outside world, just sufficient in fact to label the picture as a man or a house or a flower. If, for example, the earliest pictorial representation of houses by children from countries as different as Finland, Germany, India, France and Denmark are placed alongside one another, it is impossible to identify them correctly because they owe so little to the cultural environmental influences of the respective countries.'[2] The situation of a modern child, born into a society which provides him with pencil and paper, obviously contains both social and sociological elements. The point is that these elements may not be reflected in the drawings themselves.

It does not look at first sight as if story-telling which depends on language could have any such solitary aspects. There is, however, a clear connection between it and day-dreaming, which is also a 'self-rewarding activity', and one which is essentially solitary.

The connection of literature with day-dreaming and fantasy is much insisted on by Freud and his followers. Freud himself said: 'I believe the greater number of human beings create phantasies as long as they live.

'This is a fact which has been overlooked for a long time. The adult is ashamed of his day-dreams and conceals them from other people . . . as a rule he would rather confess all his misdeeds than tell his day-dreams.'[3]

This kind of fantasy has not been so much disregarded as Freud thought. Sir Walter Scott gives an analysis of Waverley's day-dreaming which in different language gives the same description as Freud. 'Had he been forced to choose between any punishment short of ignominy, and the necessity of giving a cold and

[2] Morris, Desmond, *op. cit.*
[3] Freud, Sigmund, *Introductory Lectures on Psycho-Analysis*, 1922.

composed account of the ideal world in which he lived the better part of his days, I think he would not have hesitated to prefer the former . . . This secrecy became doubly precious as he felt in advancing life the influence of the awakening passions; female forms of exquisite grace and beauty began to mingle in his mental adventures.' That Scott should have written this is important, because it may reassure anyone that he may accept the connection between day-dreams and literature without necessarily swallowing the whole Freudian doctrine, and because Scott is here describing the mental processes of a writer, for there is no doubt that his description of Waverley's youth is based on memories of his own.

Fantasy, as indicated by Scott and elaborated by Freud, is largely concerned with the more fundamental biological activities. Even when it becomes written fiction, it frequently treats of what was described in the sixteenth century as 'open manslaughter and bold bawdry' and is lamented today as 'sex and violence'.

Day-dreaming like night-dreaming is mainly carried on in visual images. Such images are solitary experiences. They cannot be directly shared, but have first to be translated into some kind of symbol; as animals are unable to do anything like this, it is impossible to be certain whether they dream. The eye movements and electrical rhythms associated with dreams in sleeping man have, however, also been observed in sleeping animals. It is thus not quite impossible that rudimentary and disconnected images may occur to them—perhaps connected with the sense of smell rather than with vision. Even if the possibility is rejected, the association between story-telling and day-dreaming, together with the themes with which they are often concerned, suggest that the basic impulses which lead to literature, no less than those which lead to painting, may have deeper roots than was previously suspected.

There are also certain themes which, while they are concerned with social situations, are found in so many cultures differing from each other in every possible way, that they cannot be attributed to any one of them. Tales of lost heirs and hidden princes, reversal of fortune in favour of the poor and despised and the triumphs of younger sons, fools and Cinderellas are examples. The Cinderella formula could be used in any society, known or imaginary, and if lost heirs involve some kind of hereditary rights, reversals of fortune need not be tied to any time or place. The details of a day-dream even of this universal type must be coloured by the society in which the dreamer lives. This is true even while it exists only in his mind, and once it is communicated to another person the social influences are clearly strengthened. When the story, perhaps originally merely a day-dream, becomes a commodity which can be exchanged for some kind of reward, these influences may begin to mould the form and modify the content.

The composition of a poem, a play, or a story, is not at all like day-dreaming; it demands strenuous and long-continued efforts to get it done at all. Many other motives must be called in to reinforce the delight in fantasy: the desire for applause, pride in skill, the wish to enforce some moral lesson or inculcate a religious or political doctrine, as well as the need to secure money, food, clothing or protection. It may seem as if these are so much more numerous and powerful than the original impulse that it makes little difference whether or not this is solitary or social; but in reality the alternatives lead to different conceptions of the relations between society and literature. If the basic impulse is a response to other people, it is truly social, and society, whether it is thought of as composed simply of human beings or is believed to include social 'facts', can accurately be described as 'producing' or 'creating' fiction with all other kinds of literature. If, on the other hand, most human beings are born with a tendency to draw and to day-dream, these activities must be regarded as 'non-social': while social and cultural forces direct and control the expression of the tendencies, they do not create them. They act as limits beyond which the possibility of certain kinds of activities is so remote that for practical purposes they can be called impossible; but within these limits real choices exist. Sometimes the limits are so narrow as to allow few alternatives. They are, however, never so narrow as to prohibit the appearance of literature, although they may be narrow enough to confine it to the simplest kind of hunting song or gnomic saying. Even in societies which by comparison with small, primitive groups are highly complex the absence of writing, or even a narrow limit on the number of people who can read, may make the alternatives so few that there may hardly be a choice at all. In these conditions it may look to the observer as if the sociological structure or the culture literally creates the form. It is only when they are compared with others where numerous alternatives occur that doubts about this begin to arise.

THE IMPLICATIONS OF INDIVIDUAL DIFFERENCES

Visual art even at its simplest level is linked not only with the biological constitution of the species, but with the differences between its individual members. Morris tested a group of six chimpanzees who lived together and had all experienced the 'same daily routine for some time past.' He says, 'It was quickly discovered that each animal could be identified by their drawing style. . . . These individual differences were fairly constant over a number of tests and could not be explained away by age or size differences.'[4] The divergencies went so far that one ape refused to draw at all.

Humans seem, at least to other humans, to resemble each other less than do apes. Everyone is agreed, however, that this can be attributed in some measure to the greater complexity of human society; some aspects of the difference in behaviour between any particular baron, priest or peasant in the Middle Ages were due to their respective positions in the social structure. When to these qualities are added the many ways in which everyone in the Middle Ages differed from those living in the seventeenth century or today, which are even more clearly the result of a different social environment, it is perhaps not surprising that the history of sociology consists largely of attempts to make social conditions explain not some but every aspect of human life. Their failure is perhaps best demonstrated by the present reaction against this kind of explanation.

Two American sociologists have remarked: 'Such terms as culture-pattern, subculture, social role, reciprocal role-expectations, social class, status group, mores and folk-ways, communication, human relations and many, many others are employed in such a way that individuals appear to act as group influences dictate. Unwittingly perhaps, this vocabulary has often had the accumulative effect of suggesting that the individual mainly does what is expected of him'.[5] This is true of sociology as an academic discipline. It is truer still when the terms are reinforced by the tradition which regards them not merely as a convenient way of

---

[4] Morris, Desmond, *op. cit.*

[5] Bendix, R., and Bennet, B., 'Images of Society and Problems of Concept Formation' in *Symposium on Sociological Theory*, edited by Llewellyn Gross, New York, 1959.

referring to the complex interactions of individuals but as entities which have an existence, in some sense, independent of human beings. The terms not only give a misleading impression of human psychology but they also make the entities referred to seem far more unified, far more monolithic, than they are in reality. Even the simplest and most rigid culture pattern, at least in civilized societies, offers the individual some alternatives. Even in the most authoritarian society no one but a mental defective can be completely passive.

There is no doubt that, in their more absolute forms, theories which explain everything by social structure or culture pattern give too little weight to the consequences of the differences in the biological equipment with which each individual is born. These divergences are, of course, kept within fairly narrow limits by the necessity of physical survival; but slight physical differences can have important psychological consequences. The world, for example, is not the same for a short-sighted and for a long-sighted person. All that society can do to modify this is to provide spectacles, which, while lessening biological differences, create social ones. 'Men do not make passes at girls who wear glasses'; a girl at whom men do not make passes will write a different kind of book from one who has to fend them off. Other and less obvious physical differences also make their contribution to character and personality. No group of writers, as far as I am aware, has ever tried to obliterate the differences between them. Strenuous, and generally successful, attempts are continually made to do just this for people using scientific instruments. Individual differences occasionally make this task difficult. A manual of astronomy refers to 'the extremely troublesome errors varying from individual to individual in the use of the modern transitmicrometer'.

All this may seem to be labouring the obvious, and it could be said that while humans differ, the forces which keep the divergences within limits, have the effect of causing people to differ in groups, rather than truly as individuals. Members of each group of long-sighted and of short-sighted persons will be, as far as their eyesight goes, perfect substitutes for each other. More culturally significant qualities will also be found in many, although not in all, human beings.

For literature this kind of approach would mean that there are always enough people born who can write books. Whether or not any individual actually does so will make little difference to the general line of development and none whatever to the emergence of literary forms. The influence of each particular language on the literature which is written in it, is often discussed in such terms. It is through language that the individual acquires the traditions and outlook of his culture, and its effect on him is all pervading. Day dreams may occur to some people entirely in visual images, but even a day dream, when it is told to someone else, must be told in words.

LANGUAGE AND THE INDIVIDUAL

What used to be called 'the genius of the language' dictates to some extent, and at first sight seems to dictate absolutely, what effects can or cannot be produced with it. For example, even if the literary theory had not forbidden the use of familiar speech in French classical drama, the form of the verse would have made it difficult if not impossible to say, 'She was a vixen when she went to school' or

> Grace me no graces, nor uncle me no uncles
> I am no traitor's uncle.

The influence of language is, however, the influence of tradition as much as of sociological or even of social factors. However hard a writer tries to use contemporary idiom, the main structure of the language and ninety-nine per cent of the words were produced, if by sociological forces at all, by those at work many centuries ago. But whatever it is called—historical, sociological or social—a phenomenon as vast and all-pervading as this may seem too large to be affected by any single person. Yet, in any civilized language, the introduction of large numbers of words can be traced to known individuals.

Everyone knows that the whole English-speaking world uses words and phrases because Shakespeare used them; but we are apt to forget that other and lesser writers also contributed to the prose in which newspapers are composed today.

William Whewell, realizing the need for some word to describe the activities of those occupied with the physical sciences, made the word 'scientist'. 'Agnostic' was invented by T. H. Huxley, 'determinism' by Sir William Hamilton. 'Outcome' is a

Scots word and only came into the English language through Carlyle's use of it. 'Outcome' he took from Scots, but the combination of 'wind' and 'bag' he seems to have invented himself. It is not surprising to find that a greater Scotsman, Sir Walter Scott, made such Scots words as 'uncanny', 'gruesome' and 'blackmail' current English. The word 'blackmail', the payment made by those living near the Highland Line to chiefs for protection against attacks by others clans or wandering robbers, first appears in *Waverley*. When Waverley hears the word he asks 'What is blackmail?' and receives a long explanation.

The language in which Scott's medieval characters conversed is not now much admired; but it has had an even greater influence on the English vocabulary than his Scots. 'Raid', now so happily combined with 'air', is the Scots form of an old English word not used between Lindsay of Pittscottie's *Chronicle of Scotland*, written about 1550 and *The Lay of the Last Minstrel*. Scott not only revived the rare and obsolete word 'henchman' but changed its meaning. It seems to have originally meant a horse groom, subsequently a page of noble birth; in both these senses it was obsolete by 1650. Scott, by associating it with 'hanchman', a word said to have been used in the Highlands, altered the meaning to the one it bears today. 'Stalwart' is the sixteenth-century Scots form of the Old English 'stalworth', and 'slogan' the Lowland form of a Gaelic word, both revived by Scott. The Scots word taken from contemporary or archaic Scots may be regarded merely as a special case of contact between cultures, known to be one of the main factors in the introduction of new words; but the deliberate revival of obsolete words is surely an instance of individual choice. Still more are the phrases taken from the Waverley novels including 'passage of arms' and 'free lance', both unknown to the Middle Ages. Although 'passage' was used for a combat in the sixteenth century, Scott appears to have been the first to combine it with arms. 'Free lance' is so familiar today that it is quite forgotten that it originally meant a man with a lance. It is said that we use the word 'present' as synonymous with 'gift' because of Sir Thomas Malory's imperfect grasp of French. This seems even less connected with sociological factors than deliberate inventions.

The revival of old and the invention of new words and phrases give a rough guide of the extent to which a single individual can influence the culture into which he is born. Small, perhaps, when viewed against the aggregation of institutions, habits, rules and traditions today called culture, but even there perceptible. This suggests that the process through which a literary form emerges is also the work of innumerable individuals rather than of immense anonymous forces, that it resembles a coral rather than a volcanic island. The impression is strengthened by the individuality shown by some writers in the combination of words, called 'style' in literary criticism.

This is such a well-known and platitudinous phrase that its significance for the sociology of literature may be overlooked. There is now an idea that prose is a more socially conditioned form of writing than verse. It is perhaps easier to see in what period any piece of prose was written than it is to place a poem, but even in prose sensitive readers can discriminate between one writer and another, and some are distinguished by an individuality so intense that it is impossible not to recognize it. It has been said of Apuleius that his Latin 'in its sum, is entirely his own: a Latin never written, much less spoken, by mortal man besides'.[6] This indeed might be, and indeed often has been, attributed to the social situation of the cosmopolitan world in which Latin was mixing with languages spoken by other races in the Roman Empire. Similar words have, however, been used about Sir Thomas Malory. *The Cambridge History of English Literature* says of his style: 'It entirely escaped the stamp of its century', and R. W. Chambers in his book *On the Continuity of English Prose* separates Malory from all other writers, saying that he 'remains as a beautiful inland lake, cut off from the outer world'. That he did not mean it altogether as a compliment makes it all the more likely to be true. Vinaver, indeed, has shown that Malory began, as did other writers of prose romance, by turning a poem in his own language into prose, not by translating a French story, as had previously been thought. The poem was the alliterative *Morte d'Arthur*, and Vinaver thinks it left traces in the style even of the later books of Malory's version.[7] On the other hand, the mood and atmosphere of the book is remarkably unlike that of the poem.

Individual style is not confined to European writers. Sir George

---

[6] Todd, F. A., *Some Ancient Novels*, 1940.
[7] Vinaver, Eugene, *Introduction to the Morte d'Arthur*, 1947.

Sansom says of Murasaki, 'The difference in point of language between the early romances and Murasaki is astonishing. . . . In some ways, of course, she profited by improvements made before her day, but no Japanese work gives so strong an impression of individual style as hers, and there is no doubt it was largely her personal achievement which made the contemporary language a fit medium for sustained artistic effort.'[8]

There are, of course, limits to the eccentricities of style. It must remain comprehensible to at least a few of its author's contemporaries. And, as has already been pointed out, certain effects cannot be achieved in some languages. Here again 'limit' seems to be an accurate description, and if sociological and historical factors set these limits, their influences on which choices will be made within them seem weaker than that of individual characteristics.

NON-SOCIAL ELEMENTS IN THE EIGHTEENTH-CENTURY NOVEL

Non-social elements can be plainly seen in the eighteenth-century novel. The marked individuality of the writers has already been sufficiently discussed. The element of fantasy and day-dream is not so obvious, but it exists, not only in *Robinson Crusoe*, but in the latter novel of manners, as well as in medieval romance and modern science fiction.

There is no difficulty in discerning it in Richardson; indeed, there are moments in *Clarissa* where it becomes intrusive. How near his novels were to day-dreams for Richardson himself is shown by his letters, in which he discusses his characters as if they were real persons, even quoting from them, as if this supplied evidence, independent of his own opinions.[9]

Fielding's attitude to his work was in strong contrast to Richardson's. His books are deliberate intellectual constructions, far removed from what is ordinarily regarded as day-dream. But they also incorporate universal themes, and make use of fundamental human experiences—too much use, it used to be thought. *Tom Jones* from one point of view a realistic novel of eighteenth-century life, from another is a variant of the story of the lost or

---

[8] Sansom, George, *op. cit.*
[9] Richardson, Samuel, *Letters*, edited by J. Carroll, 1964.

hidden heir; perhaps also of the common fantasy of childhood, that the child is in reality born of people more splendid that his parents. It has also something of the ultimate European day-dream, the dream that everyone's story will end happily. *Amelia,* too, may have something of this in the fairy-tale solution to Captain Booth's financial troubles, but otherwise it contains little either of fantasy or of universal themes. This may sound odd, as horrible prisons and injustice are themselves such themes. But Fielding does not make them so; his purpose was too serious, his eyes too firmly fixed on his own time. It is not only that the jails are far less horrible than the concentration camps of the twentieth century, or even that the prisoners seem to be having a better time than they would have in a modern prison, but that the evils are caused not so much by wickedness as by inefficiency. The magistrates are corrupt, but Fielding seems to think their ignorance of the law quite as serious as their readiness to take bribes. Such universal themes as appear are love, marriage and jealousy, and are centred on Amelia herself.

The book is thus an example of a sociological novel. It is obvious that there are such novels. *War and Peace* seems to have been inspired by a sociological theory. Dickens was concerned with social reform. Mrs. Gaskell, in two of her books, not generally considered her best, dealt with the relation between employers and workers. This kind of theme, however, does not appear in the novel until it had been established as a form of entertainment. Once this had been done, writers began to use it to present a point of view or suggest improvements, just as truly religious themes cannot be found in romance until this form was well established. Nor are the books even of the most sociologically minded of novelists mere reflections.

10

The Novel and Society

The evidence for the biological basis of visual art, and the connection between fiction and day-dreams, go far to illuminate the
nature of the relations between the novel and society. The
material of the crude day-dream is universal, frequently biological experience, and fiction cannot go too far from such themes
without ceasing to be romance or novel, and becoming allegory,
report, pamphlet, or prose poem. There are indeed universal
themes which are sociological. For example, the theme of the
individual against society, whether he is outlaw, criminal or saint.
The dream of absolute power is another instance, illustrated by
Marlowe's *Tamburlaine* as well as by many a mediocre piece of
fiction verging on the horror comic. The universal theme must
be interpreted in contemporary terms; but even so it sets limits
to the extent to which contemporary sociological conditions can
transform fiction. These limits are seldom thought about, and
they are indeed unimportant for most purposes, but when discussing the relations between the novel and society it is necessary
to remember them.

The temperament and ability of the writer are, on the other
hand, of the utmost significance. They may, in their effect on
literature, work in the same direction as sociological and traditional factors; on the other hand, they may, to however slight an
extent, counteract them. In either case they make it difficult to
discover the precise influence such factors have had. For example,
attempts to explain Fielding's novels by the conditions of eighteenth-century society must fail, because even if the literary tradition is included they cannot allow for his reaction to *Pamela*. We
do not know what his novels would have been like if this book

had never been written. Everyone would agree that he could hardly have written *Joseph Andrews*, but it is possible to maintain that he would have written *Tom Jones*. There is, however, no way of testing this, and we are therefore quite unable to assess what precise effect any sociological factor, or all of them together, had on Fielding's work.

Up to this point individual temperament—the difference in personality between one man and another, rather than differences in ability—has been stressed. But there is also, and it is more important for literature, the quality we call literary genius.

No sociological causes can be detected for the birth of people with the ability to produce great literature. Some partial explanation may be given for individual temperament. Literary genius, however, remains a mystery. Attempts can be made to explain it by analogy with other human traits which are better understood (such as predisposition to certain diseases), as a combination of genetic and environmental factors. But all those who have tried to do this have admitted that there remains something inexplicable. For any study of the relations between literature and society, literary genius is simply there, as much a fact as that men have always lived in societies. It has consequences however, just as the social nature of human beings has consequences. Everyone, even the most convinced social determinist, would agree that it is impossible to predict when a genius will be born, or what he will write. But it is not always realized that this means that it is also impossible to explain what has happened in the past. No rational judgement can be made as to what the English novel would have been like without Fielding, and it is still more impossible to decide what Fielding's work would have been like without Shakespeare. This kind of influence is, of course, part of the literary tradition, and is often included in the 'sociological background' of a writer. But as we cannot understand the traditional element, without considering the qualities of certain individuals, and as these qualities have never been completely explained, there is something inexplicable in the sociological background itself.

When we are faced not with the background, but with the work, this element is accentuated. The greater the work the more it seems to belong to the writer and the less to the society in which it was written. The attempt to interpret books and plays by ideas developed long after their authors are dead shows a recognition of the impossibility of explaining them through their 'age'. Much of modern Shakespearian criticism is an example of this type of argument. None of the early eighteenth-century novels are so great that even social determinists have to resort to determination by future, rather than contemporary sociological factors, but the attempt to make *Robinson Crusoe* into an allegory of classical economic theory is, in a way, an acknowledgement that it cannot be explained by the society in which Defoe lived.

The element of indeterminism introduced by the influence of individuals on literary events, disconcerts many critics and historians of literature. This is partly a matter of tradition. All theories which seek to explain literature by sociology are modelled, directly or indirectly, on classical physics. This is true of all Marxist theories, for if Marx's social determinism was originally inspired by Hegel, it was confirmed by the theories of nineteenth-century science. Taine declared in his introduction to *The History of English Literature*: 'Here as elsewhere we have but a mechanical problem; the total effect is a result depending entirely on the magnitude and direction of the producing causes. The only difference which separates these moral problems from physical ones is that the magnitude and direction cannot be computed in the first as in the second.'

Nearly all critics, even those most anxious to explain literature in sociological terms, would repudiate this; but they are strongly influenced by the idea that to admit that there exists an element of indeterminism or chance in their subject, leads to a dead end. It seems to them that it means no explanation can be given, or even sought. And indeed it is true that, if the factor of literary genius is really used in any discussion of the subject, instead of merely receiving a respectful mention, no precise and detailed account can be provided of the sociological factors which allowed the novel to develop.

On the other hand, a general sketch or model of the relations between the novel and society can be suggested. This would start with the human tendency to fantasy and daydream, a tendency which is so universal that it seems to belong to biology rather than to sociology. The social nature of human beings means that these day-dreams are socialized into anecdotes and short stories. In some societies conditions exist which allow the composition of long narratives. These conditions, at the same time, limit the narrative to certain forms and subjects. The mere appearance of a long narrative, whether epic, novel or romance does not mean that it will continue to have an appeal beyond the moment for which it was produced. A necessary condition for this is, as far as we can see, the birth of a writer capable of producing great literature. Even while keeping within the limits set by sociological factors, he will transcend them, by giving superb quality to a hitherto mediocre form. This will give rise to a literary tradition, which will, to a greater or lesser extent, alter the effect of all future sociological factors; they become different from what they would have been without it.

The emphasis laid on the contribution of the individual may seem unnecessary because no one appears to dispute the importance of at least some individual writers, in spite of the many historians who hold that no single person can have any real effect on the course of political or social history. Yet the fact that books are written by people, if taken seriously, makes more difference than may appear at first sight. It means not only that solitary experiences which fall outside the sphere of social influences play some part, however small, in the genesis of literature, but also that the immediate circumstances surrounding the individual become more important, and large sociological factors less so. To put it another way, sociological factors, as far as they impinge on literature, are transformed into social circumstances. For example, the class systems of England and France as they affected the novels of Richardson and Madame de la Fayette lose their generalized characters by becoming entangled with personal circumstances and individual temperament. There are, it is true, some conditions in which a sociological factor is so important that it overshadows all others; slavery for a slave would be an example. Another more modern instance is totalitarian dictatorship. These extreme cases, however, seem to prohibit literature altogether rather than to allow or encourage the invention of literary genres.

Some kind of writing can indeed be explained in sociological terms. When someone tells us he has sent his book to a publisher we instantly understand what he has done, because we know about the organization of the book trade; but this does not tell us why he wrote it in the first place. If, however, we hear that he is a professor who has been commissioned to write a textbook the whole transaction becomes comprehensible as a result of the interaction of two social institutions: the British educational system and the publishing industry. Even the most detailed knowledge of the institutions will not, however, explain why this professor consented and another refused because he was too busy with his own researches—or day-dreams. A comparison of their social circumstances may give us the reason, but on the other hand it may afford no clue at all; and if the book is a poem or a novel, instead of a textbook, it certainly will not provide a complete explanation. Even when, as has happened, a novel has been commissioned, it has frequently turned out to be quite other than was expected. To the cases of *Robinson Crusoe* and *Pamela* can be added the commission given to Trollope by the editor of *Good Words*, a magazine inspired by rigid evangelical piety. Trollope attempted to comply with these standards, but found it impossible to satisfy the editor. *Rachel Ray*, one of Trollope's most characteristic novels, was, however, the result of his attempt to write something different.[1]

One of the difficulties recognized by social determinists as well as by others is that it is not possible to discover every significant element in circumstances. A social determinist might say that although this means we cannot in practice explain complicated situations, by analogy with other situations a combination of sociological factors with social circumstances can account for them. This may lead to a more and more detailed examination of the lives of writers, but gives little or no help towards understanding the sociology of literature.

The opposite assumption—that choices are not entirely determined by social or sociological factors—seems to make at least some of the interactions between society and literature easier to understand. One of these is the influence which literature and literary models have on living persons. An instance is the story of Arthur which affected the manners of the Middle Ages in at least two ways: tournaments were modelled on what were believed to be the rules at Camelot; and those knights susceptible to such things tried, in some cases successfully, to behave in a way becoming the contemporary representatives of Lancelot and Galahad. Romance was not, of course, the only influence in changing the idea of what a knight should be; but the evidence

[1] Sir Karl Popper drew my attention to this example.

seems to show that chivalry appeared in literature before it did in life.

It has lately been suggested that these fantastic tales, as they are generally called—except by medieval historians—had, in England, an effect on political as well as social history by encouraging the dislike of the barons for the character and conduct of King John. Holt says of this, 'To a large extent men still accepted the exercise of royal patronage and personal influence. Magna Carta scarcely touched it, and the ancient law and custom, on which the barons fought, was here on the King's side rather than their own. But law and tradition were not their only resource. They had a common background in the imaginary world of Arthur's court and the Grail, of Tristan and Alexander, of Charlemagne and Roland . . . John must have seemed an enemy, not because he broke what they took to be the law, but because in their eyes, he had ceased to exercise a tolerable and honourable lordship judged by the standard of current literary images.'[2] To explain this kind of effect by saying that the society or the culture of the time created the images and the images then reacted on the society, is simply saying that society influences society; hardly an illuminating remark.

The way in which literary forms lost their attraction for the more talented writers, often described as the exhaustion of a form, also seems comprehensible in terms of known facts about human psychology. There are, of course, instances of literary forms or poetic metres being made unsuitable or unacceptable by some social or cultural change, but there are others for which no such explanations can be found. The disintegration of blank verse in the playwrights who followed Massinger and Ford is an example. It has been attributed both to the lack of talent (a purely individualist explanation) and to social changes of various kinds. Neither, however, seems to explain why writers, successful in other metres, were quite unable to write blank verse. Sir John Suckling is an instance of this odd disability. The simple psychological fact that a continuous stimulus tends to lose its effect seems to throw some light on this phenomenon. Writers cannot go on doing the same thing over and over again; if they do, they cease to produce anything worth while and their audience prefers to read not them but earlier writers.

[2] Holt, John, *The Northerners,* 1963.

Another aspect of the way in which certain forms become unusable is the impact of the masterpiece. A really great poem, play or novel can so excite the imagination of other writers as to found a school or movement; but it can, on the other hand, be so overpowering that it destroys the form in which it was written.

Murasaki seems to have created and destroyed the Japanese novel by a book so great that no subsequent piece of fiction could escape its influence. In the middle of the eighteenth century Lord Elibank said, 'Shakespeare had put a stop to great tragic writing in England,'[3] because his plays could never be surpassed. If tragedy in blank verse was substituted for 'great tragic writing', many modern critics would agree.

F. L. Lucas says of the writers of the Silver Age in Latin, 'It was not merely this literary invasion of the barbarians that made Silver Latin less classical; it was also the mere fact that it followed the supremely classical Golden Age of the Augustans. They had said so much and said it so well, that their posterity found themselves faced with the dilemma of saying consciously the same as they had or saying consciously something different. Imitation is poor inspiration and means dullness; being different for the sake of being different, is demoralising and means extravagance. The Imperial writers became either melodramatically wild like Lucan or ultra-classically tame like Statius; just as Chinese poetry became swamped with its own classical tradition.'[4]

This approach through the individual also seems to explain, better than any form of social determinism, how it is that the novel has appeared in societies so unlike each other. If sociological conditions are limiting, rather than determining factors, dissimilar conditions may impose similar limits. Limits in different societies may, as it were, overlap. This would also explain how it is that characteristics supposed to be peculiar to one period can be found in others. 'Realism' in medieval romance is one example and the way in which the realist novel of Richardson, Fielding and Smollett was immediately followed by the 'Gothic' novel, a revival of romance, provides another.

The connection of fiction with day dreaming, an individual and solitary activity, also gives some hint why fiction has developed into an important form of literature in some cultures and not

[3] Quoted in *Boswell in Search of a Wife*, edited by F. Brady, and A. Potter, 1957.
[4] Lucas, F. L., *Seneca and Elizabethan Tragedy*, 1922.

in others. Day-dream and fantasy are the root of many other human activities, but fiction is nearest to them in their crude and original forms. In this original form most cultures tend to frown on them, and to direct the impulses behind them to more serious ends by education. If this is done successfully, fiction will be outside those limits which are set by traditional as well as by sociological factors. If, for example, a group of people really believe in a religion which regards the biological material of day-dreams as sinful, one can be fairly certain that they will not produce novels. This could be used as an explanation of why no novel or romance was written in Puritan New England, and suggests one reason why there was no Scottish novel until the hold of Puritanism on Scotland had been loosened. A purely technico-logical education might have the same effect by making the day-dream seem useless and therefore sinful from the technological point of view.

Few societies are, however, as homogenous as Puritan New England, or as a modern technological state might become. Although Chinese education, both in China and Japan, did not encourage fantasy of any kind, and although the subjects of European medieval romance were disapproved of by the Church, there was in all these societies a class which was not exposed to the full force of the educational system. Even so the novel did not appear in China until the Mongol invasion had disrupted the famous examination system, and it was afterwards associated with Taoism, the religion of myth and miracle, rather than with Confucianism. The general disorganization of life in the early Middle Ages meant that education, in its academic sense, was largely confined to priests. And although in the twelfth century Catholic Christianity was wholeheartedly accepted in France and Great Britain there were obviously degrees of wholeheartedness. Chrétien de Troyes was clearly less wholehearted than Anselm or Lanfranc. Medieval Christianity also, like Taoism, allowed some rein to fantasy, in the lives of saints, and through its belief in angels and devils.

Although fantasy is the basis of all imaginative literature, it must, if it is to grow into anything more than a fairy story, be subject to some kind of intellectual discipline. This may consist in something we might not at once recognize as 'intellectual'; for example, the knowledge of fighting and of the code of chivalry limited the duels and battles in early romance to something not too far from the possible. A knight could have a magic sword, but he still could not fight more than a reasonable number of men at once. The wholesale slaughter of some Oriental romance or the ultimate weapon of modern science fiction would have made the story uninteresting to its audience.

The failure of Islamic romance to develop into the novel may be partly due, as previously suggested, to the Islamic interest in history being too involved with religion to allow fantasies about it to develop. This may have had the further effect that Arabic stories were never considered serious enough, by their authors or their audience, to require criticism either in the light of experience or of artistic standards. *The Tale of Genji* shows, however, that at least one of these disadvantages could be overcome by genius. The Japanese attitude to history was neither too serious nor too religious to inhibit fantasies about it; but it is hard to see what discipline Japanese culture had to offer as a help towards the production of a serious novel.

The same factors—biological, sociological, social and individual—must operate in other forms of literature, as well as in the novel; but there is no reason to suppose that they necessarily have the same relations to each other. Sociological factors may be highly important in the emergence of the drama, for example. The theatre, wherever it has appeared, seems to have arisen from religious ritual, a sociological phenomenon. The performance of a play is, moreover, a social activity, while reading a novel is not.

The nature of politics and of practical affairs in general seems to make the role of the individual less powerful than it is in any kind of literature. Although there is no doubt that something of the same effect results from the birth of people with particular qualities, at particular moments of time, there is more difficulty in attributing an historical event to one person. Besides the statesman or general responsible for what seem to be major decisions, a multitude of other people are always involved, and a host of minor decisions made by them contribute towards the result of the major ones. Only occasionally is there any difficulty in identifying the individual responsible for a book, and when there is, it is usually for quite other reasons.

Apart from this limit on the power of individuals in real life, there is, as Popper has pointed out, a certain logic in events themselves.[5] In any situation, whether historical event or personal dilemma, an understanding of the situation goes a long way to explain the actions of the people concerned in it. An example chosen by Mandelbaum to illustrate the existence of social 'facts', that of a man going to his bank to change a cheque,[6] seems to be rather an illustration of this situational logic. The cashier and the client behave in the way they do because of the logic of their situation. If instead of some habitual action a situation containing a problem is considered, it seems sensible to say that some solutions are impossible, made so by the situation itself. It may make sense to talk of a novelist's problems in the same manner; but only of his problems as a salesman, not of his problems as an artist. Defoe's situation, after he had failed in business and become too discredited for serious journalism, explains why he turned to writing fiction, but not why he wrote *Robinson Crusoe*.

A novel is also always to some extent a fantasy, an escape from a situation, rather than a solution to it. This remains true even of a novel designed to expose or illuminate some social problem.

Whatever the exact nature of the individual's contribution to 'history', there is no doubt of his importance in literature. A recognition of the element of chance which this introduces has some advantages in addition to its explanatory value. It provides a safeguard against the dangers of viewing the literature of any period merely a part of some imaginary social 'whole'. This can lead those who are enchanted with the literature into believing that there was some mystic rightness in the social structure, and those who are repelled by the social structure or atmosphere into refusing to read the literature. No doubt a society which allows great literature is superior to one that prohibits it; but this characteristic can be combined with others of a most unpleasant kind. It is more encouraging to believe that a cruel, a decadent or a frivolous culture need not necessarily contaminate all the work done within it.

To remember that books are written by people also seems to offer some guidance, in certain perplexities of the moment, about what has been called 'the two cultures'. For example, it seems clear that too close an identification of literature with society must be

[5] Popper, Karl, *The Open Society and Its Enemies*, 1945. *The Poverty of Historicism*, 1957.

[6] Mandelbaum, Maurice, 'Societal Facts', *The British Journal of Sociology*, 1955.

an obstacle to its wide enjoyment. If people are told that in order to appreciate a great writer it is necessary to understand the society in which he wrote, many busy scientists and technicians may decide not to bother, and many housewives and factory workers may feel that it is all too difficult for them. Sociological theories of literature tend to raise barriers between the ordinary reader and literature, although it is his heritage as much as that of any critic or expert.

Index

5

8
19

30